3

The Popular Antiques Yearbook

THE POPULAR ANTIQUES YEARBOOK

Current trends and prices of everyday antiques

Edited by Huon Mallalieu

Phaidon · Christie's

Oxford

Phaidon · Christie's Limited, Littlegate House, St Ebbe's Street, Oxford, OX1 1SQ

First published 1985
© Phaidon · Christie's Limited 1985

British Library Cataloguing in Publication Data

The Popular antiques yearbook: current trends
and prices of everyday antiques.——1985–.
——(Christie's South Kensington collectors series)
1. Antiques——Periodicals
I. Series
745.1'075   NK1125
ISBN 0 7148 8023 X

Design, phototypesetting and origination by Gecko Limited, Bicester, Oxon.
Printed in Great Britain by Butler & Tanner Ltd, Frome, Somerset.

Contents

A note to the reader

Unless otherwise stated, all the objects illustrated in this book were sold at Christie's South Kensington on the date and at the price indicated in the caption. Where the photograph shows one of a pair or part of a set sold as one lot, the price indicated is the price paid for the whole lot. Prices of objects sold at Christie's King Street include the buyer's premium of 8 per cent.

The measurement given in the captions is always the height of the object, unless it is indicated otherwise.

Overall responsibility for each chapter rests with the person who has written and signed its introduction. Queries and inquiries from users of this book will be welcomed, and should be addressed either to the author of the relevant article or to the author of the chapter introduction, at Christie's South Kensington, 85 Old Brompton Road, London SW7 3JS, telephone number (01) 581 2231.

Finally, a word of caution: each price recorded in the book is unique, and represents what one individual was prepared to pay at auction for a specific object on a particular date. We have made every effort to choose representative objects, to explain individual prices and to illuminate current trends, but the fact remains that prices do vary, particularly at auction, often in ways that defy prediction or explanation. Readers are therefore reminded that no price in this book should be taken as representing a fixed value for any object or type of object.

Managing Director Christopher Elwes takes one of the weekly South Kensington furniture sale.

Foreword

Thousands of lots, hundreds of sales – year in and year out the antique and the not-so antique, fine art and kitsch pour into Christie's South Kensington, and I hope will continue to do so ad infinitum. But what a task for our experts, to be told that they had to produce a Yearbook. With the masses of material they have to hand, the hardest decision was not what to put in, but what to leave out. So by definition, this Yearbook is not a record of prices realized or just of 'record prices'; it is a practical guide, explaining the differences in price for apparently similar objects. These can often be alarmingly different, and therefore price lists can be misleading. So this is not only a price guide for the popular antiques market, but a price guide to the antiques and works of art which can be found daily, in antique shops and markets, in provincial auction rooms, in your own attics and cellars and, above all, at Christie's South Kensington.

For we are the only major auctioneer to specialize in 'everyday antiques'. The result is that every week there can be up to 15 different auctions in our Old Brompton Road salerooms, and each one provides the specialist dealer or collector with plenty of choice, even in the more unexpected subjects, and we have plenty of those – from garden furniture and tools to radios, Disney cartoons and tinplate toys.

It is the incredible volume catalogued by our specialists every week that makes them supremely qualified to write this Yearbook. Each week, they are confronted by objects apparently similar to those sold the week before, and so making comparisons in this way is second nature to them.

This year Christie's South Kensington celebrates its 10th anniversary. Statistics for those 10 years show that we have handled 1.5 million lots in nearly 6,000 sales for a total of £126 million. We are a proud of being able to offer specialized auctions in this market and pleased that we can still provide the fastest service. I am only sorry that this book took so long to be conceived.

W.F. Brooks
Chairman

Introduction

by Huon Mallalieu

A wide range of antique price guides and market surveys is now published each year, and it might seem perverse to add to their number. However, we feel that there is a gap between the strictly limited guides, which tell all about a small field, but do not then link it to happenings elsewhere, and the general surveys, which by aiming at comprehensiveness succeed only in imparting such useful information as 'secretaire bookcases range from £300 to £3,000', or 'prints have increased in value by 130%', together with a run of illustrations the size of postage stamps.

We do not aim to be comprehensive, rather to concentrate on individual items within a representative spread of categories, comparing like with not quite like, and thus showing why particular prices were as they were. Although investment in antiques and works of art is possible, it is often chancy; the whole fascination of the business lies in the fact that no two items are ever exactly the same, and thus no wise buyer will ever treat antiques as if they were stocks and shares. A salutory lesson to this effect is given here in the article on Modern British Etchings on page 231, and in the diary extract printed on page 12 overleaf.

It is the business of an auctioneer to try to set reasonable estimates on the objects that he handles, and to hope that these will be exceeded by a small margin. If he consistently undervalues his wares, in time he will come to look as foolish as if he were always optimistic. This is one of the differences between the auctioneer and the dealer, who has to price his goods fairly but also exactly. Luckily no one is infallible, despite the widespread use of that unfortunate word 'expert', because if everyone knew the price of everything and was right on every occasion, there would be no bargains, and ultimately no antiques business.

Too close a concentration on a limited field can also have

I saw one just like it on TV last week' is a phrase heard more often than the cuckoo in spring. But did you? Things aren't always what they seem, and like needs to be compared very closely with like . . .(Photo Bill Warhurst, courtesy Times Newspapers.)

unfortunate consequences. The seemingly unconnected markets in nineteenth-century paintings and fans, for instance, can have effects on each other. A fan decorated with a Chinese scene may be worth so much to one collector, purely seen as a fan, but double that to a dealer or collector in the currently booming market for China Coast paintings. Thus we have tried to indicate general trends which may link diverse markets as well as discuss individual prices and characteristics within them.

C.F. Tunnicliffe, 'The Swing Bridge', etching, published in an edition of 75, 1928. 8 × 11 in. current auction estimate c. £500. Photo courtesy Gaston & Cook.
'Tunnicliffe etchings continue to find their way into each auction and fetch very little for lack of any support. It looks as if the Tunnicliffe market was merely a gamblers' market like so many at this time and commercially the most was made out of it when sales were possible and it is not proved at all that sales of this artist's work would have continued if less had been published during the boom. They probably never were prints to appeal to the general public any more than have his watercolour drawings and oil paintings handled by other firms.'
My thanks are due to Messrs. H. C. Dickins of Dover Street, London W.1., for permission to quote from the diary of H. C. Dickins. He was the agent and publisher for Arthur Briscoe and C. F. Tunnicliffe, and this extract shows how quickly the bubble of the 1920s collapsed. It was written within a month of the Wall Street Crash. It is pleasing to see that Tunnicliffe's work now has a strong appeal for the general public.

A price is only exact for one individual object on one particular day. If (heaven forbid!) something has been miscatalogued in a sale, it may instantly be worth more than has just been paid for it, should the knowledgeable buyer wish to re-sell it with the true description. Equally a major exhibition or publication can easily alter price levels in a very short time. Sales themselves are as individual as the items which make them up. A strike on the underground, a snowstorm or a power cut might mean the prices on a particular day bore no relation to those realized a month before or a month later. On the other hand a good snowstorm could persuade potential bidders to make an extra effort to attend in the hope that no one else would turn up.

Perhaps the most notable example of this occured in 1940 shortly before Christie's was bombed out of its King Street premises. The dealer Louis Meier, who died in 1984, found that owing to excitements elsewhere he was the only bidder at an important porcelain sale. He ran out of money at lot 19, and one wonders how this sale would have appeared in a traditional price guide.

On a less dramatic occasion I remember sitting through a sale of watercolours one hot and soporific September afternoon. Bidding was sluggish, and lot after lot was bought in. At last something sold to a lady dealer, whose name was duly announced by the auctioneer. 'No, no,' she protested, 'it's Jenkins now'. He peered down from the rostrum at her for a moment and asked: 'Do I understand that we must congratulate you?' before conducting the room in a round of applause. After that bidding was brisk and almost everything sold. Once again I doubt whether a traditional guide would explain the difference in prices between the earlier and later parts of the sale.

In certain instances prices can be determined by the needs and desires of one or two individuals, but this most often happens in the upper reaches of the art market, or within tightly specialized fields, or both. For the last decade prices for the prints of the Norwegian artist Edvard Munch have been governed by the competition between two very rich American collectors. For some time auctioneers and dealers have been speculating with much trepidation as to what will happen to prices when each of them has acquired a good example of every Munch print – which cannot be long now.

However, there is a ray of hope. This year a totally new buyer walked into Christie's King Street by chance and paid more than £50,000 for a Munch. He claimed never to have heard of the artist before, but to have liked what he saw. Perhaps this random purchase will prove to be the start of a collection which will govern prices in its turn.

At less elevated levels prices can be boosted or maintained by a single good dealer with an exhibition in mind, or with a good client in hand. Yet another cautionary tale comes from a friend who is in the business, but not a picture specialist. For some time he has been buying up the work of a particular artist, at perhaps £150 a time. He mentioned this interest to two dealers, who then happened to attend the same sale at Phillips . . . In future he must expect to pay £350 or more if his collection is to expand further, because others have noted the freak price and acted accordingly. The lesson from that is: if you are ahead of the market, be very discreet until you want prices to rise.

Equally, prices may be kept down by the activities of a ring. To my mind the law in this area has now been shown to be a thorough ass, and until a more rational and practicable code is produced the only defence of a vendor's interests at auction is the professionalism of the auctioneer. It is not only dealers who may contravene the Auction Bidding Agreements Act, but also any private individuals who agree not to compete against their friends. This year we have seen a leading museum director announce his flouting of the law as it stands, from the highest motives, and the most successful – and widely praised – ring of all time could be said to have been operated by a group of German museums and dealers to secure their heritage at the great von Hirsch sales in 1978. More recently, the highest price ever for a work of art – £8,100,000 for the Henry the Lion Gospel Book sold at Sotheby's in December

1983 – was paid by a similar consortium of German museums and dealers.

Thus, I would submit that one of the strengths of the *Popular Antiques Yearbook* is that the writers have not only handled, studied and catalogued the items with which they deal, but also attended or conducted the sales, and where necessary discussed anomalies with the buyers and other experts. Although, naturally, the bulk of our examples come from Christie's South Kensington or Christie's Scotland, our writers have noted important prices achieved by other auctioneers and by dealers when these help to give a fair picture of the market. For the same reason a few illustrations have been brought in from outside sources.

Naturally, too, there are personal opinions here, and you may well not agree with them. While imposing a general format on the book, we have endeavoured to allow individual voices to be heard. In their everyday working lives cataloguers must often put commercial considerations before aesthetics or personal tastes. This book would be pointless were they to do only that in their articles. Price and value are not, after all, synonymous. The one, with the provisos mentioned above, is a matter of fact and record, the other is governed by all sorts of unquantifiable considerations and associations. A family Bible containing the births and deaths of your ancestors may be immensely valuable to you, but still have a price of only a few pounds. In our articles we deal with prices, but where possible we have also kept values in mind. An obvious example is the article on early postcards (page 165).

Since this book is not intended to be a comprehensive record, it has been difficult to decide what should be included and what left out. Here we have tried to let the events of the year 1984/5 dictate the subjects. You may be disappointed to find that your own speciality has not warranted a mention. However, since this is a yearbook, it may well be covered on a subsequent occasion. In any case the principles of looking for quality and learning to see what is before you are common to all areas of antique collecting, and a survey of the market in one field may illuminate that in another.

In choosing illustrations for the book, we have acted on the maxim that more is not necessarily better. Our aim to encourage people to see what is before them would not be well served, we feel, were we to present them with huge numbers of illustrations so small that there was practically nothing to be seen in them anyhow. At the expense of sheer numbers, therefore, we have tried to ensure that illustrations are of a good size and quality, that they all have a point to make, and that they have as much commentary as they need in order to make sense of the bare price information.

You will find certain repetitions in this book, and they are not only inevitable but also necessary. Several of the categories depend on overseas buyers and have therefore been affected by the currency fluctuations of the year. Many of our writers have emphasized the need to be firm with oneself when assessing quality, and rigorous when inspecting condition. It is easy enough to over-persuade oneself as to merit when buying, and it is the way of the world that little sympathy is wasted on someone who has bought a dud. If you are a dealer or an established collector, you should need no advice from me, but if you are a new collector and your means are limited, you should always go for the best things by second-rank artists and craftsmen, rather than spending perhaps more on poor work purely because it is by a big name.

In our articles there is a repeated emphasis on quality, rarity, age and condition. In my opinion the greatest of these are the first and the last. A thing may be quite modern and have quality, which makes it stand out in an age of mass production – and in an age of mass production it will probably eventually gain rarity because so many things are thrown away.

It is always worth looking for quality among the currently unfashionable. Around 1900 the family of some friends of mine abandoned their house in the Shetland Islands for a more comfortable property on the mainland. They had two 'long' sets of dining chairs, but only one would fit on the boat. So the unfashionable Chippendale set was burnt on the shore, and the late nineteenth-century reproduction Chippendale set is still in the house in Fife. Subsequently the Victorian set would have been despised, but now, because it too had quality in the making, it is in demand again (see p. 23). However, it is nowhere near as valuable as the contents of that bonfire would now be, as a comparison of the chairs below will show.

Two from a set of six reproduction Chinese Chippendale dining chairs, 19th century. Mar. '85, £1,500.

The real thing – two of a set of eight George III mahogany dining chairs. Christie's King Street, Dec. '84, £41,040.

Just occasionally rarity is enough on its own. Given the space it would probably be a good investment to lay down a Sinclair C5 in factory condition at the moment. Condition would, however, be an important factor in determining the price thirty or so years hence. Condition, after all, can make the difference between thousands of pounds for a Rembrandt etching, and quite literally nothing at all.

Some markets are subject to the whims and vagaries of fashion, particularly if they are new collecting fields. Since our article on wristwatches went to press it has become apparent that the first fine careless rapture of buyers is giving way to a more careful and selective approach. In June sales only the very highest quality watches were creating enthusiasm. The early days of any market are the ones when a discriminating collector can do best. Often after the first surge of prices there is a levelling off or even a fall, before a second and perhaps even more dramatic rise. During such a pause it is sometimes possible to secure really good examples.

An opportunity for buying well if your nerve was steady and you liked the work of the ceramic designer and potter Clarice Cliff, came midway through the period covered by this survey. In November her prices were very high, in March few people seemed to want to know, and in May price levels were back to those of November. Those who are ready for such hiccups are the people who will form the best collections and profit most financially.

A fairing: 'Revue'. Christie's King Street, Mar. '73, 750 guineas.
At the time unrecorded, this fairing made a record price. Today, in spite of its rarity, it would probably make no more than £100 at auction.

In the 1970s there was a great surge of interest in fairings – the sort of things which were supposed to have detained Johnny so long at the fair. These humorous little porcelain figures, mostly made in Germany and Bohemia, and sold at 6d each, became a booming collector's market – and then a drug on the market. They are not rare or of particularly high quality, but they have an appeal, and one day, doubtless they will be fashionable again. If you do like them, you should be buying the best now, before other people recover their confidence. At the moment South Kensington does not even accept them for sale.

This pattern was very apparent in the revival of interest in Victorian paintings from the late 1960s to the 1980s. In about 1973, for instance, it was possible to buy a painting by John William Godward for £7,000, which might only have been worth a few hundred five years previously, but which was shortly to soar to £70,000. At present it is only a Godward of exceptional quality that would realize this price, and there are signs of a more discriminating approach, with a levelling off of prices for all but the best Victorian paintings.

At other times markets which have been boosted and puffed for years will ultimately decline again because they do not contain enough works of the very highest quality. The best, of course, will still sell, but lesser stuff, which has risen on its coat tails, will no longer find a ready market. At an elevated financial level, there are signs that this is now happening in the market for Impressionist paintings.

For a good many years Impressionists have been among the most saleable commodities. Really poor and repetitive Renoirs and Monets have made six figure sums, because collectors throughout the world had been persuaded by marketing and publicity that anything by these great masters must be great art. Unfortunately this is not the case. For the long-term good of their reputations these painters should really have burnt a fair part of their oeuvre. The pricing of their work has long been due for reappraisal, and the unsold casualties among lesser examples in recent major sales in London, New York and Paris indicate that it may be with us at last.

In this book we have put a fairly strong emphasis on the eighteenth, nineteenth and twentieth centuries. This is natural because Christie's South Kensington was set up just over ten years ago to cater for the large trade in lower-priced antiques, or near antiques. Given the increasing sophistication of the operation at Christie's London headquarters in King Street, St. James's, and the vast increase of business there, it was no longer worth the commission to sell the sort of things with which we are concerned as if they were by Chippendale or an Old Master of Renaissance Italy. After all, it can take as long to write an accurate catalogue description of a biscuit tin as of a Chippendale commode.

At South Kensington and Christie's Scotland, or indeed Christie's Amsterdam or Christie's East in New York, it is possible to deal with humbler items economically, and in general expeditiously. No other auction organization in the

Television and the newspapers generally present the idea that everything old is automatically good, and highly expensive, but dealers and auctioneers know that an awful amount of the antique goods that they will be offered is just plain bad. Byron dismissed the idea of 'the good old days' with a wry 'all days that are old, were good', and certainly in the antiques market old does not invariably mean good.

Here we have a small group of really weak paintings of the sort that frequently appear in sales and shops, and sometimes, amazingly, they still make money – good examples of inferior work riding the current boom in Victorian paintings.

F.V. Hagen, 'A Camel Rider at Prayer,' oil on canvas, indistinctly signed. 15½ × 10½ in. June '85, £20.
It may be Orientalist (see page 224), but . . .

Florence Blakiston Allwood-Matthews, 'The Great Hall, Karnak', oil on canvas, signed and dated 1888 on reverse. 18 × 14¾ in. June '85, £60.
. . . Oh dear!

After Sandro Botticelli, 'Tondo', oil on canvas. 17 in. diam. June '85, £65.
A very long way after.

F.E. Jamieson, 'Loch Awe', oil on canvas, one of a pair. 20 × 30 in. June '85, £250.
This sort of thing is known as a 'furnishing painting'. They were sold or given away with poor quality furniture for front parlours at the turn of the century. People seem to want them again.

F.E. Jamieson, 'Sheep by a Lake', watercolour, signed. 11 × 15 in. June '85, £30.
Jamieson is as bad in watercolour as in oil painting. Note how he has avoided painting the feet. This is often a give-away as they are quite difficult to paint.

world handles such quantities of material covering the middle and lower ranges of the market, and it is these areas which provide the raison d'être – and the contents – of this book.

Over the ten years of South Kensington's existence, the various markets have changed, often dramatically. In looking through the earliest catalogues of the firm, I have constantly been made to wish that in 1975 I had more spare money and greater acumen. In 1970 I wrote a not entirely serious Antiques Alphabet for *The Observer*. In it I used the old trick of 'Ephemera, see Junk . . . Junk, see Ephemera', and for some time afterwards I was plagued by witty friends inviting me to tour their local ephemera shops. The pretentious euphemism of fifteen years ago has become the straight-faced usage of today, and at South Kensington there is now even a Department of Ephemera – which is neither a junk nor an ephemeral department.

Time has his revolution, and the blooming of new collecting fields can be a matter of intense irritation. The high prices currently paid for toys may be a joy for many people, but for those who, like me, went with rubbing hands in search of their childhood lead soldiers and clockwork trains, only to find that they had been donated to a jumble sale by unthinking parents, each triumphant record price is a new frustration.

Often it seems that the more commonplace and mass produced an object was originally, the rarer and more desirable it will ultimately become. An obvious, if juvenile, example is the Mickey Mouse watch. At one time on every childish wrist, the majority were smashed and thrown away in months. The few working survivors now sell for many more pounds than the few shillings they cost new.

The tools of craftsmen were so often objects of craftsmanship in themselves, that it now seems extraordinary how many were abandoned without thought. An old wood and brass brace or plane is much more satisfying to work with than a modern metal and plastic equivalent, and this should surely have given a clue as to future value.

From superannuated cards to long-demobbed bayonets, and from photographs to microscopes, everything that was once neglected now has its collectors and its price. Yesterday's junk is today's ephemera, and no doubt tomorrow's heritage. Where is my pith helmet, where is my first safety razor, and, which is more and most of all, where's my model Coronation coach?

It would have been nice to have held on to a few things. In about 1973 I put a pair of desert scenes by Lamplough into a watercolour sale, and they were bought in. On a subsequent occasion the auctioneer managed to squeeze a bid of £30 from a reluctant room for them. I was pleased at the time, but now editing pages 224–5 I am rather galled.

The very first sale at Christie's South Kensington, which was a marriage between Christie's King Street and the long-established Debenham Coe, was held on 3 February 1975,

As an antidote and complete contrast to the pictures on p. 15 here are a couple of exceptionally good old pieces – and prices.

1. *English late 15th-century chasuble, sold by the Duke of Norfolk and bought by the Victoria and Albert Museum (see page 146).* July '84, £8,000.

2. *Mid-17th-century ladies' mules.* Feb. '85, £5,500.

and during the following month or so the firm offered many things which made prices that are now mouthwatering. A Hester Bateman punch ladle dated 1776 made £33 (now perhaps £200); a Staffordshire 'Washington' figure £80 (£600 today); another Lamplough desert watercolour struggled to £22; a late Georgian mahogany bow-fronted chest of drawers at £55 (perhaps £1,000 today); and at the top end of the market, a fine and large pair of famille rose fish-bowls, Ch'ien Lung, 24 in. diam., £2,500. The last went to one of the top London dealers, Marchant, who say that they were in good condition, and that they should make £20,000 to £30,000 today.

In ten years' time this book will no doubt provoke the same nostalgia and self-kicking.

This book, like most price guides, is firmly based in the world of auctioneering. Because of the immense publicity given to the auction houses in recent times, which is a revival of the public fascination with the salerooms in the Victorian period, all too many people look askance at the prices charged by antique dealers, which can seem high by comparison with results in the rooms. More often than not this is unfair. A specialist dealer may well be able to contribute more scholarship and expertise to his stock than even the most knowledgeable auction house staff. He may also have had to pay for restoration or reframing. Quite often it is possible to find bargains among the old stock of a dealer, because he has not repriced it to reflect more recent trends.

Dealers and auctioneers, for all their occasional sparring, are essential to each other, and the public needs the services and strengths of both. It has been estimated that some three-quarters of the lots that go through Christie's South Kensington are bought by dealers, and it is of course common practice for dealers to bid at auction on behalf of their clients. There are good auctioneers and bad ones, brilliant dealers and duds, and it is up to the would-be buyer to find out for himself which is which. Dealers and auctioneers can be invaluable allies, but the watchword must always be 'caveat emptor'.

Anyone who wishes to make serious forays into the antiques market must read both widely and deeply, and above all must learn to look. One of the purposes of this book is to suggest items and areas that are worth looking for. I hope that it will also provide a guide as to the way things should be looked at.

The signatures to articles do not cover everyone who has contributed to this book in one way or another. It would not have existed were it not for the enthusiasm of the Chairman and the Managing Director of Christie's South Kensington, Bill Brooks and Christopher Elwes, nor if it had lacked the guiding hand of Bernard Dod at Phaidon Press. Many of the photographs have been specially taken by Messrs. A. C. Cooper or by Ted Holmes at Christie's South Kensington, with the help in one extremely urgent situation of Bob Masters. Almost everybody on the staff of Christie's South Kensington has been dragged in at some point, but my particular thanks are due to Nicholas Pitcher and David Allison who have acted as co-ordinators and whippers-in, despite being very busy men in their own departments.

Debbie Harman and Victoria Wolcough have provided essential support from the Press Office – next door to one of the more comfortable temporary offices in London – as has my wife, Fenella, in one of the more chaotic offices run from home.

There are times when it seems unwise to throw anything away. Perhaps old metal dustbins will also one day have their collectors. Already they can be art . . . Woodcut by Chris Wormell, reproduced by permission of the artist and Times Newspapers.

1. *Furniture*

Introduction
by Hugh Edmeades

Perhaps the most frustrating, but at the same time the most fascinating, part about deciding on a price for buying or selling a piece of furniture is that there are no hard and fast rules by which to work. The reason for this is twofold: firstly no piece of furniture is exactly the same as any other, and secondly the state of the market is forever fluctuating – and not always upwards. While at one moment one style or type of furniture may be highly fashionable, and therefore much sought after, the next it may be a drug on the market. Witness the lamentation often heard in the auction rooms from potential vendors who have just been given an estimate . . . 'Oh, but it must be worth more, because I paid more than that for it six months ago!'

However, no matter what the state of the market may be, there are various points to bear in mind when buying furniture which obviously influence the potential market value. It is surprising how many people expect to be given an instant estimate when they have given, in their opinion, a detailed description over the telephone. It is equally difficult to form an opinion from a photograph of an item, even when it is a colour photograph. You can only begin to judge something accurately when you can actually see it and handle it. Make sure you can inspect it in a good, preferably natural, light and that it is in a position where you can look at it from all angles including behind and underneath. In crowded auction rooms this is not always easy to achieve, but don't be afraid to ask a porter to help you to see something properly.

The first thing to notice about any piece of furniture is the proportion; nothing affects a price more adversely than the proportions being wrong or unpleasing to the eye. Ask yourself: 'Is the top half too wide for the bottom? Are the legs long enough for the rest of the piece?' and so on. Only when you are satisfied that the piece is in proportion, or for that matter not, should you look at it more closely. Then you should take note of the type of wood used. No matter what it is, whether it be a rare variety, or a more common one such as mahogany, walnut or oak, the important facts to consider are the type of grain, the depth and richness of colour, and the patina. The more complex and interesting the grain, the more desirable the object becomes, and a heavy-handed restorer can destroy not only the potential value, but also the intrinsic beauty, of a piece by over-zealously French polishing and thus removing at a wipe the natural maturity of the wood.

Both the standard of proportion and the quality of the wood can be assessed relatively quickly and easily. However, a study of the decorative features takes slightly longer and should not be rushed, because it is the small details that can turn a seemingly ordinary piece into something special. Any carving should be crisp and restrained. This is also true of marquetry work, too much of which tends to distract the eye and hide the beauty of the wood into which it is laid. If an item has decorative mounts, beware of plain gold-painted metal purporting to be ormolu. The mounts are one place where you can find makers' names or marks. Signed pieces are more interesting and by nature more desirable – so be careful when you find a name or a label, because you cannot take it for granted that it has always been there.

These, then, are some of the more important points to bear in mind when confronted by any piece of furniture in which you could be interested. Most of them are gone into in greater detail in the following articles. Remember, no matter how strong or depressed the market may be, these points are always relevant in helping you decide whether a piece is good, bad or indifferent.

During the 1984/85 period, it can be safely said that, as a

general rule, prices for most styles, types and periods of furniture showed a healthy increase over the corresponding months of '83/84. Naturally in the space allotted it is impossible to cover every movement in the world of furniture prices, but in the following pages we hope to highlight some of the more noticeable ones.

Run-of-the-mill Georgian brown furniture, as was to be expected, continued to attract keen competition, but equally naturally it was items of the higher quality of the period that showed the most dramatic rises. The chair, No. 1, was one from a set of fourteen in the style of Robert Manwaring, which sold for £66,960, an increase of more than 2,000% over their last appearance at auction in 1971. Paid by an American, the price is an example, albeit extreme, of the continuing desire for English furniture from across the Atlantic. Perhaps it should be said at this point that the relative strength of the US dollar against the pound made conditions very favourable to Americans buying in this country for much of our period.

Progressing into the nineteenth century and the Victorian era, 1984/85 may prove to have been the time when Victorian furniture really began to emerge from the shadow of previous periods, and finally to be accepted not only as a collectable, but also a saleable, style of furniture in its own right. A splendid example is No. 2. Of all the styles the Victorian cabinetmakers loved to work in, the Gothic has proved to be the most popular this year. No. 3, of small size by Victorian standards, needed some major restoration to the top, whereas No. 4 is an example of a pair of cabinets which were not only of the highest standard, but were virtually in mint condition.

Typical of the Victorian age is the balloon-back dining chair (No. 5) which must be singled out for its increase in popularity. As is made clear on page 22, sets of chairs are expensive items regardless of their age; consequently it is

1. *Set of 14 George III mahogany dining chairs, including two open armchairs. Sept. '84, £66,960 (house sale at Kingston Russell, Dorset).*

2. *Victorian walnut games/work table inlaid with Tunbridge ware. 24 in. wide. May '84, £750.*

3. *Victorian amboyna, pollard oak and ebonized centre table. 46 in. wide. Feb. '85, £1,900.*

4. *Pair of Victorian satinwood and amaranth banded display cabinets. 61 in. wide. Mar. '85, £6,200.*

impossible to gauge with certainty whether the increase in demand for balloon-backs is merely part of the general trend, or a desire for Victorian designs in their own right. The evidence tends to point to the latter, if Davenports, for example, are anything to go by. As can be seen in the article devoted to these peculiarly Victorian pieces, Davenports appear regularly on the market, making it easy to chart any increase in demand. It is very interesting to note that the example here, No. 6, was sold after our article had been written, and it fetched a disproportionately higher price than the most expensive mentioned therein, which only goes to show how desirable they are and doubtless will continue to be.

Much of what has been said of Victorian furniture can also be said of Edwardian pieces. Compare the prices of Nos. 7 and 8, noting the dates of sale. This type of furniture, with its inlay on rosewood ground, was produced in large quantities at the turn of the century, and the high prices they now fetch will undoubtedly prove to be a sore point with our parents and grandparents who have disposed of such things with relief, believing that they could never be admired again.

Over the last few years there has been a gradual increase in demand for reproduction furniture such as the chairs, No. 9. The maker had paid particular attention to accuracy in copying Chippendale's design for a ribbon-tied back, but even though the quality could have been of a higher standard, this did not affect the bidding. On the other hand the quality of craftsmanship of the tables, No. 10, was quite superb. In 1977 they had realized £600, so you can judge for yourself just how lively the reproduction market is at the moment.

At this point, a few words should be said about oak furniture. By comparison with other woods, no doubt owing to its sombre and provincial appearance, oak is not expensive. There was scant evidence of any appreciable increase in this market this year, with the notable exception of dressers, of which No. 11 is typical. To contradict our argument that oak is inexpensive, but in support of our claim that reproduction is popular, is No. 12. While on the subject of provincial furniture, Windsor chairs (No. 13), especially those made of yew, have always been popular and their popularity increases year by year.

To conclude this all too brief summary of the year 1984/85, it can be said that the desire and competition for furniture showed a marked overall increase. Supply kept up with demand, and as a consequence there was a plethora of goods on offer, which in turn meant that people could buy selectively, preferring those items that were not in need of restoration. As always there are exceptions to every rule. No. 14 not only had bits of veneer lifting, but some bits were missing altogether. The top was badly water-stained and only one of the four original handles had survived. But, no doubt, careful restoration will confirm its potential as an example of English furniture-making at its finest.

5

6

7

5. *Set of 8 Victorian walnut balloon-back dining chairs. Feb. '84, £1,300.*

6. *Victorian burr walnut Davenport inlaid with boxwood arabesques. 24 in. wide. Apr. '85, £3,400.*

7. *Late Victorian rosewood and inlaid side cabinet. 48 in. wide. June '83, £350.*

8. *Late Victorian rosewood and inlaid side cabinet. 54 in. wide. Mar. '85, £1,200.*

9. *Set of four Chippendale-style mahogany dining chairs. Sept. '84, £1,900.*

10. *Pair of George III-style mahogany tripod tables. 13 in. diam. Aug. '84, £2,200.*

8

9

10

12

11

13

11. *George III oak dresser, the drawers banded with mahogany and inlaid with boxwood and ebony stringing. 74 in. wide. Mar. '85, £4,400.*

12. *Elizabethan-style oak draw-leaf refectory dining table. 78 in. long. Apr. '85, £2,200.*

13. *Harlequin set of 7 George IV yew and elm Windsor armchairs, stamped William Wheatland. Nov. '84, £3,500.*

14. *George III mahogany Pembroke table inlaid with satinwood and rosewood bands within boxwood lined borders. 29 in. wide. Mar. '85, £5,200.*

14

Dining Chairs (1)

When buying dining chairs always remember that the 'longer' the set, the higher the average price per chair. Sets of six appear most often, so in longer sets, which are not only rarer but intrinsically more desirable, especially if they include two 'carvers' or armchairs (Nos. 1–4), the price per chair increases dramatically.

The price achieved by No. 1, however, was not solely due to the fact that it was a set of ten, but even more to the unusual design of the backs, with satinwood tablets and pierced latticework. The design of No. 2 is much more standard, although the rope-turned back rail is always a popular and sought after feature. This can also be seen in No. 3, which although later in date has the added decorative feature of inlaid brass work on the top rail. However, the telling feature in both No. 3 and No. 4 is not so much the backs, as the legs. The use of the sabre leg, whose graceful curve is the epitome of the Regency style, is a

more desirable feature than the rather simple turning of Nos. 1 and 2.

Although by the middle of the 1830s the turned leg was again in use (Nos. 5 and 6), No. 5 is embellished by 'lappeting' and No. 6 by 'reeding'. The former is a good example of my point about the desirability of 'long' sets even when the design is on the dull side. This is not true of No. 6. Had three of the eight not been reduced in height, they would undoubtedly have fetched a higher price. *Hugh Edmeades*

1. *Set of ten, mahogany, George III.* Aug. '84, £8,500.

2. *Set of eight, mahogany, George III.* Aug. '84, £2,600.

3. *Set of eight, mahogany, Regency.* Feb. '85, £3,200.

4. *Set of eight, mahogany, Late Regency.* Feb. '85 £2,800.

5. *Set of eleven, rosewood, William IV.* April '84, £2,200.

6. *Set of eight, rosewood, William IV.* Jan. '85, £2,000.

1

2

3

4

5

6

Dining Chairs (2)

Perhaps the most reproduced of all designs for dining chairs are those of Thomas Chippendale. All the sets illustrated here date from the nineteenth century, all are made of mahogany and all appear to be vaguely similar at first glance. Leaving aside the number of chairs to each set, what are the salient features to look for?

The first thing that you should study in any detail is the splat: the more complex this is, the more desirable the chair (No. 1). The top rails should be full of movement (No. 4), and any carving (Nos. 1 and 3) is an additional bonus. Look out for small decorative features, such as the 'paper-scroll' finials on No. 3.

After the backs, look at the arms on the carvers. These too should have plenty of movement, as in Nos. 1 and 5, but not Nos. 3 and 6.

The seats are also important: see how the maker of No. 3 has taken the trouble to add a serpentine movement to the front, and notice how generous are the seats of Nos. 1 and 5 (don't be put off by the fact that they need restuffing). By contrast, the seats of No. 6 are mean.

When you move down to the cabriole legs, the more exaggerated the scroll, the better. Compare Nos. 1, 2 and 5 to Nos. 3 and 6. Any carving on the knees and on claw and ball feet should be crisp and precise. Here the best examples are Nos. 1, 2 and 4.

Finally, look out for trade and makers' labels or stamps. Although not the most complex in design, the quality of craftsmanship in No. 5 was outstanding, and I was not surprised to find 'Gillows, Lancaster' stamped on the underframe.

Hugh Edmeades

3

4

2

1. *Set of ten, mahogany.* April '84, £6,000.
2. *Set of ten, mahogany.* July '84, £4,500.
3. *Set of eight, mahogany.* Dec. '84, £2,200.
4. *Set of eight, mahogany.* Feb. '84, £2,400.
5. *Set of twelve, mahogany.* Aug. '84, £5,600.
6. *Set of twelve, mahogany.* Jan. '84, £2,200.

1

5

6

Eighteenth-Century English Bureaux

Although the word bureau is often wrongly applied to other types of writing furniture, it is generally accepted to describe a piece which has a narrow rectangular top above a hinged sloping front with an arrangement of drawers below.

By the beginning of the eighteenth century walnut had succeeded oak as the most popular wood with furniture makers and their clients, owing largely to the influence of the Dutch craftsmen who had settled in England under the Restoration and William and Mary. Walnut, with its varied grain and rich colouring, dominated the first quarter of the century, and Nos. 1–3 all date from that period. Not surprisingly all have had their bracket feet and handles replaced. Although No. 1 is the most provincial – well veneered on the front but not the sides – it has the advantage of a well rather than a drawer below the slope, and this accounted for the higher price, despite the superior craftsmanship of Nos. 2 and 3. Note how good quality reproductions (No. 10) compare very favourably in price.

As walnut had succeeded oak, so by the middle of the century mahogany had become the fashionable wood, and so it continued until the end. Nos. 4–6 are typical George III bureaux. The prices are much the same, differences being mainly due to the colour and patina of the wood. No. 5 had the attraction of smallness, No. 6 had satinwood crossbanding in its favour, but No. 4 made the most because of the deeper richness of its mahogany.

From the same period is No. 7, a much restored piece – note the 'easy-glide' castors – but still it realized a very respectable £800.

Of course other woods were still used, and No. 8 is a superior oak example. The value is enhanced by the arrangement of two short and three long drawers and by walnut crossbanding. The fluted angles are a particularly popular feature, and also to be found on mahogany and walnut examples.

Finally take a good look at No. 9 Straightforward mid-Georgian mahogany bureaux don't come much better. The colour and patina are superb, the size ideal, the drawers graduated and the handles and escutcheons cast in a Rococo style rather than a monotonous swan-neck pattern. The interior is fitted with drawers and pigeon holes with a fret-carved central door and, most importantly, every part is original. Hence the price. *Hugh Edmeades*

1

2

1. *Walnut, George I.* 36 in. wide. June '84, £1,900.
2. *Walnut, George I.* 36 in. wide. Apr. '84, £1,450.
3. *Walnut, George I.* 36 in. wide. Dec. '84, £1,500.
4. *Mahogany, George III.* 39 in. wide. Jan. '84, £1,200.

3

4

5. *Mahogany, George III.* 36½ in. wide. Aug. '84, £1,000.

6. *Mahogany, George III.* 39 in. wide. Dec. '84, £800.

7. *Mahogany, George III.* 42 in. wide. Nov. '84, £800.

8. *Oak, George III.* 42 in. wide. May '84, £750.

9. *Mahogany, George III.* 36 in. wide. Feb. '85, £4,800.

10. *Walnut, reproduction.* 30 in. wide. May '85, £1,500.

Pedestal Breakfast Tables

With only a few notable exceptions, there was no appreciable increase in demand for late Georgian/Regency breakfast tables on quadruped legs throughout the year.

The average 54 in. wide examples (Nos. 1–3) continued to sell in the £1,000 to £1,500 range, whereas the later Regency examples (Nos. 4 and 5) with too thick tops and exaggerated bases do not yet warrant a four-figure price. One of the most obvious features of these is size, as in No. 6, which although only 6 in. wider than No. 1 and 2, fetched 25 per cent more.

The one notable exception is No. 7. At first glance it is not dissimilar to No. 1, but the enormous price difference is due to several factors. Primarily again, the size is rare. Although the top is nicely crossbanded as in No. 1, note how the corners are more generously rounded, and how the graining, patina and colour are of far superior quality. Looking at the column one might think it rather plain; however, this 'plainness', as in No. 6 too, is a positive feature, being neither too tapered as in Nos. 1, 2 and 3, nor too bulbous as in Nos. 4 and 5.

Finally one can see how well the legs are proportioned to the top and sweep gracefully to the floor, far more so than in No. 1, where they are too arched, and Nos. 3 and 5, where they are too splayed. The additions of reeding and simple brass block caps and castors combine to make this table a near perfect example and thus a highly desirable and sought after piece. *Hugh Edmeades*

1. *Mahogany, Regency.* 54 in. wide. Dec. '84, £1,500.
2. *Mahogany, George III.* 54 in. wide. July '84, £1,500.
3. *Mahogany, George III.* 54 in. wide. Oct. '84, £1,100.
4. *Mahogany, Regency.* 57 in. wide. Feb. '85, £750.
5. *Mahogany, Regency.* 46 in. wide. Dec. '84, £800.
6. *Mahogany, Regency.* 60 in. wide. Feb. '85, £2,000.
7. *Mahogany, Regency.* 66 in. wide. Oct. '84, £9,500.

1

2

3

4

5

6

7

George III Mahogany Tallboys

As a safe guide to price, the majority of George III mahogany 'tallboys' or chests-on-chests, can be said to fetch between £1,000 and £2,000 as in Nos. 1–4; but what are the points that make one worth more than another?

Initially, before studying any detail, look at the obvious. See how well proportioned Nos. 1 and 2 are as compared with the rather dumpy appearance of Nos. 3 and 4. Nos. 1 and 4 still have their original ogee bracket feet, whereas those on Nos. 2 and 3 have had to be replaced. The drawers should be well arranged and slightly graduated; notice how the three short drawers in No. 3 are too cramped and out of proportion. However, the one saving grace of the latter, which none of the others has, is the inclusion of a brushing slide at the top of the base section.

Once the obvious has been noted, start looking for the additional decorative details such as the moulding on the cornice (Nos. 1, 2 and 4). The maker of No. 4 has gone one step further and added blind fretwork carving to the frieze. Finally, the handles and escutcheons should be studied. Even if these are not original as on Nos. 2 and 3, make sure that the replacements are in keeping and proportion to the drawers – those on No. 3 look distinctly mean and out of place.

It is only when you find all these features on one piece that the price increases dramatically. No. 5 is one such example. Beautiful proportions, original ogee bracket feet, well graduated drawers, a brushing slide, a dentil moulded cornice, blind fretwork on the angles as well as the frieze, and original and well cast swan-neck handles and escutcheons.

Hugh Edmeades

2

1

5

3

4

1. 50 in. wide. June '84, £1,800.
2. 39 in. wide. Dec. '84, £1,300.
3. 44 in. wide. June '84, £1,000.
4. 44 in. wide. Nov. '84, £1,400.
5. 44½ in. wide. Nov. '84, £2,808 (Christie's King St.).

Secretaire Bookcases

These are always popular since they combine the functions of display, writing and storage. Because of this popularity, be on your guard against buying 'marriages' – that is, be sure that the top and bottom sections started life together. There are various ways to ascertain this. If possible look at the construction of the backs: are they similar? Do the grain, colour and patina of the wood of the two match? If the top of the base is veneered all over, then it is likely to be a marriage, since if the base had been meant to carry an upper storey, then there would be no need to veneer the top part. When inspecting the base, pay particular attention to the fitted writing drawer. Is this original, or has it been made up from an ordinary drawer?

Naturally, no matter how happy a marriage or successful a conversion, the mere fact that the piece is not an original will depress the price. But what are the positive features to look for? Apart from the obvious – age, type of wood and condition – the piece must be well proportioned. No. 1 is not only beautifully proportioned, but also has astragal glazing with the added feature of flowerhead

motifs where the bars cross. No. 8 by contrast certainly is not, the top being too squat for the base. No. 3, although not badly proportioned, suffers from very dull glazing bars. Although No. 6 has delicate Gothic arched glazing, the arrangement of the drawers spoils the appearance, especially by contrast with Nos. 4, 5, and 7. The great appeal of No. 2 is the size, an example of small being beautiful.

The same is true of No. 9. Although this is a satinwood example, and built within the last thirty years, it is small, well glazed and ideally proportioned, and the price proves that it is not only 'antiques' which attract keen bidding.

Hugh Edmeades

1. *Mahogany, Regency.* 46½ in. wide. Feb. '84, £3,000.
2. *Mahogany, Regency.* 36 in. wide. Dec. '84, £2,400.
3. *Mahogany, George III.* 36 in. wide. Feb. '84, £1,900.
4. *Mahogany, George III.* 42¾ in. wide. Jan. '85, £1,600.

1

2

3

4

5

6

7

8

9

5. *Mahogany, Regency.* 42½ in. wide. Nov. '84, £1,600.

6. *Mahogany, Regency.* 42 in. wide. Jan. '84, £1,500.

7. *Mahogany, Regency.* 44 in. wide. Jan. '84, £1,500.

8. *Mahogany, Regency.* 42 in. wide. Mar. '84, £1,100.

9. *Satinwood, 20th century.* 31 in. wide. Feb. '85, £2,250.

Davenports

A Davenport is a small writing table with a sloping flap, or enclosed slide on which to write, above a solid case of drawers, usually to one side. In the late eighteenth-century records of the firm of Gillow the entry "Captain Davenport, a desk" is generally believed to have been the origination of the term. This is probably Henry William Davenport, a member of the Capesthorne family, who died in 1834.

It is unusual to find 18th Century Davenports, since they only became popular in the Regency period. The Davenport of this period is relatively plain in design (see No.9), the decorative qualities usually being limited to the choice of wood. It was not until the Victorian era that this type of furniture of questionable utility really enjoyed its heyday.

In No.1 we have an early Victorian example, which while retaining a Regency simplicity of form, gives way to a more florid taste with the decorative use of figured walnut. This transitional piece realised a handsome price of £1,600. In the slightly later No.2, we have lost the plain boxed form and progressed to a more practical shape, it is no longer necessary to slide the desk top in order to obtain a knee hole and write at it. The use of scroll supports to allow for this easier use, has not influenced the maker to elaborate on the plain sloping flap.

A far more successful variation on this development can be seen in the hinged serpentine folding flaps of Nos.3 and 4. The £700 paid for No.2 was surprisingly high for the rather crude interpretation, particularly when compared to the prices of Nos.3 and 4. These two almost identical examples (one open, one shut), show a successful resolution of the development of the projecting desk into a harmonious form. It is interesting to note how much better the use of figured wood suits the curvilinear design in Nos. 3 and 4 compared with the geometrical lines of No.1. The combination of the above points and the additional spring loaded 'pop-up' stationery compartment, a piece of classical Victorian gadgetry, make Nos. 3 and 4 desirable examples of Victorian furniture.

Interesting interpretations of the form can be found in other Victorian styles. The romantic historical revival of old English oak is represented in No.5. The eclectic application of sixteenth-century and seventeenth-century motifs to this Regency form, creates a bizarre hotch-potch. Despite the dubious aesthetics, this is an interesting piece of Victoriana.

No.6 shows a more intelligent use of decorative motifs; for instance, the elegant relationship between the inlaid palmette and the shape of the support. The Aesthetic Movement of the 1880s was a reaction to the decadent state of design implicit in No.5. Unfortunately the ebonized ground is unfashionable today, indeed such pieces are difficult to house outside a comprehensive decorative scheme. This goes some way to explaining why No.6 fetched half the price of No.5.

Moving towards the Edwardian era, we come to No. 7, an altogether dainty example, with classical inlay, slender legs and use of rosewood creating an overall lightness of effect. It is somewhat lightweight by Regency and good Victorian standards, but pleasing on its own terms.

To finish on a high note, No.8 is the apotheosis of the Victorian treatment of the form, a restrained confidence, combined with fine craftsmanship and choice of veneers, make it a splendid example.

Robert Copley and James Graham-Stewart

2

3

1

1. *Figured walnut, Victorian.* 23½ in. wide. Feb. '85, £1,600.

2. *Figured walnut, Victorian.* 21 in. wide. Jan. '85, £700.

3. *Figured walnut, Victorian*, 23 in. wide. Mar. '84, £950.

4. *Figured walnut, Victorian.* 22½ in. wide. Sept. '84, £1000.

5. *Carved oak, Victorian.* 29 in. wide. July '84, £700.

6. *Ebonized, Aesthetic Movement.* 24 in. wide. Mar. '84, £350.

7. *Rosewood, Edwardian.* 23 in. wide. Feb. '85, £700.

8. *Figured walnut, Victorian.* 25 in. wide. Dec. '84, £1,900.

9. *Rosewood, Regency.* 19½ in. wide. Apr. '83, £1,650.

4

5

6

7

8

9

Boulle

If I was asked, which of all the great types of French furniture has proved the most durable, the word 'Boulle' would leap to mind.

Although the technique of using tortoiseshell as a material for marquetry had been devised by the Italians in the previous century, it was not until the seventeenth, during the reign of Louis XIV in France, that one man brought the technique to such perfection that since then any item inlaid with tortoiseshell marquetry, be it a piece of furniture, a clock or a tea-caddy, has been given his name.

André-Charles Boulle (1643–1732), with the assistance of such designers as Jean Berain, became one of the leading cabinetmakers to the Sun King's court, as can be judged by a visit to the Wallace Collection in London. His workshop was continued by his son, Charles-Joseph Boulle, and it was there that Etienne Levasseur not only provided 'Boulle' pieces for Louis XVI, but also trained his own son so that top quality 'Boulle' would continue to be produced well into the nineteenth century, by which time there were other workshops producing 'Boulle' of varying quality. Demand for tortoiseshell inlaid furniture has continued, and even today, in Spain, large quantities are being manufactured. So when one is buying 'Boulle' one must bear in mind that it could have been made at any date from the reign of Louis XIV to that of Juan Carlos I.

Before even trying to establish the age of an item, make sure that the 'tortoiseshell' is indeed tortoiseshell, since there are pieces where the maker has simulated the material in paint. This was particularly common during the latter part of the last century when materials were in short supply. More recently, a form of resin has been used. This is relatively easy to detect, primarily because it is often too bright a red to be the real thing, and secondly because if touched with a red hot pin it will melt.

To help you date the item, take a careful look at the quality of the inlay. If it appears to be uniform and precise, probably it dates from after the second quarter of the 19th century, because up to that time, the materials were cut by hand. With the advent of technology, machines were invented that could mass produce 'sheets' of marquetry from a particular design. Hand-cut examples are much more desirable, not only because of their age, but because of their individuality.

The most common material used to divide the tortoiseshell in Boulle pieces is brass, but pewter, ivory, silver and other materials were also used. Be prepared to pay relatively more for a piece inlaid with something other than brass because these are rarer, and so appear on the market less often.

Apart from the marquetry, the majority of Boulle items are embellished with various mounts. Again the quality varies enormously and is an important factor when it comes to price. Look for bold and heavy ormolu mounts, rather than light and skimpy pieces of gilded metal which have often been added at a later date and so seem out of place.

So when you are buying an item of Boulle, there are many points to bear in mind: satisfy yourself that each part of the piece, be it the shape, the colour, the marquetry or the mounts, is of sufficient quality to merit the price you may have to pay.

Finally, bear in mind the condition. You will often find that the brass or tortoiseshell has become detached from the carcase and is sometimes totally missing; remember that it is expensive to have individual pieces recut when it comes to restoration. Again, satisfy yourself that the expense of the restoration work will be justified, should you wish to re-sell the item. Where possible consult a restorer before actually buying.

No. 1 is a good example of the restrained use of marquetry decoration. Note how the maker has taken the trouble to inlay the sides as compared to Nos. 3 and 4 where you see a profusion of uniform scrolls and arabesques, but only on the front. Shape is an important factor – note the graceful outline of No. 2 compared to the harsh outlines of Nos. 4 and 5. See how skimpy the mounts appear on Nos. 3, 4 and 5 compared to the bold examples on No. 2. Articles were often made in pairs (Nos. 3 and 7). Be prepared to pay up to three times as much for a pair as for a similar single item.

Hugh Edmeades

1

1. *Bureau, late 17th century.* 41 in. wide. Dec.
   '84, £19,440 (Christie's King St.).
2. *Bureau plat,* mid 19th century. 50 in. wide.
   May '84, £1,500.
3. *One of a pair of cabinets, mid 19th century.*
   34in. wide. Feb. '84, £3,000.
4. *Bonheur-du-jour, late 19th century.* 36 in.
   wide. May '84, £1,200.
5. *Card table, late 19th century.* 35 in. wide.
   Nov. '84, £1,200.
6. *Bureau à cylindre, late 19th century.* 35 in.
   wide. Mar. '85, £1,100.
7. *One of a pair of cabinets, Napoleon III.* 29. in.
   wide. May '85, £1,600.

3

4

2

5

6

7

George III Mahogany Serpentine Chests

Many features on English furniture of the eighteenth century were borrowed and adapted from the French. In all the examples of serpentine chests shown here, unlike their French relations, curvilinear outlines are restricted to the top and the front. This is generally the case, but in some instances the sides of the top are shaped, and more rarely the carcase as well.

The use of fluted canted angles in No. 1 overcomes the problem of transition from curved front to straight sides. There are several methods of decorating the canted angles so as to emphasize the front and draw the eye away from the plain sides, the rarest being the use of inlay. The ogee bracket feet in No. 1 are fairly bold for the close fitting top, but basically it is an 'honest' piece, dating from the 1760s, with the exception of course, of the knob handles.

No. 2 is a fake, made up out of some old pieces. The top was of good quality – note the serpentine outlines on the sides – but unfortunately it does not sit happily on the carcase. The canted eared angles of the top do not correspond to the fret carved angles flanking the drawers. Above the drawers there is a brushing slide (sometimes plain wood or inset with baize); this a popular feature, and replaced the folding tops found on bachelors' chests earlier in the century. The size in this particular chest is paramount, 46½ in. wide being much too large for popular taste. It is, therefore, of little surprise that No. 3, at only 36 in. fetched £1,800 as opposed to £650. Having said that, No. 3 had only been reduced and reconstructed rather than made up out of odds and ends.

The use of figured wood, and how it is employed, is also instrumental in influencing the price. No. 4 is particularly successful in this respect, as the flowing grain complements the front well. It is a very simple but subtle piece and has not suffered any alterations, merely reinforcement to the bracket feet.

A lot of serpentine chests were made as gentlemen's dressing chests. No. 5 is an example of this, the top drawer with a fitted interior with lidded compartments and an easel supported mirror. In this instance the drawer was covered by a brushing slide, which could be pushed back to reveal the compartments. The condition was not very good, with pieces of veneer missing, but overall it was of good quality and size. The boxwood lines and the rosewood crossbanding are probably later additions. The potential for it is good – a little restoration will go a long way – hence a price of £3,000.

No. 6 dates from the end of the George III period. It is interesting to note how the undulating apron enhances the overall effect. The longer leg also makes it higher than its predecessors. The only defects on this piece are the 'associated' (not originally for this piece, but of the same age) top, and the knob handles. It realized £3,800.

Finally, beware of copies. No. 7 has the appearance of a George III chest, but was made during the early part of this century. *Robert Copley*

1

2

1. 41 in. wide. Feb. '84, £1,600.
2. 46½ in. wide. Sep. '84, £650.
3. 36 in. wide. Nov. '84, £1,800.
4. 43½ in. wide. Oct. '84, £4,104 (Christie's King St.).
5. 36 in. wide. Feb. '85, £3,000
6. 38 in. wide. Mar. '85, £3,800.
7. *Reproduction*. 38 in. wide. Apr. '85, £900.

Chiffoniers 1800–1850

It was in the Regency drawing room that the chiffonier first came into its own. It served as a small decorative bookcase.

No. 1 shows a typical example, with the useful addition of a secretaire drawer. Characteristically of the early Regency, it borrows its decoration, namely anthemions, vitruvian scrolls and paw feet, from a variety of antique sources. For a piece that combines so many characteristics of the form, the £2,000 was by no means expensive.

Despite the neat appearance of No. 2, it had been made up at a later date, possibly from the top section of a clothes press or a similarly less saleable item. The oddly placed scallop shelves are an easily added refinement. The fact that they are presently in vogue, and the ease with which they can be recreated from larger pieces, makes chiffoniers a prime target for the faker. Nevertheless, the end result was an elegant furnishing piece; it still made £1,000.

By comparison, No. 3, a rather plainer but unsullied piece, proved more desirable at the end of the day. The size and condition of No. 4 led to a lower price of £950.

Moving on from the Regency, No. 5, dating from the 1830s, lacked any applied decoration, relying on minimal carving and the use of a burr wood. The prices of £750 on this and No. 6 reflect the state of the market in early '84. It is reasonable to presume that they might have realized between £1,000 and £1,500 a year later.

The use of lacquered panels and ornate mounts was more expensive for the cabinetmaker, so it was not surprising that the extremely successful combination in No. 7 produced £5,500. The overall condition was by no means pristine, but this did not outweigh the advantages.   *Robert Copley*

1. *Rosewood, Regency.* 29 in. wide. Dec. '84, £2,000.

2. *Rosewood, early 19th century.* 35½ in. wide. Sept. '84, £1,000.

3. *Mahogany, Regency.* 28½ in. wide. Mar. '84, £1,600.

3

2

1

4: *Rosewood, Regency.* 53 in. wide. Aug. 84, £950.

5. *Birds-eye maple, Early Victorian.* 41 in. wide. Jan. '84, £750.

6. *Rosewood, William IV.* 43½ in. wide. Jan. '84, £750.

7. *Rosewood, Regency.* 56¾ in. wide. Mar. '84, £5,500.

Pembroke Tables

The use of a proper name in the description of a piece of furniture usually derives from an initial commission. Thus, in the case of Pembroke tables, Thomas Sheraton in his *Cabinet Dictionary* describes them as being 'a kind of breakfast table from the name of the lady who first gave orders for one of them, and who probably gave the first idea of such a table to the workman', namely the Countess of Pembroke (1737–1831).

In my opinion the finest item of furniture that we sold in 1984 was a Pembroke table (No. 1). It shows an excellent combination of the simple qualities of English cabinetmaking in the latter stages of the eighteenth century, with inspiration from the French Rococo movement. The graceful serpentine top, the shaped frieze and the lightly fluted slender cabriole legs, are all features synonymous with the Hepplewhite period.

Although No. 2 had the serpentine top, the rather severe base was not original, and this, with the variation in the colour of the mahogany, gave the table a disjointed appearance. No. 3 is probably the sort of table the Countess had in mind and is similar to Thomas Chippendale's designs for breakfast tables. The fractional difference in price between Nos. 2 and 3, despite the former's dubious construction, is accounted for by the serpentine top on No. 2 and the rather mean flaps on No. 3.

No. 4 is the standard design which immediately springs to mind when the term 'Pembroke table' is mentioned. In date and quality it compares well with No. 5, but the large price difference is not only due to the fact that the latter is made of satinwood, but also because it has an oval top which runs a close second in desirability to the serpentine top as in Nos. 1 and 2.

Pembroke tables lend themselves well to decorative features such as marquetry or painting, and this enhances their value. Nos. 4 and 6, although of similar construction, show a marked difference in price simply because No. 6 has been decorated with painted floral sprays, albeit at a later date. No. 7 has again been embellished with subsequent floral painting, but here the satinwood and the

oval top make it more desirable than No. 6.

The size of Pembroke tables, as of most types of furniture, also plays an important part when it comes to pricing. Both Nos. 8 and 9 have one or more of the decorative features already mentioned, but are considerably smaller than the other examples: even though they date from the Victorian and Edwardian eras, their prices compare very favourably with the earlier examples, and this is largely due to their dainty appearance.

No. 10 is the only Pembroke table

illustrated with a central form of support as opposed to four legs. Despite the rich patination of the mahogany and the excellent quality of craftsmanship, it fetched only £600, illustrating that, as a general rule, the centrally supported tables are less popular.   *Robert Copley*

1. *Mahogany, George III.* 40 in. Mar '84, £4,000.
2. *Mahogany, early 19th century.* 42 in. Dec. '84, £1,100.
3. *Mahogany, early George III.* 36 in. Oct. '84, £1,000.
4. *Mahogany, George III.* 38 in. June '84, £550.

5. *Satinwood, George III.* 38 in. House sale, Yotes Court, Kent, Apr. '84, £2,052.

6. *Mahogany, George III.* 40 in. Aug. '84, £900.

7. *Satinwood, George III.* 38 in. July '84, £1,500.

8. *Rosewood, Victorian.* 28 in. Nov. '84, £750.

9. *Satinwood, Edwardian.* 28 in. Oct. '84, £750.

10. *Mahogany, Regency.* 41 in. Sept. '84, £600.

Later Dutch Marquetry

If you like your furniture to be in original condition, then with the exceptions of Nos. 1–3, you can ignore these illustrations, simply because the marquetry decoration has been added at a later date. Most Dutch furniture made in the late eighteenth century and early nineteenth century relied for its effect on the shape of the piece and the grain of the wood, as in No. 1, which is an example of a piece that escaped the late nineteenth-century Dutch craze for smothering all earlier types of furniture with marquetry. No. 2 dates in design, construction and decoration from this period, whereas No. 3 is original only in that it is an example of a modern piece made in Italy to cater for the demand for marquetry furniture, based on earlier designs such as No. 4.

However, having said that, there is a lively and buoyant market for 'later inlaid' Dutch furniture, and the price is largely dependent on the quality of the marquetry detail. Comparing Nos. 5 and 6, you might think that there is too much detail on the former, but at least here you find birds and butterflies rather than

just the monotonous foliage of the latter. In No. 7 the birds and butterflies have room to fly and to breathe, but the skimpy inlay on the drawer fronts and uprights flanking the mirrors has only been added for the sake of it.

Neither was seat furniture safe from the marquetry craze (Nos. 8 and 9), and although the detail on the latter is of good quality – note the musical instruments – the comparatively low price was surely due to the fact that benches are not comfortable to sit on.

The most common piece of later Dutch marquetry seen on the market is the bureau. Of those illustrated here (dating from the late eighteenth/early nineteenth century), note the lack of shape in No. 10 and how little of the original veneer has escaped the inlayer's knife. It compares poorly with Nos. 11 and 12, where not only do the fronts have some movement, but also the marquetry is much more restrained. Both these points are pertinent to No. 13, but notice here how, rather than simply inlaying the drawers individually, the ebeniste has treated the front as a whole and has added the marquetry 'sans traverse', thus giving the piece a far more unified and pleasing aspect.

Hugh Edmeades

1. *Oak bureau*, late 18th century. 41 in. wide. Jan. '85, £850.

2. *Ebonized cabinet*, late 19th century. 44 in. wide. Mar. '85, £4,500.

3. *Walnut and oak bookcase*, 20th century. 101 in. wide. Mar. '84, £1,300.

4. *Walnut display cabinet*, 19th century. 62 in. wide. June. '84, £3,800.

5. *Walnut corner cabinet*, 19th century. 40 in. wide. Jan. '84, £2,400.

7

8

6

10

9

11

12

13

6. *Mahogany escritoire*, 19th century. 41 in. wide. Nov. '84, £1,500.

7. *Pair of mahogany consoles*, 19th century. 30 in. wide. Feb. '85, £1,900.

8. *Set of 8 walnut dining chairs*. Aug. '84, £2,200.

9. *Mahogany settle*, 19th century. 69 in. Feb. '85, £1,000.

10. *Walnut cylinder bureau*. 39 in. wide. Jan. '85, £2,000.

11. *Mahogany cylinder bureau*. 48 in. wide. Mar. '85, £3,200.

12. *Walnut bureau*. 47 in. wide. Mar. '84, £3,200.

13. *Mahogany bureau*. 51 in. wide. June '84, £3,800.

Nos. 10–13 are all 18th/19th century.

Miniature Furniture

Most miniature furniture was executed by apprentice cabinetmakers, under instruction to produce replicas of standard size pieces. In miniature, as with normal size furniture, the standard of craftsmanship inevitably varies, but since the apprentices were making test pieces, it is generally high.

The illustrations shown are all the work of Joseph Nolan (1878–1948), who was a member of the Nolan family firm of coachbuilders in Dublin. The pieces were not made as apprentice furniture, but as a hobby.

When they came up for sale considerable interest and idle fascination was shown not only by the usual furniture buyers, but a broader spectrum of potential collectors. It is interesting to note that the prices realized on the five items correspond to their size; the larger they were the more they fetched. This is certainly not a coincidence, but one must bear in mind that Nos. 1, 2 and 5 are all better or closer representations of eighteenth-century pieces, while the bookcase, No. 3, has only a tenuous link

in design to an original. In fact in that respect, the bureau, No. 4, with its squat cabriole legs, is a bit of a muddle, neither an eighteenth-century nor an Edwardian design, but an Edwardian interpretation of a Georgian design. In the same October '84 sale a miniature South German walnut commode of three drawers with lozenge pattern inlay, dating from the eighteenth century, was also on offer. It was not of the same high quality as the Nolan pieces, but had age on its side. However, the £650 that it realized illustrates that in this field age doesn't always go before beauty.   *Robert Copley*

1. *Mahogany bookcase inlaid with chequered lines and thuya bands.* 31 in. Oct. '84, £1,000.
2. *Mahogany linen press lined and banded with satinwood.* 22 in. Oct. '84, £800.
3. *Mahogany bookcase with thuya and rosewood bands.* 23 in. Oct. '84, £750.
4. *Mahogany and inlaid bureau.* 16½ in. Oct. '84, £600.
5. *Mahogany and inlaid longcase clock.* 21½ in. Oct. '84, £420.

1

4

2

3

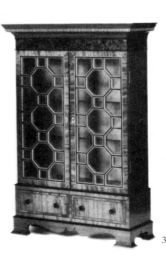

5

Card Tables

Before the advent of radio and television, one of the principal entertainments in the home was playing card games, so the demand for pieces of furniture on which to play these games was enormous, which accounts for the large numbers of such tables that appear on the market these days. Because of this, the price of a card table is largely due to its decorative qualities rather than to rarity or age. Hence, No. 1, although the most 'antique' of those illustrated here, fetched the lowest price. In design it is similar to No. 2, but notice how the addition of cabriole legs and inlaid decoration on the latter increases the price. Comparing No. 3 with No. 4, the £300 price difference is due not only to the painted decoration, but also to the fact that No. 4 is veneered in satinwood rather than mahogany. The preference for a centre pedestal support during Queen Victoria's reign is seen in No. 5. This example is made of rosewood, but more importantly, note the quality and the crispness of the carving on the nicely shaped frieze and on the scrolling feet. You might find it surprising that the higher price was paid for the youngest table, No. 6. This is stamped Edwards and Roberts and is of the quality one expects of that firm, and proves that quality of workmanship can be a more desirable feature than age. So far all the examples have had the simple hinged foldover tops; I have included No. 7 to show a good example of the 'envelope' top card table with its four-hinged quartered top. Again, comparatively speaking, of no great age, the quality and decorative features more than compensate.

Hugh Edmeades

1. *Mahogany, early George III.* 30 in. Mar. '85, £650.
2. *Mahogany and inlaid, mid-19th century.* 31 in. Dec. '84, £1,000.
3. *Mahogany, George III.* 36 in. Oct. '84, £700.
4. *Satinwood, George III, later painted border.* 36 in. Jan. '84, £1,000.
5. *Rosewood, Victorian.* 36 in. Mar. '84, £650.
6. *Rosewood and inlaid, Edwardian,* 36 in. Mar. '85, £1,300.
7. *Thuya wood and ebonized, late 19th century.* 22 in. Feb. '85, £600.

Miscellany

1. *Victorian velvet upholstered sociable of trefoil shape*. June '84, £1,300.
   Victorian modesty at its height: people could sit in close proximity, but actual physical contact was awkward.

2. *Bathchair*. Jan. '85, £380.
   Unusual to find one dating from 1930s in such perfect condition. Somebody was planning on a comfortable retirement.

3. *Dutch Giltwood child's sleigh, carved with figures, animals and cornucopia, and painted with rural scenes*, 19th century. June '84, £1,350.

4. *Bavarian carved walnut hat and stick stand, 19th century*. June '84, £1,550.

5. *Chinese rosewood opium bed, 19th century*. 78 in × 50 in. wide. Feb. '84, £1,100.

6. *A pair of pine columns with Ionic capitals*. 115 in. Nov. '84, £1,150.
   Architectural fittings such as these and the Renaissance style door are increasing in popularity, not only with interior decorators but specialist firms offering such items.

7. *Siamese red and gilt lacquered howdah*. 81 in × 34 in. wide. Dec. '84, £1,600.

8. *Florentine blue painted and gilded doorcase and door of Renaissance style*. 106 in. Feb. '84, £1,900.

9. *Mahogany campaign chair*. Dec. '84, £500.
In David Lean's film of *Passage to India* it is
possible to spot an almost identical chair
in the sitting room of the schoolmaster
Fielding.

10. *A full-sized ebonized and giltwood billiard
table, stamped Waring & Gillow*. Oct. '84,
£19,000.
Quite literally, you could not give full-
sized billiard tables away fifteen years
ago. This piece is obviously exceptional,
but even plain and stolid tables now find
new homes.

11. *Not a Louis XVI secretaire à abbatant, but a
safe, fitted with 2 doors*. 56½ in. × 32 in.
Oct. '84, £1,950.

12. *Early Victorian mahogany weighing chair*.
38½ in. wide. Dec. '84, £1,500.
These chairs are often called Jockey Scales
– it would have been quite a jockey who
weighed the 16 stone plus that this chair
was capable of weighing. It was
purchased on behalf of an American
Museum.

13. *Victorian burr walnut Davenport in the Louis
XV style, of serpentine and bombe outlines,
inlaid with marquetry and tulipwood bands
and applied with gilt metal mounts*. 26½ in.
Mar '85, £4,400.
A most unusual and rare piece.

14. *French mahogany framed gaming table, the
inlaid top depicting racing*. 72 in. square.
Oct. '84, £2,800.

15. *Fixtures and fittings of a jewellers' shop*. Oct. '84.
The 41 lots, which varied from showcases
to neon light signs to mahogany and acid
etched glass panelling, totalled over
£45,000.

2. *Western Ceramics and Glass*

Introduction
by Paul Barthaud

In the pages that follow, we have chosen to concentrate on areas which represent items which you are likely to find, and which are types of their markets. We have highlighted not only the established markets, but also new and potential ones.

Two of the established markets are eighteenth-century blue and white porcelain, and wine glasses. Many of these pieces have been prized collectors' items from new, and this year has seen high prices being paid for good examples as fewer pieces come onto the market and fewer still are in fine or perfect condition.

Newer markets which have developed over, say, the last ten years would include Bohemian glass, Samson and Wemyss. These are primarily highly decorative objects which reflect the current fashion for colourful antiques. Samson porcelain and Bohemian glass are both worthy of more serious attention and have the potential to evolve into long-lasting, established markets.

Royal Doulton figures are an even newer market which is attracting large sums of money for single pieces. It is broadly based and is unlikely to suffer the fate of that in Fairings, which seemed to wither for lack of both buyers and objects after having peaked very quickly between 1980 and 1982. It is too early to predict how the market for Doulton will develop, or how far prices will continue to rise. If it continues to attract more Continental buyers, then we will certainly see new record prices over the next twelve months. I feel that this market now has too much support – and money – tied up in it, to see a serious downturn in prices within the next two years. After that time this too might be considered as being established and its long-term future would be assured.

I am often asked by people who are 'interested in antiques' for my opinion on what they should buy. My

1 & 2. *Seated porcelain figure.* Oct. '84, £35.
  The price for this figure, which was sold as a part lot with two other porcelain figures (p. 57, Nos. 13, 14), , is not why it is illustrated here. It is shown as a warning to the unwary. The enigmatic smile should not prevent you from looking at the base where one finds that the mark has been removed. This figure may well be resold as Samson or Continental or Chinese. The mark probably read 'Made in Japan'.

reply is that they should first like the object. This statement of the obvious conceals sound economic advice. If you have bought an object which you enjoy looking at and handling, then when you come to dispose of it there is a good chance that other people (now potential buyers) will also appreciate it and pay a good price accordingly, but if, after studying the market, you have bought for investment an absolute horror which you yourself dislike, then there is a good chance that nobody else will like it either, and it will not have increased in price when you come to sell.

3

4

3. *Very rare Staffordshire equestrian figure of Sir Robert Peel facing to the left and wearing top hat and tails, with the name in gilt. 13½ in. Feb. '85, £3,500.*
This is a world record price for a single Staffordshire portrait figure. There is a variant in which the figure wears a cloak over one shoulder. This version realizes between £150 and £250, and four were brought to us for sale in the week following the sale of this figure. If there is a moral to be drawn then perhaps it should be to study photographs of expensive objects with care and not make hasty comparisons.

4. *Royal Doulton group of the Flower Seller's Children, HN 1342. 7¾ in. May '85, £80.*
This group was produced in five variations between 1921 and 1949. It is not of the type which I would describe as rare, and this is reflected in the price. However, it does have charm, and is supposed to have been sketched by the designer, Harradine, on the cuff of an evening shirt when he observed these children while passing through Piccadilly.

5. *Opaque twist wine glass, the bell bowl supported on a knopped stem and high conical foot. 7 in. Feb. '85, £65.*
This type of well-proportioned period glass will always find interested buyers, although it is unlikely to show an enormous increase in value over the short period.

6. *Pair of amber-flash oviform jugs cut with oval panels, engraved with named buildings between facets. 9¾ in. Apr. '85, £180.*

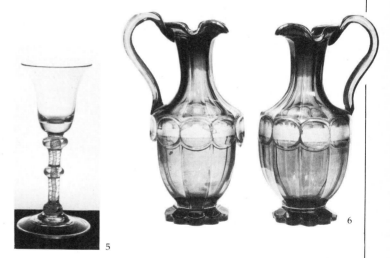

5

6

Having decided on the 'what', the next question is usually 'where'. I would recommend the first-time buyer to go to a reputable specialist dealer or saleroom, and to ask for as much detail as possible with regard to authenticity and condition. Contrary to popular opinion there are very few 'bargains' to be had in street markets or antique fairs – unless you have a specialist knowledge which is superior to that of the stall holder!

A market which has increasing prices dependent on the condition of the objects is open to some abuse by the unscrupulous. This year has seen further improvements in restoration techniques on ceramics with the use of modern chemicals and compounds. There is now no easy way to spot good restoration, which can fool both the experienced and the novice, but I would suggest that you beware of a 'bargain', and are not satisfied with the often used phrase that 'it was purchased as perfect'. Also do not be misled by the suggestion that restoration can produce an article which is as valuable as a perfect example. Restored or not, the piece is still damaged and should be priced accordingly. Nevertheless, a 'good' restoration will leave an item, particularly a figure, looking more presentable, and naturally this will help the price.

My own view of the art market is biased. I find its shifting prices and judgements a constant source of fascination, and the popular misconceptions an equally constant source of amusement. You do not have to be 'trained in fine art appreciation' to like or to own any of the pieces illustrated in the following articles. All you have to do is use your own judgement as to what is attractive, and not be put off by specialists (including me) when we pronounce some things fine and others ordinary. It is all a matter of opinion shaped by established traditions and personal taste. If, for example, you like plain white biscuit porcelain figures then buy them. Just because they are unpopular at present does not damn them forever. Who can tell whether a later edition of this book may not write them up as the new market of the year?

I have used the word 'market' frequently and this is intentional. To examine, say, the price of a single Samson vase which may sell for £200 against an estimate of £40, and conclude that there is a substantial increase in the prices of Samson would be incorrect. It would only show that that particular vase had sold very well. But a series of prices with the same difference of estimate to final price could mean a reappraisal of this market was under way. Thus there are many generalizations in the following articles, which may appear to be incorrect from a reader's personal knowledge of an individual price. This simply underlines the fact that there are no absolute, hard-and-fast rules about prices in the art market.

English Blue and White Porcelain of the Eighteenth Century

1. *Worcester leaf-shaped pickle dish with tendril handle and raised veining, painted with a bird and butterfly among flowers, painters mark, c. 1758. 5 in. wide. Jan '85, £480.*
   Although this dish is about the same date as No. 3, and only slightly larger, this is a more uncommon shape with a more elaborate pattern – thus a two times multiple in price.

2. *Lowestoft feeding-cup of bucket form painted with flowering shrubs in a fenced garden, the top and spout with flower-sprays, painter's numeral 5, c. 1765. 3 in. Christie's King Street, Feb. '84, £670.*
   This is a rare shape which is reflected in the price.

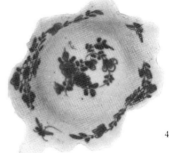

The range of porcelain produced in England during the eighteenth century was very wide, from utilitarian chamber pots to decorative figures, some of which are very thickly made and clumsy. Most people can appreciate the coloured wares; with their rich burnished golds and bright enamels they make the blue and white examples appear dull by comparison – at least on first impression. I would say that the appeal of blue and white porcelain to buyers is at a deeper level, the cobalt (which produced the blue colour) combining with the 'soft' glazes to give a pleasing 'feel'. It is these qualities, as well as rarity, which combine to produce high prices.

There was probably no porcelain made in England prior to 1745, and most buyers are not interested in pieces produced after 1785. This seems a narrow area on which to concentrate – but do not be misled! Within this time factories came and went with great rapidity. For example, the Bristol factory, termed 'Lunds Bristol' to differentiate it from later concerns, was only in production for about three years. It produced some beautiful blue and white wares – particularly sauceboats, which are very rare, with an example selling at Christies' King Street in 1982 for £1,620.

To be able to recognize the products of this period is a skill which can be acquired by reference to museums, specialist dealers and auction previews. But then to attribute them to their exact manufactory is extremely difficult and often produces disagreements between specialists. I do not intend to open the Pandora's Box of 'who made what', but I will make some general points as a guide

to buying. There are several excellent specialist books to help with a study of the subject, but your best education will be your own mistakes!

Of the surviving pieces currently on the market the largest proportion were produced by the Worcester factory, with printed examples far outnumbering the earlier painted pieces. You can identify a piece as being printed by close examination of the design. If you can discern straight lines in the make-up of the picture, then it is a printed example. This observation will directly affect the value, with printed items at a level of, say, two-thirds of similar but painted examples. However, as with any generalization, there are exceptions, and some rare prints realize high prices. The various printed designs, their background and identification is, in my opinion, such a large area that it could constitute a market on its own merits, but this is for the future perhaps.

The major influence on designs was Chinese, with some charming scenes of Oriental figures in river landscapes or at leisure in gardens. Even the animal subjects have an Oriental feel, with birds perched on pierced rockwork among bamboo and chrysanthemums – not an average English garden view. In commercial terms these more elaborate designs are preferred to simple floral subjects.

The products of the more obscure, and potentially rarer, factories are not automatically more expensive. In January 1985 we sold a Penningtons Liverpool milk-jug for £75, and a Worcester milk-jug printed with a common pattern for £50. But for every one example of the Liverpool jug you will find ten of the latter. So this price comparison should not be seen as a reflection on the quality of the products of the smaller factories, but as an illustration of buying trends. In general the large number of potential buyers of Worcester porcelain will provide a better market than buyers for smaller factories. This preference – fashion, trend, whatever – allows a newcomer to choose an area of the market which not only appeals to him as an individual, but also suits his pocket. It also means that if the choice later proves to have been in advance of the market, he will see an appreciation in price of the purchases. Using this example we could say that the blue and white porcelains of Penningtons Liverpool, and the other Liverpool factories, appear to be undervalued and that careful buying of good examples would be advantageous. However, no such buying patterns have emerged this year for an individual factory.

Dated pieces always meet with strong bidding. This is not only because an actual date is a better guide to the year of manufacture then details of design, shape or other important facts, but one dated piece can be used to attribute similar items accurately, and is therefore an important 'yardstick'. The majority of pieces do not bear factory marks, and those items which are marked should still be questioned. The crescent mark used on Worcester porcelains from about 1750 is consistent, but was copied by Lowestoft and other factories, and I have even observed it on Continental wares.

In general terms the products of the 1750s are more expensive than later examples. The early pieces are painted designs of good quality with dark, strong tones of blue. The later pieces tend to be printed, with a decline in the blue from about 1775, giving a weak or watery appearance with a feeling of mass production.

Auction reports in the newspapers might give the impression that all eighteenth-century English porcelain is expensive. This is incorrect. Certainly some fine pieces of Chelsea or Worcester can realize thousands of pounds, and yes the market for blue and white examples has been very strong this year, but with prices for quality pieces starting from about £200 I do not feel that it is prohibitive – but then I'm not impartial. Not many areas of the antiques market today stand comparison with eighteenth-century English blue and white porcelain. Currently you can purchase rare, if slightly imperfect, examples for £50 or less. However, this may not last . . .
Paul Barthaud

5

6

7

3. *Worcester geranium moulded butter boat painted with two butterflies among flower sprays, painter's mark, c. 1758. 3 in. wide.* Mar. '85, £220.

4. *Worcester geranium moulded butter boat painted with flowers and trailing foliage, painter's mark, c. 1758. 3 in. wide.* Jan. '85, £200.
No. 4 is more desirable as it is larger and has a better design. The lower price could be explained by the time lapse of three months at a time of rising prices.

5. *Two Lowestoft spirally moulded cream-jugs painted with flower sprays, c. 1765. 3½ in. wide.* Jan. '85, £100 (left) and £45 (right). This is a good comparison for the difference in prices due to damage.

6. *Worcester shell-shaped sweetmeat dish painted with a bird perched on pierced rockwork, c. 1758. 5 in. wide.* Mar. '85, £280.

7. *Worcester shell-shaped sweetmeat dish, c. 1755. 6 in. wide.* Christie's King Street, Oct. '84, £324.
Nos. 6 and 7 were both chipped in the same

area of their rims and to a similar extent. The dish sold at King Street is more desirable in terms of size, moulding and date. The other dish was a stronger tone of blue. Allowing the 8% buyer's premium added to the former this gives a price difference of about £50.

8 & 9. *Worcester documentary miniature root pattern saucer inscribed C + S 1758, 3 in. diam., and a miniature sugar-bowl and cover en suite, painter's marks, c. 1758, 2 in. diam.* Christie's King Street, Oct '84, £4,320. 18th-century Worcester miniatures are rare and highly desirable, and with the date on the saucer this lot realized 60% more than the top estimate.

10. *Worcester egg-cup painted with trailing flowering branches beneath a cell-pattern rim, crescent mark, c. 1765. 2½ in.* Christie's King Street, Oct. '84, £486.
A good example of a rare shape attracting strong interest even though there was a repaired chip to the foot.

8   9   10

English Blue and White (cont.)

11   12   13

14

15

16

11. *Worcester pleated baluster cream-jug with double scroll handle painted with an Oriental fishing from a river island, another in a sampan beneath pendant willow branches, painter's mark, c. 1745 (slight chip and crack to lip). 3¾ in. Christie's King Street, Oct '84, £454.*

12. *Worcester moulded oval sauceboat painted with a pagoda beneath a pine-tree and fisherman in a sampan, painter's mark beneath the handle, c. 1754 (two slight rim chips). 6 in. wide. Christie's King Street, Oct. '84, £389.*

13. *Worcester spirally moulded milk-jug of 'Chelsea Ewer' type with scroll handle, painted with trailing flowering branches on one side enclosing diaper-pattern, crescent mark, c. 1765. 3½ in. Christie's King Street, Oct. '84, £594.*

14. *Bow powder-blue ground egg-cup painted with two ogival panels of flowers divided by similar circular panels, mock-Oriental four-character mark, c. 1760. 2½ in. Christie's King Street, Dec. '84, £702.*
    This Bow example is arguably rarer than the comparable Worcester piece illustrated (No. 10).

15. *Worcester shallow saucer-dish painted with the Dragon Pattern, crescent mark, c. 1765. 7¼ in. diam. Christie's King Street, Oct. '84, £864 (Phelps Collection).*
    This price was 50% above the top estimate and reflects the increased interest aroused by sales of collections.

16. *Caughley miniature part dinner-service painted with grasses and houses on domed river islands comprising two quatrefoil sauce-tureens and covers (one cover chipped), two sauce boats (one foot chipped, the other cracked), four oval dishes in two sizes and 21 plates (three with minute rim chips), most pieces with blue S mark, c. 1785. Christie's King Street, Feb. '84, £2,052.*

17. *Worcester shell-moulded oval sauceboat painted with an Oriental in a garden and another fishing from a river island, crescent mark, c. 1760. Christie's King Street, Oct. '84, £432 (Phelps Collection).*

18. *Worcester shell-moulded cream-boat with Lamprey handle and moulded entwined dolphins beneath the lip, blue crescent mark, c. 1765. 3½ in. wide. Christie's King Street, Oct. '84, £972 (Phelps Collection).*

19. *Worcester baluster mug printed with a loose bouquet of flowers, (slight crack to rim, minute star crack to base), c. 1765. 4¾ in. Christie's King Street, Oct. '84, £173 (Phelps Collection).*

17   18   19

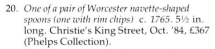

20. *One of a pair of Worcester navette-shaped spoons (one with rim chips) c. 1765. 5½ in. long. Christie's King Street, Oct. '84, £367 (Phelps Collection).*

21. *Worcester sauce-spoon (slight rim chip to bowl), c. 1770. 5¼ in. long. Christie's King Street, Oct. '84, £238 (Phelps Collection).*

22. *One of a pair of Blind Earl sweetmeat-dishes with twig handles (one with slight rim chips, both with buds chipped), c. 1760. 6½ in. long. Christie's King Street, Oct. '84, £972 (Phelps Collection).*

23. *Worcester oviform teapot and cover with faceted spout and loop handle painted with three birds in a tree, the reverse with a loose bouquet and scattered flower-sprays (cover damaged), painter's mark, c. 1758. 4¼ in. wide. Christie's King Street, Oct. '84, £562 (Phelps Collection).*

24. *Worcester cylindrical mug painted with an Oriental in a garden and another standing by a vase of flowers on a table within ogival cartouches reserved on a cracked ice ground (crack to top of handle), crescent mark, c. 1765. 4¾ in. Christie's King Street, Oct. '84, £702 (Phelps Collection). This lot realized 54% more than the top estimate.*

25. *Worcester flared cylindrical tankard with strap handle painted with the Root Pattern (star crack to base, firing crack to top of handle), painter's mark to base of handle, c. 1755. 5½ in. Christie's King Street, Oct. '84, £732.*

26. *Worcester patty-pan painted in a pale blue with two fishermen, the reverse with three foliage sprays, two different painter's marks, c. 1754. Christie's King Street, Oct. '84, £2,592. Unrecorded pattern.*

27. *Bow oval meat-dish painted with the Golfer and Caddy pattern, c. 1760. 10½ in. wide. Mar. '85, £220.*
    This dish was thickly potted with 'staining' to the glaze and a rim chip. This did not dissuade the market from bidding almost double the estimate of £80–£120.

28. *Worcester bowl painted with the Twisted Root pattern, painter's mark, c. 1758. 4 in. diam. Mar. '85, £500.*
    This pattern is fairly rare, and is always popular when offered at auction. The estimate was £300–£400.

29. *Worcester teabowl and saucer painted with the Cormorant pattern of a bird on rockwork with a fisherman in the distance, painter's mark, c. 1754. Saucer 4¾ in. diam. Mar. '85, £280.*
    This is a good example of where quality can overcome some of the market resistance to damage. The saucer was broken and glued, and the estimate reflected the condition. The bird in the pattern, although in an unlikely twisted stance, gives a feeling of movement which is a delight to the eye.

English Delft

1. *Lambeth delft blue-dish portrait charger, painted predominantly in blue with King William enriched in yellow and manganese within a yellow line and blue-dash rim, c. 1690 (cracks and rim restored). 13¼ in. diam. Christie's King Street. June '85 £2,788.*

2. *Lambeth delft blue-dash portrait charger, painted predominantly in blue with Queen Anne, the orb and sceptre enriched in yellow, standing in a green field flanked by sponged trees, c. 1705 (restored). 13¾ in. diam. Christie's King Street, June '85, £2,899.*

3. *Bristol blue-dash Adam and Eve charger, the ill-fated couple to either side of a massive tree hung with striped fruit and surrounded by sponged green trees, c. 1720 (chipped and cracked, glaze flaking to rim). 13½ in. diam. Christie's King Street, June '85, £781.*

These illustrations show the general trends in decoration and subjects of English delft across the major part of the period of production.

The commemorative influence was very strong from the earliest years, and currently prices can be seen to be very high. Royalty subject chargers tend to make the highest prices on a regular basis. No. 4 is a good example of a rare factory, Brislington, coupled with a desirable subject. The estimate of £800–£1,200 reflected poor condition, yet it still realized a quite remarkable £10,593.

The rarest item illustrated, No. 7, clearly shows the influence of the Italian Maiolica, with its broad lines and classical and mythological subjects. This piece was also dated, which is important for attribution (a far from easy exercise with English delft) of similar objects. The price of just under £20,000 was double the top estimate.

Drug jars (albarelli) were produced in large numbers. The wet drug jars were spouted, and the jars for dry drugs were oviform, cylindrical or waisted. Winged cherubs are often found as decoration on these jars. Dishes and plates form the largest category of surviving pieces, and shaped items such as shoes or wall pockets are rare.

The prices at the lower end of the market, under £100, have not shown an increase in the last twelve months. However, large dishes of fairly simple design in the £120–£150 bracket are proving increasingly popular. We may see this area improve in price during the next year.

Paul Barthaud

4. *Brislington delft charger, painted in blue and yellow with a portrait of Charles II within a border of tulips, c. 1680 (riveted). 13½ in. diam. Christie's King Street, Mar. '85, £10,593.*

5. *London delft charger, painted in blue, manganese and yellow with a portrait of King William seated below looped curtains, c. 1690 (triangular crack, minor rim chips). 13¾ in. diam. Christie's King Street, Mar. '85, £2,676.*

6. *Bristol delft dish, painted in blue, green and manganese with a butterfly above a rabbit in a garden, the flower-shaped cartouche within a border of stylized leaves, c. 1760 (minor chips). 13¼ in. diam. June '85, £190.*

7. *Massive London dated polychrome armorial drug-jar, painted predominently in blue with the arms of the Worshipful Society of Apothecaries, above the motto 'Opifer Que Per Orben Dicor' and the indistinct date 165(6) on a ribbon cartouche, c. 1656 (cracked round the body, restored, a triangular hole to one side filled; unrecorded). 14¼ in. Christie's King Street, June '85, £19,650.*

8   9

10

11

8. *Liverpool delft blue and white cornucopia wall vase, lightly moulded and painted with a bird perched on a branch below a shell and leaves, c. 1760. 8 in. June '85, £380.*

9. *Liverpool delft blue and white cornucopia wall vase, c. 1760. 8 in. June '85, £320.*
This selling of a pair of objects in separate lots was not some clever ploy on the part of the cataloguer to increase the prices. Within the space of two weeks, two separate clients brought in their pottery wall pockets and, by pure chance, they made a matched pair facing in opposite directions.

10. *London delft dish, boldly painted in iron-red, green, blue and yellow, c. 1750 (restored). 13½ in. diam. June '85, £170.*

11. *Bristol delft blue and white dish, painted with an Oriental figure fishing on an island with boats, buildings and trees in the foreground and distance, c. 1750. 10 in. diam. June '85, £100.*

12. *London delft blue and white shoe, with yellow heel and the base dated and inscribed E.S. 1759 in manganese (restoration and clips). 6¾ in. wide. Christie's King Street, Mar. '85, £1,561.*

13. *Lambeth delft blue and white drug-jar, for U SAMBUC named on a cartouche with winged cherubs flanking a scallop shell above and with a winged cherub's head below, c. 1740. 6¾ in. Christie's King Street, June '85, £223.*

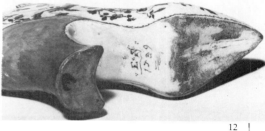

12

14. *Lambeth delft blue and white wet-drug jar, with scrolling strap handles for S: E: CORALLIS named on a cartouche with a winged angel's head above, c. 1680 (clips to foot and some glaze flaking). 7 in. Christie's King Street, June '85, £546.*

15. *London delft blue and white drug jar, named for CONF.DE.OVO within a strapwork cartouche, c. 1680 (rim flaking). 7½ in. Christie's King Street, June '85, £563.*

16. *Liverpool delft blue and white dish, painted with the Taking of Portobello, the border with bunches of grapes, c. 1741 (slight crack to well, glaze flaking to rim). 11¾ in. diam. Christie's King Street, June '85, £1,338.*

17. *Lambeth delft ballooning plate, painted in blue, green, yellow and manganese, c. 1785 (minor glaze flaking to rim). 11¾ in. diam. Christie's King Street. June '85, £1,450.*

18. *Bristol delft blue and white dish painted with an Oriental maiden standing by rockwork in a fenced garden and with a boy attendant to the side, c. 1740. 11½ in. diam. June '85, £130.*

13   14   15

16   17

18

Staffordshire Portrait Figures

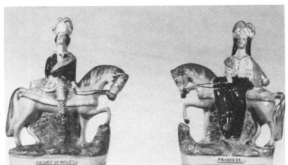

its own right. In December 1984 this model made £600.

A desirable portrait figure should have sharpness of line which allows an immediate recognition of the subject. The decoration is important to price, with a preference for figures with a lot of dark blue and gold. High quality pieces tend to date from before 1860. After this, owing to the re-use of moulds, figures tend to lose definition around the head and hands, and the colouring is sparse and poorly applied – particularly on pieces from the end of the century.

There are fakes on the market. Very modern examples are easy to spot with a lack of weight, incorrect colouring for the model and an even, all-over crazing of the glaze. There are also the products of the Sampson Smith factory which are less easy to recognize. This factory existed from 1846 to 1963 and used some of the original moulds to produce copies – not fakes. They are, however, sometimes sold as nineteenth-century. They are difficult to recognize, but hard bright colours and a wide use of green and yellow on the base can be indicators.

Buyers, in what might seem a purely local market, are surprisingly widespread. This year has seen a very strong interest not only in America, but also Canada and France, particularly for

Napoleonic and French Royal subjects. Even religious figures, the poor relations of the market with prices often under £40, will find buyers overseas – in Ireland. For the other subjects a bid of £100 is unlikely to succeed.

Paul Barthaud

The term 'Staffordshire' covers the various pottery and semi-porcelainous wares produced in and around the five towns of the Potteries, of which the largest is Stoke-on-Trent, over a period of some 200 years.

It is possible to attribute some pre-1840 figures to specific makers such as Sherratt, Walton and Salt, but the vast majority of portrait figures are currently unattributable. In contrast to the market in other European ceramics, prices are not dependent on 'who made it', but 'who it is'. Once you have identified a figure – there are books and lists – you can determine the price range by individual quality.

The market concentrates on particular subjects. The most sought after pieces, with consistently high prices, are Crimean and Military Figures, with Theatrical, Royal, Sporting, Political and Religious subjects following in descending order. These are broad headings and do not exhaust the types which you may discover. For instance, there are certain rare animal portraits such as the elephant, Jumbo. This remarkable beast was killed by a train in 1885 after a series of events which would make a book in

1. *Benjamin Franklin on an oval base entitled 'The Old English Gentleman'*. 16 in. Aug. '84, £320.
   A good example of renaming. If a model did not sell well, it was given a new name with greater appeal. I have also seen examples of an aged Wellington renamed 'Grandfather'.

2. *Lady Hester Stanhope and Doctor Meryon* 7¼ in. Aug. '84, £200.
   The eccentric Lady Hester travelled widely in the Middle East with her physician, and was considered a 'prophet' by the desert tribes.

3. *Rare pair of equestrian figures of the Prince of Wales and the Princess Royal (some restoration)*. 10¾ in. Mar. '84, £150.
   These have a theatrical feel, with the plumed headdress and the decorative bands along the horse's sides. They show that display and appearance were as important as producing an 'accurate' model.

4. *A pair of rare well-coloured and well-modelled figures of Victoria and Albert*. 9½ in. Mar. '84, £700.
   This charming pair of figures was unrecorded. Thus our estimate of £250 to £350 was trounced by the price.

5. *Rare Obadiah Sherrat group of Romulus and Remus (some restoration and minor damages)*. 6¾ in. June '84, £800.
   Not a portrait, more of a representation. It does, however, show the differences between the pre-1840 figures and the later models illustrated here. This is more crudely modelled but has a feel of movement which is lacking in later pieces.

Samson

The name of Samson as a producer of porcelain and, to a lesser extent of enamel, has more pieces attributed to it than almost any other single manufacturer or factory. At every 'antiques fair' and in many antique shops you will see at least one piece attributed to Samson, and a suggested date of production as nineteenth century. If you ask the retailer about such an article you will probably receive a limited reply; for example, 'it's French' or 'it's as good as Chelsea'. This information, which is usually incorrect on both points, is not an attempt at anything underhand, but reflects a genuine lack of knowledge about the maker.

The factory, which was in family ownership until 1964, may have been started as early as 1845. It is known to have been in full swing towards the latter part of the nineteenth century with, in 1873, some 20,000 original models providing the basis for copies of most major European factories as well as most Chinese porcelain wares, in particular famille rose.

The known trademarks, registered in 1900 and in use from about 1905, are reproduced at the end of this section. However, at the request of the customer these marks could be omitted altogether, or others substituted in their place, so that some Samson wares reproduce the marks of the manufacturers they are copying. Also, these marks were applied over the glaze, and can be removed. The presence of a small bare area of glaze around, for example, the rear edge of a base would suggest that a mark has been removed, and such an item should be treated with extreme caution as it has may be a deliberate forgery. Thus the presence or absence of a Samson mark is not a reliable guide.

The mark of a gold anchor, copied from the eighteenth-century Chelsea factory, is not enough for a secure attribution to Samson. Contrary to popular opinion, but from observation, I would conclude that such marked examples can be more correctly attributed to other French or Italian producers. This mark was noticeably absent among the lots at the Samson stock sale held at Christie's King Street in 1979.

1

1a

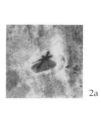

2

2a

3

1 & 1a. *Finely painted Samson semi-eggshell ruby-back plate.* 8 in. diam. Christie's King Street, Mar. '85, £238.
This plate is copying a Chinese original of about 1725, which should be worth some £2,500. The reverse shows that it was unmarked; the paper label should be ignored. The white area in the centre is slightly blue which is characteristic. The enamel colours on the front are different in tone to the Chinese.

2 & 2a. *Samson 'Meissen' rectangular tea-caddy and cover painted with Chinese figures and pink lustre scrolls.* 4½ in. Feb. '85, £85.
The base shows the factory mark. This base is unglazed and the mark could be removed.

3. *Typical original Meissen tea caddy, painted by C.F. Herold and with later silver mount.* Christie's King Street, Oct. '81, £1,000.

4 & 4a. *Samson figure of a young man wearing a yellow floral coat and turquoise hat, seated on a tree stump with a dog at his side, ormolu base.* 7 in. Feb. '85, £170.
The Samson mark is clearly to be seen on the bottom edge of the figure. Compare this with a genuine Meissen mark (No. 5a). Yes, people do get them confused.

5. & 5a. *The Meissen original.* 6¼ in. Christie's King Street, Oct. '81, £850.

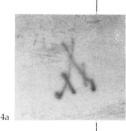

4

4a

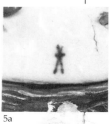

5

5a

Samson (cont.)

6

7

7a

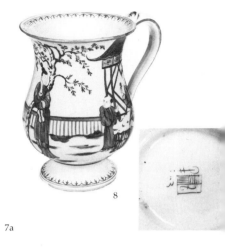

8

If we now look at the commercial position of Samson porcelain, with the above problems in mind, the question arises: 'How does one assess the commercial market where there is uncertainty as to what is genuine?' The reply must be – with difficulty! The individual nature of much of the Samson output precludes direct price comparisions, for the same object, from one year to another. This year there has been a general indication that prices have increased for typical models, such as pairs of 'Shepherd and Shepherdess'. An average 1985 price at auction for a pair of such figures in good condition is currently between £100 and £150, whereas earlier in 1984 £100 would have been top price. The copies of Chinese famille rose and famille verte porcelains have shown a more noticeable increase, which could reflect 'overflow' of money which cannot find enough period Chinese originals to meet demand, particularly from America. These types of Samson copies can be identified by the blue tinge to the glaze, and the slight difference in the colours of the enamels. Pieces, especially figures, which have been fitted onto gilt bronze mounts are very difficult to attribute to Samson, rather than to the original factory. It is certain that such items are in possession of major collections and museums with the wrong attribution.

The demand for Samson porcelains is widespread. The current purchasers at auction will be mainly dealers supplying a demand for decorative porcelains at a fraction of the cost of an original design but of a quality which, from a distance, will confound most experts.

Paul Barthaud

6. *Samson octagonal plate with flowers in the famille rose style.* 8¾ in. diam. Feb. '85, £30.

7 & 7a. *Samson plate painted with exotic birds and insects.* 8in. diam. Feb. '85, £40.
The reverse shows a gold Chelsea mark. It is debatable whether this type of anchor marked item was produced by Samson, but the market currently accepts the attribution. I often have this type of object brought to me as having been made at Chelsea, particularly when it has been purchased some years ago, but the differences are many. The style of painting, colours and the border are the most obvious.

8 & 8a. *Samson bell-shaped mug painted with Oriental figures.* 5½ in. Mar. '85, £50.
The base shows the mock Chinese mark. I have only observed this in red overglaze enamel. There is thick pooling of glaze in the well of the foot.

9 & 9a. *One of a pair of Samson armorial campana tulip vases painted with flower sprays and white scrolls on square bases (one cover broken).* 11 in. Feb. '85, £110.
A comparison with No. 8 reveals that the mock Chinese marks are totally dissimilar in detail, although of a similar overall appearance.

10 & 10a. *One of a pair of Samson candlesticks modelled with putti holding baskets of flowers and standing before flowering trees.* 8 in. Jan. '85, £90.
A typical Derby model but with important differences. The flowers are 'sharper' and more elaborate, and the gilding is too bright. The reverse shows the Samson mark. This particular mark is more commonly found on enamels.

9

10

10a

11 & 11a. *Pair of Samson groups of dancing figures in 18th-century dress on oval gilt scroll bases.* 8 in. Jan. '85, £120.

The mark on the figures is often mistaken for Derby.

12 & 12a. *One of a pair of Derby groups of Toilette, depicting a young lady polishing the shoes of a gentleman.* c. 1830. 7¼ in. Dec. '85, £320.

Note the difference in the faces and hands on this model to No. 11. The base of this group shows the clear Derby mark which is closest to the Samson example.

11 11a

12

12a

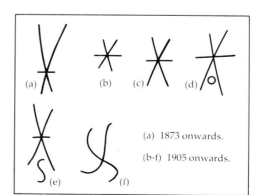

13

13a

13 & 13a. *Samson figure of a standing bearded Immortal wearing an iron-red dragon decorated robe.* 10 in. Sold along with No. 14 and the figure illustrated on p. 46, Oct. '84, £35.

The mark on the base, which is unglazed, is not a recognized Samson mark.

14 & 14a. *Samson famille verte figure of a seaked Immortal on a rectangular base.* 7 in. Sold with No. 13 and the figure illustrated on p. 46, Oct. '84, £35.

Note again the unglazed base.

15. *Samson marks registered in 1905.*

14

14a

(a) (b) (c) (d)

(e) (f)

(a) 1873 onwards.

(b-f) 1905 onwards.

15

Royal Doulton Figures – A New Market

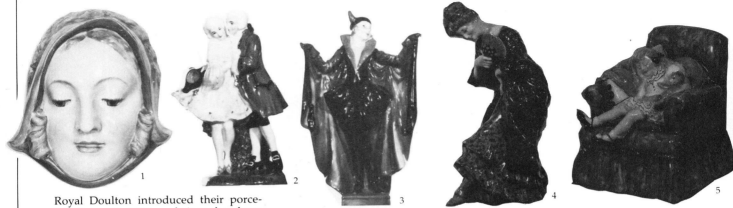

Royal Doulton introduced their porcelain figures in 1913, and since then have produced over 2,000 models, with 300 different subjects in production at one time. It was not until 1981, however, that an auction market developed with, for the time, the startling price of £100 being realized by some of the 1930s 'Bathing Beauties'. This is a relatively new market which has stemmed from buyers in America, Canada and Australia, fed primarily on London sales and fanned by the Royal Doulton International Collectors' Club.

Auction prices in this market, like any other, are subject to the usual forces of fashion, design and of course rarity. This last, and most important point in commercial terms, is easier to gauge with Royal Doulton figures than with almost any other 'collectable'. On almost all figures there will be an HN number with which, from a reference book, one can obtain the dates and the length of production, and this can be used as a good guide to the numbers produced, and thus to rarity. Therefore 'Cicely' (HN1516), which was in production from 1932 to 1949, realized £580 in September 1984, while 'Old Balloon Seller' (HN1315), which was in production between 1929 and 1978 sold for £40.

The reason for a figure being in production for only a short period was straightforward – it did not sell well! It is amusing to consider that 'Polly Peachum' (from the Beggars Opera), which was in production for 27 years and met with little interest at 16 shillings, can now command prices of £100 plus. Production of models at Royal Doulton was not on a hit or miss basis. Prototypes were made and were put to one side if they were felt to be a poor likeness or a shade immodest. These prototypes, although not intended to, did occasionally reach the market. An example is the figure of a young girl in a chair (No. 8) which realized £520.

Condition of all these figures is very important when assessing values. A hairline crack in even a rare example can reduce the price by 50% or more. The increasing prices have led to clever restorations with heads, arms and fingers being re-glued and sprayed to hide the cracks.

The price range is wide, starting at about £15. This year has seen a measurable movement in price with, for example, the 'Butterfly Girl' (HN720) realizing £260 in March 1984, and £450 in November 1984. Both figures were purchased by London dealers.

It is to be expected that, with this market being based primarily on trans-Atlantic buyers, there will be a continued rise in prices. At the time of writing the dollar is still very strong. I will be surprised if there are not record prices to be seen among rare figures over the next twelve months. *Graham D'Anger*

1. *Sweet Anne (HN1593), wallmask*, c. 1933. Nov. '84, £450.
   Good price as wallmasks are rare.
2. *The Perfect Pair (HN581)*, 1923–38. 7½ in. Jan. '85, £420.
   Possibly made for Tatler and Eve magazines.
3. *Marietta (HN1341)*, 1929–49. 8¼ in. Apr. '84, £220.
   Figure from the comic opera *Die Fledermaus*.
4. *Lady with Fan (HN335)*, 1919–38. 9 in. One of a pair with Lady with Rose, Nov. '84, £350.
   A very good price for this early figure, as it was badly damaged.

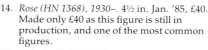

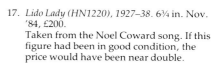

5. *Sleepyhead (HN2114), 1953–5.* 4¾ in. Nov. '84, £420.
   This is a more recent figure but is rare. The price was fair as it had a large crack.

6. *Tony Weller (HN346), 1919–38.* 10½ in. Oct. '84, £100.
   An early figure but not painted, which explains the relatively low price.

7. *Doreen (HN1389), 1930–8.* 6 in. Oct. '84, £480.

8. *A young girl seated in a chair.* 5 in. Oct. '84, £520.
   This figure never went into production.

9. *Crinoline (HN21), 1913–38.* 6¼ in. Oct. '84, £1,200.
   This is one of the highest prices we have had for an early figure.

10. *Dreamweaver (HN2283), 1972–6.* 9 in. Nov. '84, £120.
    One of only a few figures to have a matt finish.

11. *Tête-à-Tête (HN799), 1926–38.* 5½ in. Nov. '84, £480.

12. *Katherine (HN74), 1917–38.* 6¼ in. Jan. '85, £520.
    An early figure designed by C. J. Noke. In January this was a good price, but six months later at the time of going to press would only be considered a fair one.

13. *Sweet Anne (HN1318), 1929–49.* 7 in. Oct. '84, £90.
    One of seven models which vary in colour. This price is average.

14. *Rose (HN 1368), 1930–.* 4½ in. Jan. '85, £40.
    Made only £40 as this figure is still in production, and one of the most common figures.

15. *Lady April (HN1958), 1940–59.* 7 in. Jan. '85, £140.
    This figure was cracked.

16. *Polly Peachum (HN549), 1922–49.* 4½ in. Sept. '84, £110.
    Old, but a common figure, taken from the Beggar's Opera.

17. *Lido Lady (HN1220), 1927–38.* 6¾ in. Nov. '84, £200.
    Taken from the Noel Coward song. If this figure had been in good condition, the price would have been near double.

18. *Sairey Gamp (HN558), 1923–39.* 7¼ in. Sept. '84, £190.

19. *Mr Pickwick (HN556), 1923–39.* 7 in. Sept. '84, £140.

20. *The Fat Boy (HN555), 1923–39.* 7 in. Sept. '84, £140.

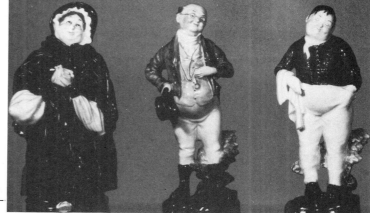

21. *Mr Micawber (HN557), 1923–39.* 7 in. Sept. '84, £130.
22. *Chelsea Pensioner.* 3 in. June '84, £480.
    The Chelsea Pensioner is unrecorded but is one of the more common unrecorded figures.
23. *Cicely (HN1516), 1932–49.* 5¾ in. Sept. '84, £580.
    An over-average price for one of the more middle of the road figures.
24. *Sunshine Girl (HN1344), 1929–38.* 5 in. Sept. '84, £600.
    One of two models, probably inspired by the musical comedy *Sunshine Girl.* This example had a hair line crack on the leg in a bad place, which lowered the price for a rare figure.
25. *Roseabell (HN1620), 1934–8.* 6½ in. Sept. '84, £350.
    Only in production for five years; but if this figure had been in good condition, the price would be near double.
26. *Penelope (HN1901), 1939–75.* 7¾ in. Sept. '84, £140.
27. *Butterfly (HN720), 1925–38.* 6¼ in. July '84, £450.
    A good price for the commonest of the four models.
28. *Sketch Girl.* 7 in. Mar. '85, £1,000.
    This sketch girl was specially made for the magazine *'The Sketch', c.* 1923–8, hence the high price.

21

22

23

24

25

26

27

28

Wemyss Piggies go to Market

At Christie's in Glasgow, the Scottish Pottery auctions attract a particularly enthusiastic following, especially for Wemyss ware.

Scottish nobility were among the very first patrons of Wemyss ware, and when Robert Heron bought the Gallatown Pottery in Fife in 1883 he renamed it after a nearby castle, home of the Earl of Wemyss. Initially the factory was very much a family affair. Heron's sister, a keen and talented amateur artist who painted wildlife and flowers, influenced the factory's style of decoration, and so too did her friend, Lady Grosvenor, after whom a type of vase was named. But it was a young Bohemian, brought by Robert Heron from Austria, who de-

1

2

veloped the distinctive style of decoration for which Wemyss became so well-known. Karel Nekola trained local decorators to paint the factory wares with, among other designs, pink cabbage roses with dark green foliage. It is this decoration which most easily identifies Wemyss.

Naturally, the less common forms of decoration make pieces particularly attractive to collectors. A large china pig door-stop left a few disgruntled hopefuls when it sold in 1983 for £1,500 – at that time a record for Wemyss – but, unusually, nestling amongst the cabbage roses were a few thistles and shamrocks (No. 1). The market is greedy for pigs. A large grunter with sponged decoration made £1,100 (No. 2), while a much smaller example with roses took £600.

A sought after piece in August 1984 was a circular plaque painted with widgeon on a shoreline, which realized £620. It was painted by Nekola in 1908, but just two years later illness forced him to withdraw from the factory, and he worked from home until his death in 1915.

Edwin Sandland assumed the artistic direction of the pottery in 1916. He continued to produce such popular lines as character jugs – The Fair Maid of Perth fetched £620 in a sale at Earlshall, Fife, in September 1983 – and pieces painted wth mottoes (No. 3). Sandland also introduced new forms of decoration including the now popular chrysanthemums painted on a black ground.

The demand for Wemyss was beginning to dwindle. Sandland imported porcelain tea services from Stoke, which

his artists decorated with dog roses, but the factory's decline continued. T. Goode & Co., major retailers of Wemyss, cancelled their order, and in 1928 Edwin Sandland died. Two years later the Depression extinguished the factory's kilns.

The Bovey Pottery of Bovey Tracey, Devon, which employed Karel Nekola's youngest son, Joseph, bought the factory's moulds and for a while continued to decorate pieces in the Wemyss style. In the late 1930s a Czechoslovakian called Jan Plichta became the sole proprietor until the factory ceased production in the early 1940s. Interestingly, one of Plichta's most successful lines went to market at Christie's in London in March 1985: a pig in clover decoration, which sold for £500.

Paul Howard,
Christie's Scotland

1. *Large pig door-stop. c. 1900.* 16¾ in. long. Oct. '83, £1,500.
   Although slightly damaged this fine beast made its money because of the thistles and shamrocks among the cabbage roses.
2. *Large pig door-stop. c. 1900.* 17¾ in. long. Mar. '85, £1,100.
   This pig with sponged decoration might have made more had the tail not been restored.
3. *One of a pair of cauldrons with Gaelic inscriptions on green grounds, with impressed Wemyss mark.* 5 in. Mar. '85, £220.
4. *Cylindrical mug painted with sweet peas below a green rim.* 5½ in. Mar. '85, £150.
5. *Preserve food jar and cover painted with a swarm of bees and a hive within a green border.* 5½ in. Apr. '85, £60.

All these pieces were sold at Christie's and Edmiston's, Glasgow.

3

4

5

Eighteenth- and Nineteenth-Century British Decanters

Mallet, club, shaft and globe, prussian, ship and bell are all names applied to shapes of decanters. Mallet decanters, for instance, so-named for their similarity to a stonemason's mallet, with shouldered bodies, are usually simple in decoration, with little or no decorative cutting, although there are examples to be found with detailed engraving, usually of foliage or fruiting vines. English decanters generally tended to be of a functional nature rather than decorative, the glass being quite thick and heavy in weight, suitable for daily use. The Irish manufacturers at Cork, Dublin and Waterford tended to produce thin, mould-blown decanters, made in large quantities from a standard mould and exported to the Continent and America. Many decanters from the Cork factory, 1783–1818, were marked 'Cork Glass Co. (No. 12). During the late eighteenth and early nineteenth centuries, particularly in England, it became fashionable to elaborate glass table ware, and decanters were no exception. In fact, their very size offered the craftsmen wonderful opportunity to display their skill and variety in cutting. Diamonds, fans, prism and step-cutting were typical forms of cutting – in some elaborate examples all can be found on one decanter.

Helene Venning

1. *Pair of mallet-shaped decanters with mushroom stoppers, early 19th century.* 10 in. June '85, £75.
The applied rings to the necks and the cut vertical flutes to the lower section of the bodies are typical features.

2. *Mallet-shaped decanter with mushroom stopper, early 19th century.* 10½ in. June '85, £40.

3. *Prussian shape decanter with mushroom stopper, 18th/19th century.* 10 in. June '85, £50.
Illustrates the popularity in Britain during the late 18th and early 19th centuries for heavy cut decanters. Step cutting to the shoulder and fans became popular characteristics.

4. *Narrow-shouldered decanter and stopper, c. 1820.* 8 in. May '85, £40.

5. *Narrow-shouldered decanter and stopper, c. 1830.* 9 in. June '85, £55.
Similar to No. 4, with step-cutting to the neck and shoulders, and cut with a band of diamonds above flutes.

6. *Pair of square-shaped whisky decanters with faceted ball stoppers, cut with hob-nail diamonds, late 19th century.* 10 in. Apr. '85, £85.

7. *Square-shaped spirit decanter with stopper cut with ovals, c. 1860.* 10 in. Mar. '85, £45.

8. *Narrow shouldered body decanter with stopper, mid-19th century.* 10½ in. Feb. '85, £40.
Similar to decanters made around 1770 cut with large facets.

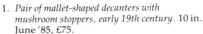

9

10

9. *Three tapering decanters with spire stoppers each with an applied ring to the neck, mid-Victorian.* Mar. '85, £110.

10. *Two cylindrical decanters with stoppers, with three facet cut rings to the necks, the bodies with moulded drapes, and with flower-moulded stoppers, c. 1860. 9¾ in. and 9½ in.* May '85, £95.

11. *Pair of mallet-shaped decanters with target stoppers, engraved in diamond point by Laurence Whistler with Godmersham Park and the Temple Godmersham Park within circular scrolling foliage cartouches, the target stoppers with a horse, one signed with initials LW. 10¼ in.* House sale at Godmersham Park, June '83, £4,536 (including premium).
Although the engraving is modern, the high price reflects both the quality of the decoration and also the venue of the sale.

12. *Pair of Cork Glass Go. engraved decanters with moulded bulls-eye stoppers, and moulded flutes at the base of the bodies, c. 1800.* Christie's King Street, 1980, £240.
These are very good examples of Cork decanters, typical of their style and decoration.

13. *Ale-carafe, with cylindrical body and tapering neck, c. 1770.* Christie's King Street, 1980, £260.
This carafe illustrates the early shapes used; simple in construction and with restrained decoration.

14. *'Lynn' decanter of mallet-shape (left), body lightly moulded with horizontal ribs, with high kick-in base, c. 1775, and serving-bottle (right), with lightly moulded panels, early 18th century.* Christie's King Street, June '85, £500 and £150.

11

12   13   12

14

English Eighteenth-Century Drinking Glasses

1   2   3   4   5   6

Only after 1677, when George Ravenscroft pioneered 'lead crystal' glass, did England become a leader in the manufacture of glass. Not only was this responsible for improving quality – removing the crizzling (clouding) which had dogged makers – but it heralded a new style and decoration. Early eighteenth-century glass houses at London, Bristol, Stourbridge and Newcastle were at first experimental, moving away from the ornate and fragile Venetian style to create a range of table wares that were durable, functional, and pleasing.

Funnel bowls, baluster-shaped stems and plain conical or folded feet (No. 1) were typical features on early glasses, emphasizing richness of colour, classical form, and much greater weight than Venetian wares. Decoration was minimal, with knops and tear-shaped inclusions of air in the stems. 'Balusters' of this period were produced for the well-to-do, and are relatively rare.

There was little basic change in construction until after 1746 when the Glass Excise Act was introduced, a duty on all glass materials, according to weight. Thus the solid, heavy baluster was abandoned, and glass houses turned to decoration to beautify a new lighter type which was cheaper, but lacked the purity and brilliance of the balusters. Decoration concentrated mainly on the

stem and bowl. Air-twists were a popular and imaginative introduction, consisting of air bubbles trapped in the stem when molten, twisted and drawn into threads, and further decorated with knops, usually at the shoulder or centre of the stem (Nos. 2–3). This trend caught on quickly, and was adapted producing many opaque-twists and the seldom found colour-twists. Pale pink and red were preferred, and the rarest colour was a bright canary yellow. The opaque-twist stem glass forms one of the largest and most common groups of glasses (Nos. 4–10).

Engraving and enamelling, previously a neglected field, were a welcome and inspiring addition (Nos. 11–12). The most famous enamellers were the Beilby family, in particular William and his sister Mary, from Newcastle-on-Tyne, from the early 1760s to 1778 (Nos. 13). Glasses attributable to them are highly sought after and expensive, owing to their unmistakable quality. More common are wine glasses (No. 14) of varying shapes and styles engraved at the bowls with bands of fruiting vines, or slender ale flutes with hops and barley.

Commemorative glasses, particularly Jacobite, are always very collectable; they were often engraved with a rose in bloom and the inscription 'Fiat', symbols of the Jacobite cause (Nos. 3, 15, 17, 20).

1. *A baluster goblet, bucket bowl supported on an inverted baluster knop and basal knop stem, the foot domed and folded, c. 1720. Christie's King Street, June '84, £280.*
2. *Air-twist wine glass, bell bowl and conical foot, c. 1755. Apr. '85, £55. This is a common type.*
3. *Air-twist wine glass Jacobite significance, bell bowl engraved with a six-petalled rose-spray in bloom, stem with applied twisted knop, foot folded, c. 1750. Apr. '85, £240.*
4. *Multi-spiral opaque-twist, bell bowl and conical foot, c. 1765. Jan. '85, £55.*
5. *Opaque-twist wine glass, base of the bell bowl with bubble inclusions, on plain conical foot, c. 1765. Jan. '85, £50.*
6. *Double series opaque-twist wine glass, bell bowl on triple knopped stem and conical foot, c. 1760. Apr. '85, £80.*

7   8

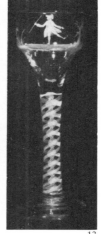

9   10   11

12   13

7. *Double-series opaque-twist wine glass, round funnel bowl and conical foot, c. 1760. Feb. '85, £60.*
An interesting feature is the moulded flutes on the bowl.

8. *Opaque-twist wine glass, ogee bowl engraved with a band of fruiting vine, conical foot, c. 1765. Jan. '85, £70.*

9. *Opaque-twist, trumpet-drawn wine glass on conical foot, c. 1760. Jan. '85, £40.*

10. *Colour-twist wine glass, with rounded bowl, the stem with an opaque three-ply spiral enclosing entwined ribbons edged in translucent blue and green, conical foot, c. 1770. Christie's King Street, Nov. '84, £600.*

11. *Colour-twist wine glass, ogee bowl engraved with floral and fruiting vine, stem with opaque white and blue corkscrew core, conical foot, c. 1765. Christie's King Street, Nov. '84, £500.*

12. *Two ale-flutes, bowls engraved with hops and barley above faceting, stems with bladed and base knops, feet folded, c. 1770. Jan. '85, £60.*

13. *Beilby opaque-twist wine glass, ogee bowl enamelled in white with a man skating on a pond, on double-series opaque twist stem and conical foot, c. 1765–70. Christie's King Street, June '83, £3,000.*

Royal births, deaths and marriages and victorious battles are also frequent embellishments.

Prices vary enormously, dictated by quality and rarity. Lack of proportion, or damage such as chips on the foot or rim, can halve the price. Obviously not everyone can afford hundreds of pounds for a 'Beilby' or 'Newcastle' glass; but there are very many beautiful and pleasing glasses at prices starting from about £45 to £50 for, say, an opaque-twist and £150 upwards for a baluster. However, the later eighteeenth-century glasses were copied throughout the nineteenth and twentieth centuries; and glasses should be scrutinized carefully for any defects. Fakes or later glasses can be identified by too clear or white a colour, as early glasses nearly always have a grey-blue tinge. Another guide, although not fool-proof, is to look for toolmarks on the bowl; all eighteenth-century glasses will have them, and some good fakes, but if there are none at all, it cannot be eighteenth-century!

The market has remained quite constant over the past few years, with high prices for balusters and rare examples, but bargains can still be found with a little effort. It is a vast subject, but one that with patience, handling, touching and careful study can only be rewarding.
Helene Venning

14   15   16   17   18

14. *Plain straight-stemmed wine glass, pan-topped bowl engraved with a band of flowering foliage, on high conical foot. c. 1765. Jan. '85, £60.*

15. *Jacobite balustroid wine glass, slender waisted funnel bowl engraved with a six-petalled rose and bud, stem with annulated beaded knop, foot domed and folded, c. 1740. Christie's King Street, Nov. '84, £200.*

16. *Air-twist wine glass of Jacobite significance, pan-topped bowl engraved with a floral border, swelling waist-cupped stem filled with spirals, foot conical, c. 1750. Christie's King Street, Nov. '84, £160.*

17. *Jacobite plain straight-stemmed wine glass, round funnel bowl engraved with a seven-petalled rose and bud, on conical foot, Newcastle, c. 1750. Christie's King Street, Nov. '84, £300.*

18. *Air-twist trumpet-drawn wine glass of Jacobite significance, bowl engraved with carnations, reverse a butterfly, on double-knopped stem filled with air-twist spirals, foot conical, c. 1750. Christie's King Street, Nov. '84, £320.*

19. *Air-twist wine glass, with bell bowl and conical foot, c. 1760 (chip to rim). Jan. '84, £40.*

20. *Double-series opaque-twist wine glass, ogee bowl later engraved with a rose-spray, in the Jacobite style, conical foot, c. 1770. Jan. '85, £40.*

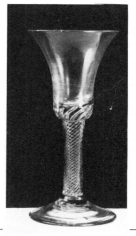

19   20

Friggers

This term should be applied to items of glass which were produced by glassmakers as a demonstration of their individual skill and imagination or for their own pleasure. They include bells, rolling pins, walking sticks, hats and pipes and are often attributed to the Nailsea glassworks near Bristol, but similar pieces were produced at other centres in England and Scotland.

These 'novelties' were made throughout the nineteenth century, often from off-cuts of glass, and the majority of surviving pieces date from the 1850s to the end of the century. There are later reproductions of bells, and possibly some pipes, but they are not common.

There is no great difference in price between the various subjects: the bells, for instance, are not worth much more than the rolling pins. However, I have not seen a full-size hat or sword offered for sale for a very long time, and these may realize in excess of £100 each. Condition is very important. A rolling pin which is badly worn may realize less than £20, but in good condition this could rise to £70 or more.

Prices have not increased greatly during the last year, which is perhaps surprising when one compares this field with other colourful wares of quality such as Bohemian glass or the later Sèvres-pattern porcelain. This may be explained by the limited number of English buyers, the relatively low volume which is purchased by Americans, and the absence of Continental buyers. The lack of increase may also be due to the poor condition of many of the pieces currently on the market.

This is, in my opinion, an area in which a new collector could build up an interesting and varied collection at reasonable prices. *Helene Venning*

1. *Tapering oviform flask, combed in white, with applied blue rim.* Mar. '85, £35.
2. *Clear glass frigger, applied with blue glass handles, trails and leaf decoration, modelled as a pair of bellows.* Mar. '85, £45.
3. *Clear glass frigger modelled as a gimmel flask, typically combed in white, with pincered borders and applied blue rims.* Mar. '85, £25.

4. *Nailsea-type bell in clear glass.* Feb. '84, £140. This is a particularly good example, the ribbed decoration enhancing a basically simple frigger.
5 & 6. *Nailsea-type bells with red (left) and blue (right) bowls.* Mar. '85, each £80. These are a more common type.

7. *Nailsea-type bell, with bowl spirally moulded at the base and handle combed in white.* Oct. '84, £100. A more interesting example than most.
8. *Nailsea-type blue salt container with traces of gilt decoration.* Mar. '85, £40.
9. *Glass rolling pin.* Mar. '85, £40. Traditionally made by sailors to give to their wives and sweethearts, these are very common and were made in large quantities.
10. *One of three coloured pipes.* Mar. '85, £85. Typical examples are in blue, green or red glass, often applied with white glass to the rims.

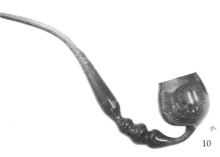

Bohemian Glass

For our purposes the Bohemian glass market dates from about 1815 to a peak of quality and inventiveness around 1850 and then declines to *c.* 1900. The term 'Bohemian' has been attached to almost all coloured glass, as well as large quantities of clear glass engraved with animals and hunting scenes. Although the factories of Bohemia were prolific this an obvious nonsense, like the widespread tendency to attribute all blue glass to Bristol.

In the early part of the nineteenth century Bohemian glass was influenced by the Viennese Biedermeier style and was popular in England. The best examples of this are tumblers and beakers decorated with enamels of Vienna, palaces and churches, but to describe these as souvenirs is to cheapen their quality. They were expensive originally, and one has to pay £150 or more for good examples now. Souvenirs were produced, in ruby glass, of the spa towns such as Karlovy Very, and Peplice, but similar beakers were produced in other countries, and later nineteenth-century examples are not uncommon from around £40.

The early nineteenth century also saw the invention of new colours, with Lithyalin, a polished and strongly marbled opaque glass, imitating agate and other semi-precious stones, in 1819, and Hyalith, producing dark red or black glass, in 1829. These types do not appear for sale by auction very often, and £100–£150 and £200–£300 respectively would be broad estimates for small examples. Metallic oxides were experimented with through the 1820s and became fashionable from the 1830s, particularly the blue and green. The 1840s saw fashions for greenish-yellow glass (annagrün), which used uranium, and yellow, coloured with antimony or silver chloride. A pinkish roseline was produced about 1850 using gold. This coloured glass found imitators in France, England and Germany – in the 1830s the French even offered prizes for the best imitations.

Another development of the 1830s was cased glass. This was produced by taking molten glass and putting it into a prepared hollow case of another colour, and then the two layers were fused together. The engraved decorations went through to the base colour, which was usually clear or white opaque, and this produced the effect of a design against a coloured background. Sometimes more than two colours were used, and the design was often further enriched with gilding or enamel. On later examples porcelain plaques painted with girls were also added.

On the mid-nineteenth-century cased glass the Gothic style showed its influence with panels cut in shapes which resembled church windows. Later in the century fashion moved away from coloured glass in general, but Bohemian still found some admirers for its quality. Today the market trend is for the dark red, rose pink, blue and green examples.

Any damage will lower the value of coloured glass. Colours can not be easily matched to disguise small cracks, and grinding of chips is never totally successful. I have observed some clever reshaping of broken vase bases by remounting onto clear glass, wood or brass. On overlay examples the gilding may be worn or rubbed. This is quite common and, depending on the extent, will not greatly reduce the price.

Bohemian engraved clear glass is unrivalled, and attribution is often based on this quality. However, these skills travelled with the craftsmen who exercised them, and many workers travelled to England, Scotland and Ireland. Two such masters were Emmanuel Lerche, who worked in Scotland from 1853 to 1906, and Frawy Tierge, who worked initially in England in 1862 and then went on to Dublin where he died in 1871. It is certain that many of the pieces which were designed and executed by such masters have been attributed to Bohemian rather than British or Irish glass houses. In the 1880s even English inventions in glass such as the 'Rock Crystal' of Thomas Webb were finished by Bohemian craftsmen.

Prices for Bohemian glass, particularly the coloured types mentioned above, have increased steadily over the last three years after the collapse of the so called 'Persian Market'. Current buyers are again Middle Eastern but also American and Japanese. The clear engraved glass is more a French and English market.   *Helene Venning*

1. *Pair of Bohemian ruby-flashed oviform vases with flaring necks, engraved with running stags in woodland. 15 in. Feb. '85, £140.*
   By the mid to late 19th century vases like these were very popular, and produced in large quantities for the European market – running deer in forests is typical of the engraving on Bohemian glass.

2. *Ruby-flashed wine goblet, with slender faceted stem. 6½ in. Mar. '85, £65.*
   Engraved to commemorate the Great Exhibition of 1851.

3. *Pair of slender oviform vases with flaring necks and bases, painted with oval plaques of young girls, the vases gilt with flowering foliage. 18 in. Nov. '84, £450.*

4. *One of a pair of white-overlay vases on green-stained lustres, the bowls painted with alternate panels of portraits and flower-sprays, below cusp-and-angle rims, the bases similarly decorated; gilt with hatched scrolls and foliage, suspending button and prism drops. 12 in. Mar. '85, £380.*

3

2

1

3.   *Oriental Ceramics and Works of Art*

Introduction
by Nicholas Pitcher

The art and antiques markets see many violent or gradual changes, with new trends emerging in all fields every year. A vase, painting or sculpture, for instance, which is thought very unfashionable at the beginning of a decade can, by the middle of it, become the most sought after commodity.

Applying this to the field of Oriental Works of Art, particularly in the mid to lower price bracket, a definite movement towards decorative qualities is seen. Oriental Works of Art obviously covers a vast field and we cannot possibly discuss it all in this chapter. We have therefore concentrated on those pieces which appear most regularly and for which there has been a noticeable upward trend – or drop in interest – during the past year.

Age, quality and rarity have always been, in my opinion, the criteria for establishing an item's potential. In general the item in question must have at least two of these features before it will realize a high auction price. For instance, if small pieces of Ming porcelain have age, but very little quality and were made in vast quantities, they will not be worth a great deal (see p. 70). Similarly, if an item is of top quality, but has no great age or rarity, this will not be sufficient to produce a high price. Usually, though, this last case does not occur, since rarity and quality tend to go hand in hand, there not being an enormous number of top quality pieces on the market. Obviously the most valuable items will have age, quality *and* rarity.

The last year, however, has seen one or two exceptions to this rule. Large pieces of Cantonese, Satsuma and Imari wares, for instance, have been making very high prices, when in fact there are many examples around and their quality is, dare I suggest, questionable to say the least. These prices are due to the enormous increase in demand for 'décor', particulary from American collectors.

1. *A pair of large Chinese blue and white pilgrim-bottles, 19th century.* 18½in. Jan. '85, £950.
   A good price considering one bottle had damage to the neck, which illustrates the popularity of this shape.
2. *Japanese blue and white gourd-shaped bottle, late 19th/early 20th century.* 8½in. Jan. '85, £70.
   An equivalent bottle of more ordinary shape would realize less than half this price.
3. *Chinese blue and white tulip-vase, 19th century.* 9½in. Dec. '84, £150.
   This was not an exceptionally high price for a tulip vase. Another decorated with figures, not flowers, was sold in Mar. '85 for £240.

4

Shapes have become very important over the last few years, most of the more popular ones originating from the early years of Oriental Art and re-used extensively in eighteenth- and nineteenth-century Chinese and Japanese ceramics. Pilgrim-bottles (No. 1), named after a leather or wood vessel used by the early pilgrims in north-west China, gourd-shaped vases (No. 2), crocus or tulip-vases (No. 3) and boat- or bucket-shaped vessels are among the main shapes to augment prices, as are any elaborate body or handle mouldings (see p. 84).

In discussing the importance of shape, animal and figure subjects must not be forgotten. Early examples have long been in demand, but today, owing both to the shorter supply of their earlier counterparts, and again to the popularity of purely decorative pieces, nineteenth- and even early twentieth-century animals and figures are eminently saleable.

As far as earlier ceramics go, collectors seem recently to have become more fussy in certain areas. For instance, Kangxi period blue and white porcelain can now be bought for less than two or three years ago, if slightly damaged or of mediocre colour quality. Only the best pieces have markedly risen in value. However, while this applies to other areas of earlier Chinese and Japanese ceramics, it is certainly not the case with Chinese export porcelain, which has soared in price over the last two years, being greatly in demand with collectors from Spain, Portugal, and North and South America. Among the famille rose wares, the tobacco-leaf design is the most popular – a pair of cracked 9in. diameter plates was sold in March 1985 for £550 – and any Chinese armorial porcelain, particularly with good arms, has been realizing very high prices (No. 4). Other popular designs are the double peacock pattern (No. 5) and the mandarin pattern. European subjects, because of their rarity, are also in great demand, probably the best recent example being a punch-bowl with cricketing scenes sold at Phillips in March 1984 for £4,000, which is, incidentally, now in Marylebone Cricket Club.

Famille verte porcelain has also been very popular over the last year; not only has this been true of period pieces from the Kangxi reign, but famille verte has also proved to be one of the most desirable palettes among nineteenth-century large vases and dishes (No. 6).

Finally, a notable drop in price has been seen for poorer-quality examples of early Han, Tang and Song dynasty pottery, while the top-quality pieces have still deservedly maintained their high levels. The lower prices for the poorer wares are due to many pieces coming on to the

5

6

4. *Part of a Chinese export armorial dinner-service,* c. 1800. Mar. '85. Pair of shallow vegetable tureens £1,800; sauce tureen, cover and stand £1,300.

5. *Famille rose 'double peacock-pattern' shaped oval meat dish, Qianlong.* 12in. wide. Apr. '85, £480.
   This is a popular pattern and the dish realized a good price despite being rubbed.

6. *Pair of famille verte jars and covers,* 19th century. 17 in. June '84, £1,300. Blue and white or famille rose examples would have realized less.

market recently from China, and are a typical instance of supply and demand dictating, once again, the course of events in the world of fine art.

All these points, in some cases to a rather lesser extent, apply also to Oriental Works of Art, the main categories of which are discussed in detail later in this chapter under Bronzes, Ivories and Enamels.

Ming — Priceless or a Bargain?

1

2

3

5

4

The news that an early Ming bottle had just been sold for £421,200 after being used as a table lamp would probably send most people scurrying to their attic in hope of finding their own Ming treasure (see No. 1). What the majority may not realize, however, is that it is perfectly possible to purchase a piece of genuine Ming porcelain for £200, or less. After all, the dynasty lasted from 1386 to 1644, time enough for large quantities to be manufactured.

The pieces illustrated here are perfectly genuine examples of Ming porcelain, but were bought at relatively low prices, for a variety of reasons. To begin with, they are all rather roughly potted and painted, which is typical of the so called 'provincial Ming' wares of the sixteenth and early seventeenth centuries. Although their naivety can produce a charming effect, they are not in the same class of potting and decoration as their rarer and more expensive counterparts.

The fact that these wares very seldom bear reign marks is also reflected in their price. 'Mark and period' pieces almost never occur in the field of lower priced Ming. The last, and one of the most important factors, is that these wares were produced in great quantities, many surviving to this day; hence supply is often greater than demand.

In many cases, when I tell people that their small Ming bowl is worth only around £100, or that they can easily buy a piece of Ming porcelain at auction for under £500, I am greeted with an incredulous stare, or, on occasions – particularly in the former case –something akin to verbal abuse. I hope therefore that this briefly explains why and that people will now be more encouraged to buy this commodity, which remains rather underrated.

Nicholas Pitcher

1. *Rare early Ming underglaze copper-red decorated vase, 14th century.* 12in. Apr. '84 (Christie's King Street), £421,200.

2. *A late Ming 'kraak porselein' dish, late 16th/ early 17th century.* 14½in. diameter. Jan. '85, £220.
   This dish had a hairline crack and small chip from the rim. A perfect example could have made up to £500. Kraak porselein is so named after the Dutch 'karaks' or carracks which were used to ship this type of porcelain to Europe.

3. *A late Ming blue and white kettle and cover, late 16th/early 17th century.* 6½in. Oct. '84, £300.

4. *Two small provincial Ming blue and white bowls, late 16th/17th century.* 2½in diam. Mar. '85, £150.
   This price was higher than would normally be expected because the right-hand bowl bore the mark of the emperor Wanli (1566–1616).

5. *Small blue and white baluster vase, mid-16th century.* 6½in. Oct. '84 £150.
   This is typical mid-Ming period provincial ware and made a little more than expected owing to its slightly unusual shape.

Reign Marks — Don't be Fooled

It is very easy to look up the reign mark on a piece of Chinese porcelain in any reference book and to memorize the various symbols of the Ming and Qing dynasty emperors' names. Much more difficult, however, is deciding whether the particular piece was actually made during the period which the mark suggests.

The habit of putting earlier reign marks on Chinese ceramics (and indeed bronzes) has been practised for many hundreds of years. Not until the twentieth century, though, was it done with intention to deceive; before that it was more a mark of respect to earlier potters, or when a piece was made in an earlier style. For example, it is quite common to find a vase of seventeenth- or eighteenth-century porcelain bearing a fifteenth-century reign mark, or a nineteenth-century bowl with an eighteenth-century reign mark on its base. Items which were actually made during the reign of the emperor whose mark appears on their bases are known as 'mark and period' pieces and the inclusion of the 'right' mark can often at least double or treble the price (see No. 11).

Proper attribution of Chinese ceramics requires a skilled knowledge of the subject, since it depends, among other things, on shape, glaze, potting and colour. The reign marks shown on this page, however, can be used as a guide as to whether an example of Chinese porcelain has the potential to be mark and period. There are, of course, many more varieties of marks, but I have concentrated here on those most often seen.

Nicholas Pitcher

1

2

3

4

Marks of the Emperor Kangxi (1662–1722) are also commonly found on later pieces:

5. *Kangxi four-character mark on 19th-century Chinese vase.* There are very few Kangxi 'mark and period' pieces known which bear four-character marks so it is a reasonably safe assumption that a piece thus marked is of later date. Compare this mark also to the Chenghua mark (No. 1), which is very similar in drawing.

6. *Kangxi six-character 'mark and period' dish.*

7. *Front of No. 6.* The mark illustrated as No. 4 is on a very similar dish – which could realize as little as half the price of No. 7, being wrongly marked.

One of the most common marks to be found on Oriental porcelain is that of the Emperor Chenghua (1465–87). Here are four examples of the mark being used on later pieces:

1. *Chenghua four-character mark on 19th-century Chinese vase.*

2. *Chenghua four-character mark on 19th-century Chinese crackleware vase.*
   The mark is scratched into a dark brown square on the base. It is extremely common and is found in this form *only* on 19th-century Chinese crackleware.

3. *Chenghua six-character mark on 19th-century Japanese dish.* A fairly common sight on 18th- and 19th-century Japanese Arita wares. The spur marks on the base are a useful hint that the piece is Japanese and therefore cannot be as marked.

4. *Chenghua six-character mark on Chinese Kangxi period (1662-1722) dish.*

5

6

7

Marks of the Emperor Daoguang (1822–51):

10. *Daoguang six-character seal mark on late 19th-/early 20th-century dish.*

11. *Daoguang 'seal mark and period' dish underglaze blue decoration.* Compare these as in No. 8 and 9.
    This dish made £170 in March 1985. A similar dish of this period, either unmarked or with an earlier mark, would realize substantially less.

12. *The mark of the Emperor Xuande (1426–35) as very frequently found on the bases of the 19th-century Chinese bronze incense-burners.*

8

9

Marks of the Emperor Qianlong (1736–95):

8. *Qianlong six-character seal mark on late 19th-century Chinese bowl.* The mark is rather badly drawn in overglaze enamel.

9. *Qianlong six-character 'seal mark and period' bowl.* The mark is very well drawn in underglaze blue, is symmetrical and is exactly in the centre of the base.

10

11

12

The Increasing Demand for Later Japanese Ceramics

Japanese porcelain has long been regarded as Chinese porcelain's poor relation, the exception being, of course, the fine Kakiemon wares of the seventeenth and early eighteenth centuries. The Japanese did not manufacture porcelain until some 400 years after the Chinese had discovered the secret and they rarely managed, apart from the early Kakiemon, Hirado and Nabeshima blue and white wares, to perfect underglaze blue decoration until late in the nineteenth century. It is this period upon which I would like to concentrate, since porcelain and pottery of the Meiji period (1868–1912) have, in the last few years, really begun to be appreciated.

Probably the best-known is Imari ware, normally associated with a distinctive red, blue and gold palette and not to be confused with various European pieces similary decorated. Imari is a port of Arita in the province of Hizan, from which the earliest Japanese 'export' porcelains were sent to their destinations in the latter part of the seventeenth century. Throughout most of the eighteenth century, the export of porcelain was curtailed, but in the nineteenth century trade with the West was reopened, and vast amounts of Imari wares were produced and sent to Europe, with a peak between 1860 and 1900.

Satsuma ware is another widely known term and refers to pottery made at a place of the same name on the island of Kyu-shu. These wares date back to the late seventeenth and eighteenth centuries when a cream coloured pottery was produced, painted in coloured enamels and gilding. The mid-nineteenth century onwards saw the same formula being used but with far more elaboration and, in exceptional cases, exquisite decoration, the gilding becoming the prominent feature. During this period Satsuma wares, varying tremendously in quality, size and shape, were produced in huge quantities for the European market. Kyoto pottery, which was similar in design, also became popular at this time. On a smaller scale are the Kaga and Kutani wares, recognizable by the combination of iron-red and green colours.

Ten years ago Japanese ceramics such as these examples would have been treated with a certain amount of derision; five years ago we would have had to tell rather disillusioned vendors that, 'we could certainly sell them for you but they are unlikely to realize a great deal.' Today, owing to the immense demand for 'decor', particularly from the American market, these pieces are greatly sought after and keenly contested in auctions around the world.

Nicholas Pitcher

1. *A large Imari vase and cover, 19th century.* 21½in. Apr. '85, £450.
2. *A large Satsuma koro (incense-burner) and cover, slight damage, mid/late 19th century.* 19½in. Jan. '85, £800.
3. *Japanese Satsuma-type pottery vase and cover, late 19th century.* 18in. Feb. '85, £55. This type of enamelled pottery was virtually mass-produced and would have realized a fraction of even this amount two or three years ago.
4. *A set of three vases, Kaga, or late Kutani, c. 1900.* 12in. and 11in. Sept. '84, £500.

1

2

3

Oriental Bronzes

1

2

3

4   5   6

1. *Two small Chinese bronze vessels after archaic originals, 18th century.* 4 × 5½in. wide. Apr. '85, £85.

2. *Chinese polished bronze incense-burner, late 19th century.* 6in. wide. May '85, £50.

3. *Two Chinese bronze mirrors, Tang dynasty (618–906 AD).* Approx. 3in. diam. Sold with two others, similar, Feb. '85, £200.

4. *Chinese polished bronze ewer, 18th/19th century.* 11½in. Apr. '85, £70.
Had this not been polished it would have realized as much as £250–350. Also the inclusion of a monogram reduces its desirability.

5. *Chinese standing figure, late Ming dynasty, 17th century.* 15in. Jan. '85, £220.

6. *Chinese seated immortal, 17th century.* 8½in. Apr. '85, £110.

Bronzes were produced in China and Japan in great quantities from the seventeenth century through to the twentieth century, and it is on these I will concentrate. Although Chinese bronzes date back to the second millennium BC, the very early examples are a very different and specialized subject.

Chinese bronzes rely greatly in shape and style on their predecessors. The decoration is very stylized, using *taotie* (animal masks) and a profusion of dragons and Buddhistic lions on patterned grounds. The shapes are often direct copies of archaic pieces (No. 1) and often use the reign marks of earlier emperors, in particular that of Xuande (1426–35) either in seal or six-character form (see Page 71, No. 12).

Prices for this type can differ; figures invariably realize more than standard vases. Incense burners, which are common (No 2), have to some extent risen in price but they can still make as little as £20–£50 each, which does not indicate a vast market movement. Using the example of an eighteenth-century Chinese bronze figure 12in. high being worth some £200–£400, the equivalent vase would probably be around £100–£150. As in some other areas, the larger the item, the higher the price.

Japanese bronzes were not produced in any great quantity until the nineteenth century, particularly the end of it when huge numbers were made, mainly for Europe. Many of these were cast with birds, animals and foliage in relief, quite often on a lobed ground (p. 75, No. 5). However, some very fine ones were made during this period, decorated in *iroe hirazogen* and *takazogen* (coloured metal inlay, either flat or in relief). Birds, flowers and bamboo were the usual decorative subjects and the beautiful craftsmanship of these must be admired.

There is much more variation in prices for nineteenth-century Japanese bronzes than for Chinese examples. A large Japanese jardinière, for instance, can realize £200–£400, a similar vase £150–£250, and some of the smaller items as little as £30. Then, fine quality inlaid

Japanese bronzes can achieve prices well into the thousands, though most are worth under £1,000 (cf. p. 75, No. 6).

The other type from this period which is always popular is the animal model, including elephants, tigers and rats. These are typical of the sort of things which appear regularly at auctions around the country (see p. 74, Nos. 1–7).

The important thing to bear in mind is that it is not age which makes value, but quality. This applies even to very early bronzes. Rough examples from the Tang and ensuing dynasties, such as the mirrors (No. 3), may still be bought relatively cheaply.

Finally, beware of both polishing and damage. Bronzes have a patina which, when they are overcleaned, disappears to become a brassy colour (No. 4). This, particularly on a good bronze, can halve or quarter the price. Look also for soldering repairs, not always easy to spot on quick inspection.

John Redford

Animal Bronzes

1

2

3

4

5

1. *Japanese tiger, late 19th century.* 13in. long. Jan '85, £130.
2. *Fine and large Japanese stalking tiger, late 19th century.* 24in. long, on rootwood base. June '84, £2,000.
3. *Signed Japanese rat, late 19th century.* 6½in. long. Jan. '85, £380.
4. *Japanese elephant, late 19th century.* 13in. long. Jan. '85, £180.
5. *Japanese group of a lion attacking an elephant, late 19th century.* 19in. long. Feb. '85, £480.

Nos. 4 and 5 were equally well cast, and it is purely the extra size and more interesting subject which explains the price difference here.

6. *Six small animals, all slightly polished, 18th century.* 2–3in. Jan. '85, £650.

7. *Large Japanese lion attacking a crocodile, late 19th century.* 22in. long. June '85, £500 (unsold).
   Although an unusual subject and of larger than average size, this group has nothing like the same quality casting as No. 2.

6

7

Nineteenth-century Japanese Bronze Vases

1

2

3

4

5

6

7

8

1. *Pair of flask-shaped vases, late 19th century.* 10in. May '85, £100.
2. *Pair of two-handled vases, late 19th century.* 12in. May '85, £120.
3. *One of a pair of vases, mid/late 19th century.* 9½in. Jan. '85, £90.
4. *Incense-burner and cover, mid/late 19th century.* 17in. Jan. '85, £180.

Although of poor quality casting, the flasks (No. 1) made nearly as much as the larger superior quality vases (No. 2) due to their more desirable shape. The other pair of vases (No. 3) are another example of the Chinese Xuande reign mark being used (see page 71, No. 12), but they are badly cast, as is No. 4, which made its price on its size only.

5. *Vase, late 19th century.* 20½in. Apr. '85, £200.
6. *Vase decorated in iroe hirazogan, late 19th century.* 13½in. Christie's King Street, Mar. '85, £350.

7. *Pair of slender vases with hirazogan decoration, late 19th century.* 8in. Mar. '85, £95.
   The same type as No. 6 but smaller, with less quality and slightly worn and polished.
8. *Koro and cover, 19th century.* 15in. June '85, £35 (unsold).
   Here the bronze is quite clearly severely degraded and the dragon finial is damaged. In perfect condition this koro would have realized £200–£300 or more.

Oriental Ivories

Although most ivory actually comes from Africa or India, it is the place and date of the carving which most dictate potential value. It is a myth that all ivories are very rare and expensive – in fact vast amounts of it are on the market and in general it must be finely carved and signed, *or* made before the nineteenth century, in order to attain a reasonably high price.

The Japanese were far more prolific than the Chinese in their carving, particularly in the second half of the nineteenth century, and their ivories can be divided into three main types. The first is the *netsuke*, which is a small carving used as a toggle to be suspended from a belt, first used in the eighteenth century but not collected in any quantity until the mid-nineteenth. The second is the *okimono*, which is simply a small decorative carving, and the third type are large purely decorative carvings, practically all of which are late nineteenth century.

The last type is in some demand at the moment, but not perhaps as much as in previous years, pieces carved out of one piece of ivory rather than in sections being much the most desirable (Nos. 1 and 2). The emphasis during the past year has certainly been on smaller *okimono* and *netsuke* of above average quality (No. 4). Good patina or wear, signatures and inlay are the features to look out for. Japanese ivories of this type can be marvellously lifelike and imaginative, as opposed to most of the contemporary Chinese examples which tend to be far more stylized.

The Japanese used other natural materials for their carvings, such as marine ivory (in most cases walrus), which is distinguished by a mottled paler grain which runs through it and which has often proved less desirable than the traditional elephant ivory (No. 3). Stag antler and bone are often confused with ivory but are worth much less (see p. 78).

There are far fewer Chinese ivories on the market, although their history of ivory carving goes back much further in time. Indeed there are very rare examples known dating back as far as 1000 BC, though most of the earlier Chinese

1

2

4

1. *Japanese sectional ivory figure, late 19th century.* 8½in. Jan. '85, £95.

2. *Two Japanese ivory figure groups, late 19th century.* 4in. and 5in. Dec. '84, £420. Although they are smaller, the 'one-piece' ivory figures, which are invariably better carved, do substantially better than the much more common sectional ivory figures.

3. *One of three similar Japanese 'marine' ivory figures, late 19th century.* 9½in. Sold together, March '85, £220.

4. *A well-carved ivory 'netsuke' of a hare, signed, late 19th/early 20th century.* Jan. '85, £260. Animal subjects in ivory are always popular, this one being particularly well carved for a late example, and with inlaid eyes.

5

6

5. *Chinese ivory figure of Shoulao, 17th century.* 8in. Dec. '84, £550.

6. *Finely carved Cantonese ivory casket, 19th century.* Dec. '84, £600.
Much of this kind of carving was produced and appears on the market constantly, mainly in the form of card-cases and small plaques, usually not exceeding £100 (see Nos. 7 and 8). The high price here was due to this being a larger piece, and a casket, which is always popular.

7

8

7. *Cantonese ivory puzzle-ball.* 3in. diam. Sold together with four similar small items. April '85, £55.

8. *Cantonese ivory card-case.* 4in. May '85, £120.
Unlike the casket (No. 6) these are typical of the many small pieces of Cantonese ivory which appear regularly at auction.

ivories regularly seen at auction date from the middle of the Ming dynasty, c. 1600. Ivories from this period can attain high prices at auction and are usually distinguishable, even to the untrained eye, by the extensive surface cracking which is caused by oils within the ivory slowly evaporating over a period of time. Chinese ivories from the 17th and 18th centuries also tend to command reasonably high prices (No. 5).

From the mid 19th century many carvings such as puzzle-balls, card-cases and similar small decorative objects were produced at Canton, all carved in the same detailed style. Despite the amount of work in these, they do not tend to realize as much as one would expect, unless the item is unusually rare or large (No. 6).

Most of the Chinese ivory figures seen on the market today are from the nineteenth century, and recently they have proved themselves to be generally less desirable than their Japanese counterparts, due to a most stylized appearance which has less decorative merit. It was not until the beginning of the present century that the Chinese began to carve ivories in anything like the quantity that had been produced in Japan since the middle of the nineteenth century. These twentieth-century pieces tend to be recognizable by the shallow carving, very white ivory and colour staining. Carvings of this type realize very little at auction compared to their predecessors, and can make between £20 and £200 according to their size.

Nineteenth- and twentieth-century ivory carvings from India, of which there are many on the market, are, at the time of writing, much less fashionable their Chinese and Japanese counterparts. These also tend to be very stylized and in some cases rather roughly carved. Thus the price of a Chinese or Japanese carving can be virtually halved for an Indian example (see p. 79, No. 22).

Finally, damage is exceptionally important in dealing with Oriental ivories as in most cases it is impossible to make invisible repairs. Even the smallest chip from a carving, of whatever quality and whether large or small, can make a vast difference to price.   *Nicholas Pitcher*

Oriental Ivories (cont.)

10

9

9. *Japanese ivory tusk carving with wood stand, late 19th/early 20th century.* 17½in. long. Dec. '84, £190.

10. *Large Indian ivory tusk carving, late 19th/early 20th century.* 28in. long. Apr. '85, £220.

Although No. 10 is much the larger of these two, the fact that it is Indian and a heavily stylized piece of carving explains the similarity in price.

11

12

13

15

14

11. *Stag antler netsuke, 20th century.* May '85, £25.

12. *Ivory netsuke of a recumbent buffalo, 19th century.* May '85, £40.

13. *Okimono-type netsuke of two figures, 19th century.* May '85, £60.

14. *Ivory netsuke of Tenaga stretching, 19th century.* May '85, £170.

15. *Fine ivory netsuke of a rat by Kaigyokusai, early 19th-century,* Mar. '85, £16,200.

Roughly carved stag antler netsuke are not popular, as is shown by No. 11. Nos. 12 and 13 are both perfectly respectable 19th-century netsuke, the former being a particularly desirable subject, but their value was much reduced, each having suffered slight damage, very important in this field (see also p. 85). No. 14 is well carved, a good subject and in perfect condition. No. 15 is a very good example of a netsuke by an artist whose work is probably more in vogue than any other at present. It is beautifully carved, with exquisitely inlaid eyes and, as always with Kaigyokusai's pieces, is made from only the whitest, purest ivory found at the centre of the tusk.

16. *Chinese ivory standing female figure, 20th century.* 11in. Jan '85, £160.
17. *Chinese ivory standing warrior Immortal, 20th century.* 11in. May '85, £120.
18. *Chinese ivory standing Immortal, 19th-century.* 6¾in. May '85, £95.
19. *Japanese ivory figure, late 19th century.* 6in. Apr. '85, £240.
20. *Japanese sectional ivory figure, late 19th century.* 8¾in. May '85, £80.
21. *Sino-Tibetan ivory deity group, 20th century.* 10in. May '85, £180.
22. *Indian ivory group, early 20th century.* 3¾in. Sold together with a small ivory carving of Gandhi, Apr. '85, £65.

Nos 16–22 show an interesting variation in price for a number of reasons. Nos. 16 and 17 are very similar, No. 16 realizing more being a female subject. The kneeling semi-clad girl (No. 19) made a good price for the same reason. The Chinese figure (No. 18), although smaller, made more than the Japanese (No. 20), the latter being sectional and with a split to the head – both carvings are low in quality. Nos. 21 and 22 both realized more than average figures of their types, the Sino-Tibetan group because of the detailed carving, and the small Indian ivory because of its subject, which is more desirable than the commonly found stylized deity.

16   17   18

19   20   21

22

Enamels

When dealing with the term Enamelware, we are mainly involved with three types – Chinese Canton enamel, Chinese cloisonné, and Japanese cloisonné.

Canton enamel was first produced in the 18th century. It involved laying enamel on a metal base, and then painting with famille rose or other colours. Eighteenth-century examples have proved increasingly popular at auction, a perfect saucer of about 8 in. making £500 or more (No. 1). However, the problem has always been that it is very easily damaged, so perfect pieces have become increasingly rare, hence the slightly inflated prices. We are now finding, however, that even damaged eighteenth-century Canton enamel is rising in price, examples realizing up to £300, which would have been excessive a year or so ago. Shape can also affect prices – the more unusual, the more it will make. However, small nineteenth-century Canton enamel can still be bought for as little as £10 (No. 2). As in other cases, large decorative nineteenth-century pieces can, however, command prices of up to £400.

Chinese cloisonné, a process which involves building wire cages to the desired pattern, laying them on a copper or brass base, and filling in with coloured enamels, dates back rather earlier. The technique was first started early in the Ming dynasty, around the fifteenth century. These with their sixteenth- and seventeenth-century successors practically always command high prices. However, it is still possible to acquire a small, pleasant eighteenth-century example around £100 (No. 3).

The point which distinguishes Chinese and Japanese cloisonné is the difference in decoration. The Chinese tended to use a very stylized design, dense meandering foliage and *taotie* (monster masks). The Japanese also use stylized designs but in a more rigid form, with many different shaped panels either on brightly coloured, plain or 'goldstone' grounds (No. 4). However, they also produced some magnificently detailed work. Indeed in the latter half of the nineteenth century some of the most

exquisite and now expensive work came out of Japan (No. 5).

The Chinese cloisonné work of the same period does not stand up to comparison. The work is still stylized, although some large and exceptional pieces were being made that deviated from the norm (No. 6). However, late in the nineteenth century they were all beginning to be mass-produced, and although some of the items illustrated here look impressive and are decorative, they can be bought for under £50 each (Nos. 7 and 8).

Finally, it is very important to stress the importance of damage in gauging price. See page 85, which illustrates a vase which would have realized well over £1,000 if perfect.

Oriental enamels are extensively collected, but it is vitally important to realize the difference between early or extremely fine and perfect pieces, and late, mass-produced or damaged ones.

John Redford

1. *Three pieces of Canton enamel, 18th century.* The dishes 5¾in. and 10in. diam. and the small bowl and cover 3¾in. diam. Christie's King Street, Nov. '84, £400, £500 and £420 respectively.

2. *Three small pieces of Canton enamel, 19th century.* Sold Jan. '85 together with 11 other similar items, £50.

3. *Chinese cloisonné belt buckle, 18th century.* May '85, £140.

1

2

3

4

5

4. *Typical Japanese cloisonné vase, late 19th century.* 10½in. Jan '85, £90.

5. *Pair of fine quality Japanese cloisonné vases with silver wire decoration on dark blue grounds, late 19th century.* 12in. Apr. '85, £2,600.

6. *Unusual large Chinese cloisonné vase, early 19th century.* 31in. Oct. '84, £2,600.

7. *An extremely common type of 19th-century Chinese cloisonné vase.* 10in. Sold with another vase (damaged), Jan. '85, £28.

8. *A group of small Chinese and Japanese cloisonné pieces of a type of inferior quality and produced in great quantities.* Sold together, Apr. '85, £140.

9. *Pair of Chinese cloisonné candlesticks.* 9in. Apr. '85, £90.
Exactly the same type of cloisonné as No. 7, but candlesticks are usually more desirable than plain vases.

7

6

8

9

Eighteenth-Century Chinese Export Porcelain

1

2

3

4

The 'Wedding Presentation' plates illustrated (No. 1) are extremely rare and there are other examples of rare and unusual pieces of Chinese export porcelain making large sums at auction, occasionally doubling or trebling this sort of price. Export porcelain was, however, made in vast quantities throughout the eighteenth century and, while it is particularly in vogue at present, by no means all is wildly expensive. Shown here is a cross section of the most popular, and indeed in some cases the most common, types.

1. *Pair of 'Wedding Presentation' plates painted in famille rose enamels. 9in. diam. Christie's King Street, Nov. '84, £9,720.*

2. *Rare Chinese export porcelain plate. 9in. diam. Christie's King Street, Nov. '83, £3,240.*
   This plate is from a very well-known armorial service, the arms being those of Okeover impaling Nicholl. Another plate from the same service was sold in New York (Feb. '85) for slightly less, being restored. In cases such as this the arms are very important. A similar plate with less prestigious arms could realize half this price.

3. *One of a set of six famille rose 'tobacco–leaf' plates. 9in. diam. Christie's King Street, May '85, £1,600.*
   'Tobacco-leaf' is the most desirable of all the standard famille rose designs.

4. *Famille rose sauce tureen, cover and stand. 9in. wide. May '85, £1,100.*
   Decorated with a fairly commonplace famille rose design, this shows the popularity of export tureens.

5. *Famille rose 'mandarin-pattern' meat dish. 16in. wide. May '85, £550.*
   This was a good price, the dish being of mediocre quality and having a small chip to the rim.

5

6

7

8

9

6. *A blue and white meat dish.* 16in. wide. May
'85, £190.
A similar dish to No. 5, but in blue and
white, which is much more common, and
also fitted for a drainer, which is missing.

7. *Two blue and white meat dishes.* 10in. wide
(with pierced border) and 13½in. wide.
May '85, £140 and £130 respectively.
Both were made at the very end of the
century, the smaller example making up
for its lack of size by having a pierced
border.

8. *Famille verte meat dish.* Kangxi period,
15½in. wide. Christie's King Street, Mar.
'85, £918.
Much less common than its later famille
rose and blue and white counterparts.

9. *Two famille rose spoon trays.* 4in. wide. Apr.
'85, £75 (left) and £130.
The more unusual small pieces of Chinese
export teaware such as spoon trays,
teapot stands and tea caddies are always
desirable, the figure decoration being
preferred to the flowers in this case.

10. *A famille rose 'kendi'.* 6in. May '85, £1,500.
A very good price, which underlines not
only the popularity of kendis, but also
their comparative rarity in famille rose.

11. *A blue and white 'Fitzhugh pattern' tureen,
cover and stand.* 13½in. wide. Christie's
King Street, Nov. '84, £918.
Made towards the end of the century this
is another of the more sought-after
designs. Fitzhugh pattern is also less
commonly found separately in iron-red
and green.

10

11

12

13

12. *One of a pair of famille rose plates.* 9in. diam.
May '85, £320.
There are many similar plates around. In
this case the enamels were unusually clear
and bright. It is worth noting that even a
small hairline crack in plates as these can
halve or quarter their value.

13. *One of a pair of blue and white soup plates.*
9in. diam. May '85, £30.
Plates of this size and type are by far the
most common of all Chinese export
porcelain. They could, however, have
realized up to £60 had one not been
repaired.

The Importance of Shape . . .

Shape has always been one of the most important influences in determining the potential price of Oriental ceramics and works of art, but perhaps never more so than in this last year, which has seen a further emphasis on decorative merit. I have tried to illustrate this point with the pieces shown here, but there are, of course, many other variations of shape which affect prices (see also pages 68 & 69). Any elaborate body mouldings, handles, unusual finials, pierced rims and covers (see p. 82, No. 7) will make a vase or dish more fashionable than its plainer counterpart. Other examples are shown elsewhere in this chapter.

1. *Imari boat-shaped shallow bowl, 19th century.* 13in. long. Apr. '85, £280.
   This is approximately twice the price that a more normally shaped Imari dish of equivalent size would realize.

2. *Pair of Kaga vases, late 19th century.* 4½in. May '85, £55.

3. *Pair of Kaga flask-shaped vases, late 19th century.* 5in. Apr. '85, £130.
   The flask-shaped bodies and butterfly-moulded handles render No. 3 much more desirable than No. 2.

4. *Three Chinese blue and white vases, mid-19th century.* 11in., 11½in. and 9½in. May '85, £40, £100 and £90.
   The shape of the triple-gourd vase and the decoration of horses on the central bottle make them more valuable than the more common baluster vase and cover (left).

5. *Two examples of the popular Chinese 'tulip-vase' shape, early/mid 19th century.* 10in. and 9½in. Dec. '84, £100 (left) and Apr. '85, £140 (right).
   The presence of hexagonal flanges on the apertures of the right-hand vase make it preferable. Had it also been painted with figures the price could have been still higher.

6. *One of a pair of famille verte lozenge-shaped jardinières and stands, early/mid 19th century.* 11in. wide, May '85, £1,000.

7. *Pair of Chinese blue and white lozenge-shaped jardinières and stands, c. 1800.* 9in. wide. Mar. '85, £918.
   Nos. 6 and 7 are both sought after shapes, but although No. 6 was made some thirty to forty years later, the prices realized were similar, the famille verte being fashionable and having unusual bamboo-moulded sides.

8   9

8. *Chinese blue and white square tea-jar,* c. 1800.
13½in. Oct. '84, £1,000.
Square-shaped jars, vases and bottles are
always in demand. This one is very much
the same date and style as the blue and
white jardinières (No. 7), and made an
exceptionally good price in spite of the fact
that it should have a matching cover.

9. *A small provincial Ming crackled celadon-glazed
stem cup, 15th century.* 3½in. Oct. '84, £150.
Stem-cups and bowls have always been
among the most favoured of Chinese
shapes. Normally rough pieces of Ming
celadon would make considerably less than
this example (see p. 70).

. . . *Damage and Restoration*

There is a great deal of variation in how much difference damage and restoration will make to price. A small chip on the rim of a large nineteenth-century vase, for instance, will not vastly reduce its price – perhaps a £500 vase would drop to £400 or £450 – since in most cases it is bought purely for its decorative merits. Small, finer or earlier collectors' pieces, however, are a different story. Good Kangxi period blue and white porcelain, for example, is much less desirable when even slightly damaged (No. 1), as indeed are most of the earlier and finer Chinese and Japanese porcelains; an eighteenth-century famille rose plate, if worth £100 perfect, will make £30 with only a small crack.

The same applies to cloisonné enamel; the better quality Japanese cloisonné in particular, as is shown here in No. 2. The finest small pieces of Japanese Satsuma ware also come into this category, whereas the prices of larger, less delicate pieces will not be so affected (see also p. 72).

If fine Satsuma ware, Japanese cloisonné and early blue and white porcelain must in effect be absolutely perfect in order to realize a top price, this is also true of ivories, although to a lesser extent. Netsuke and small ivory okimono, being by their nature intricate collectables, lose a substantial amount of their value, even when the damage is not immediately noticeable (see p. 79, Nos. 19 & 20).

An important thing to remember is that no matter how well a piece is restored – and some these days are so well done as to even pose problems to the experienced specialist – it is still to all intents and purposes *damaged*. It will invariably realize less than a perfect example – in some cases much less.

1

2 a

2 b

1. *Two very similar Chinese blue and white
   yanyan vases, Kangxi period.* 17½in. and
   18in. high, Apr. '85, £250 and £800.

2a. *A large and finely decorated Japanese cloisonné
    enamel vase (damaged).* 18½in. Dec. '84,
    £380.

2b. A part of the damage is shown here. Had
    this vase been completely unblemished it
    could have realized as much as £2,000.

4.   Silver

Introduction

By Stephen Helliwell

1. *Victorian silver match-holder by E.C.B., London 1867.* 5½ in. Feb. '85, £1,200
   This charming parcel-gilt and finely engraved chimpanzee match-holder came complete with fitted case. In fine and original condition and with gilt spectacles, clay-pipe and wine goblet, he is a great rarity, hence the high price.

2. *Silver cake-stand by Viners and Co., Sheffield 1917.* 5½ in., 18½ oz. Mar. '85, £200.
   A machine-made cake-stand with no originalities of design or hand craftsmanship, but it would still make an attractive addition to any tea-table.

3. *Silver fruit-basket by Mappin and Webb, Sheffield 1919.* 10¾ in. diam., 16 oz. Mar. '85, £350.
   This fruit-basket is of rather better quality than No. 2, and has an attractively cast and applied vine border. This charming feature ensured a price of over £20 per ounce of silver, against a price of just over £10 per ounce for No. 2.

Silver has been prized for thousands of years, as it is a most malleable metal. It can be pulled, twisted, cast and beaten into innumerable wonderful shapes and then simply polished, or decorated with engraving, chasing and gilding. The possibilities are endless – the craftsman's imagination can be stretched almost as far as the metal with which he is working.

Obviously one cannot hope to condense the history of silversmithing into a series of short articles. We have tried to select topics which illustrate current collecting trends. Silver toys, snuffboxes, vinaigrettes and the like, once sneered at as nineteenth-century clutter, are now enjoying something of a revival, and there has also been a great upsurge of interest in wine relics. Domestic silver, however, must remain near the top of everyone's shopping list. People setting up home need knives and forks and other everyday items and, with silver, they can happily combine attractive design with durability and surround themselves with pleasing yet useful objects.

Silver may well be beyond the pocket of many collectors, and some twenty years ago more and more people turned to Sheffield Plate as a cheaper alternative. Naturally this too has become expensive, and so there has been much new interest in good electro-plate. We compare the two (see pp. 98–99), and also outline briefly the pitfalls which occur for any potential buyer who may at some time be offered fake or altered pieces at seemingly bargain prices (see pp. 94–5).

The market is a sensitive barometer, recording changes of fashion – but a mere study of prices is as much use as reading yesterday's weather reports. A collector or dealer

must be aware of the earliest signs of change if he wishes to take advantage of them. To state the obvious, four main factors influence a potential buyer. The first two – rarity and age – are perhaps self-explanatory. Obviously a collector of cutlery would strive to own several sixteenth- or seventeenth-century spoons and would be prepared to pay more for an unusual type, for instance a spoon with a cast maiden's head finial than a rather more standard Apostle.

On a more mundane level, any article which is over 100 years old is exempt from VAT, and consequently once that magic figure has been reached, a piece will automatically go up in value at the current rate of tax. Linked to this, we have the presence on silver of the duty hallmark, introduced during the reign of George III in 1784 as a tax on silver. Taking the form of a silhouette of the reigning Monarch's head, it was used until 1890, when Queen Victoria was successfully petitioned by British silversmiths who were struggling against the introduction of cheaper Continental silver of lower grade. Many collectors love to see the Monarch's head duty stamp, and consequently a piece made in 1891 will often make rather less than a similar item made just one year earlier.

The other two factors which will influence a buyer are rather more nebulous – the prettiness and quality of the piece. Obviously both these characteristics are rather arbitrary and depend much on the individual's personal preferences. A typical example can be seen in the chimpanzee match-holder box (No. 1), which typifies the Victorian taste for the bizarre and unusual. Beautifully made, it aroused much interest whilst on view. Many people found it grotesque and horrible, others exclaimed over its cuteness and appeal. Fortunately for the vendor, there were several of the latter present on the sale day, and it sold for £1,200 against a presale estimate of £600–800. In a similar vein, delicately pierced cake, fruit and bonbon baskets, despised until recently, seem to be at a premium today, and, if attractive and of fine quality, make good prices despite the lack of any great age or rarity.

The interest in pretty photograph frames is felt very strongly in the salerooms and even quite badly damaged pieces will sometimes surprise us. The typical late Victorian or Edwardian pierced and stamped frames seem to be especially popular, although the blue or red velvet mounts appearing through the decoration are usually sadly stained with silver cleaner as few detach for cleaning. Any Art Nouveau frames embossed with languid maidens gathering fruit or with cosy mottoes, such as 'East, West, home's best', will attract collectors from far and wide. So great is the demand for these pieces that reproduction photograph frames are flooding the market, and one has to be careful that a modern frame has not been deliberately aged in attempt to deceive. With silver we should always have the guarantee of a hallmark, but even this is not an infallible guide to dating, as the article on fakes will show.

To conclude, if there is any advice one can give to the potential collector, it is buy what you really like. There is little point in purchasing something for its age, rarity or

quality, if, after a while, its presence begins to irritate. One is constantly looking at and handling pieces which arouse true satisfaction – they evoke much joy in the buyer, which is then conveyed to friends and other collectors. On the other hand, any slight nagging dissatisfaction may grow into a raging doubt in one's own tastes and the piece will usually be relegated to the back of a cupboard, out of sight, out of mind, or sold on, perhaps at a loss. If the collector is true to his own taste, his collection will always be a source of much happiness and growing pleasure.

4. *Edwardian silver-mounted photograph frame, Birmingham, 1902.* 8 in. Feb. '85, £130.

5. *Art Nouveau silver-mounted photograph frame by William Hutton & Sons, London, 1902.* 8½ in. Dec. '84. £220.
Late Victorian and Edwardian frames are very popular in the salerooms today, although they are often in poor condition, with stained velvet backings and holes worn through the thin silver by over-enthusiastic cleaning. These frames are often reproduced using the same die-stamps, although the modern ones lack the sharpness of the originals. While the modern frames retail at between £20 and £40 each, the originals are far more popular, even if in poor condition.

6. *Early 20th-century silver, enamel and wooden photograph frame by Carl Fabergé.* 6 in. Dec. '84, £2,800.
Fabergé's factory made thousands of small desk-top items – bell-buttons, paper-weights, blotters and photograph frames. They are invariably of magnificent quality, and one feels that his workmen lavished as much care on these knick-knacks as on the more famous presentation pieces. Although pieces by Fabergé are not rare, they invariably arouse much interest in the saleroom, and this frame made a good price despite many small signs of damage.

Silver Tableware

With the exception of the early spoons, which preceded today's tableware, knives, forks and spoons are normally considered as domestic rather than 'collectable' silver. Except, naturally, by the person attempting to match sets.

As always the famous makers such as Paul Storr and Hester Bateman are much in demand and a premium can be expected for such names. The Coburg set by Paul Storr, sold in New York (No.12) is a good example.

At the lower end of the market, a canteen of fiddle pattern can be bought for as little as £8–£12 per ounce with Old English and King's pattern being more popular. A set nicely displayed in a fitted case will always command a higher price than the items sold loose. While a composite set is generally acceptable, it will obviously not realize as much as a full set with the same maker's mark and date letter.

When looking for a complete set, it should be borne in mind that very few early examples will have matching knives, since these were usually by a different maker and sold separately. Provided that time can be spent haunting the auction houses, antique shops and stalls, a great deal of pleasure can be had by purchasing half a dozen forks or spoons at a time to create a set. There are very few silver auctions today that do not include such lots.

Depending on style and condition one can expect to pay from about £8 per ounce upwards. As a very general rule of thumb dessertspoons weigh around 2 oz. each and tablespoons and forks about 3 oz., King's pattern being a heavy design and Old English much lighter.

Fish knives and forks are always sought after, since they did not make an appearance until the nineteenth century and are not to be found in the Georgian canteens. Not quite so popular are the bone-handled fruit knives and forks, which can be purchased from about £90 upwards for six pairs. The sets with pretty mother-of-pearl handles can realize double this price.

It is the 'extras' that push up the price when matching up tableware: items such as condiment spoons, sauce and soup ladles, gravy spoons, asparagus tongs and servers. One of the reasons for this is that these, together with marrow scoops, cheese scoops, grape scissors and meat skewers, start to fall within the 'collectable' category as opposed to domestic. The last, of course, are in much demand as letter openers. With such things, unlike everyday tableware, the weight of the silver has little bearing on the price realized, except as it improves the quality of the item. For example, a pair of King's pattern grape scissors weighing 4 oz. can realize £250, whereas for £140 one can purchase six King's pattern dessert forks or spoons.

Just a word of caution: Always check for condition, and, in particular, make sure that fork prongs (or 'tines') haven't been trimmed to disguise worn points.

James Collingridge

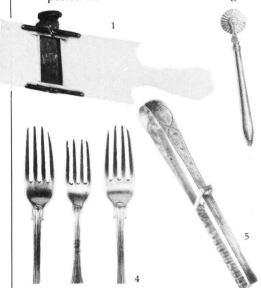

1

5

4

3

6

1. *George III silver and ivory cucumber slice by Thomas and James Phipps, London 1816.* 9 in. long. Apr. '84, £550.

2. *Victorian silver pastry-wheel by Charles Reily and George Storer, London 1839.* 6 in. long. Sept. '84, £280.
   Although not strictly 'flatware', these interesting culinary aids are rare enough to warrant inclusion, arousing much interest in collectors and museums alike. The former had the added attraction of an engraved crest, that of Baron Foley.

3. *William IV silver fiddle, thread and shell pattern table service, for 18 place settings by Samuel Hayne and Dudley Cater, London 1836.* 248 oz. Feb. '85, £11,000.
   Large table-services are very popular today, and of all the available patterns of cutlery, the above is one of the most sought after, with its elegant shell and thread edge. This service was further enhanced with an original family crest.

4. *Three from a set of six William IV silver fiddle and thread pattern table forks by Eley and Fearn, London 1835.* 14 oz. Feb. '85, £95.
   Obviously many people buy antique flatware to use, so condition must be of paramount importance. This set of forks had badly worn and damaged tines which can be shortened and re-sharpened, but this invariably spoils the balance of the pieces. The central example shows another common fault – 'burn' marks left on the silver by an elastic band. Such marks are very difficult to remove and frequently require professional 'buffing', this probably damaging the attractive thread-edge to the stem.

5. *Pair of George III silver asparagus tongs by H.I., London 1790.* Jan. '85, £180.
   Asparagus tongs are always popular – today one could use them for serving pastries or sandwiches. This pretty pair had bright-cut engraved decoration, with the bonus of an original family crest.

6. *George IV silver fiddle pattern fish-slice by William Eley and William Fearn, London 1824.* Feb. '85, £105.
   Fish slices are found quite commonly in the salerooms and frequently bear the makers' mark of Eley and Fearn, these being specialist flatware makers during the late 18th and early 19th centuries. Examples can be bought for £60–£80, but this particular slice had the added attraction of two fish engraved on the blade, hence the high price.

7

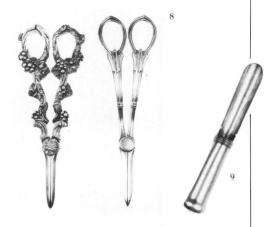

8

9

10

11

12

13a

13

7. *A selection of silver tea-caddy spoons from the late 18th and early 19th centuries.* Sold as individual lots in Feb. '85, prices ranging from £45 to £75.

Caddy spoons were made in vast quantities, many by the Birmingham 'toy makers', and standard shapes can still be bought for under £50. Novelty shapes formed as hands, flowers, eagles' heads, jockey caps and so on are much rarer and can frequently make several hundreds of pounds each.

8. *Two pairs of Victorian silver grape-scissors. Cast grape design by E.H., London 1852.* Feb. '85, £290. *Albany pattern by Francis Higgins, London 1879.* Feb. '85, £190.

Grape scissors, especially the more decorative cast examples, are popular today with collectors. The examples above were uncased — one could add on approximately 30% to the prices achieved had they still had their original fitted cases.

9. *George III silver apple corer by Joseph Taylor, Birmingham 1797.* Feb. '85, £220.

Silver collapsible apple-corers, the blades unscrewing to fit into the hollow tubular handles, are quite unusual although many examples can be found carved from sheep leg-bones. These country-made pieces cost between £20 and £30.

10. *Set of four George III Old English pattern sauce ladles, maker's mark indistinct, London 1790.* Feb. '85, £220.

Sauce or gravy ladles are still useful today and examples with shell-fluted bowls are especially popular. This set had original engraved crests, but the marks were worn with years of cleaning. Crisper marks would probably have attracted a bid of £300.

11. *French silver and bone travelling canteen, c. 1840.* Oct. '84, £220.

The 19th-century traveller would have been loath to use the eating utensils of inns and most people carried their own set. The above example still has its tooled leather case and comes complete with beaker, folding cutlery and bone and ebony salt and pepperpot — ideal for picnics or race-meetings today!

12. *Regency Coburg pattern for 18 place settings by Paul Storr, London 1819, the knives modern.* 250 oz. (weighable silver). New York, Oct. '84, $63,800 (£50,635).

Coburg pattern, an unusual variation of the more familiar King's pattern, was designed for Rundell, Bridge and Rundell in 1810, and all period pieces were made by the much collected silversmith Paul Storr. Complete services are rare, hence the high price.

13 & 13a. *Late Victorian silver canteen for 12 place settings by Elkington and Co. Birmingham, 1895.* 173 oz. (weighable silver). Mar. '85, £4,800.

This canteen was decorated with stamped 16th-century style figures amidst fruit and flowers, and was remarkably complete, including dessert knives and forks, fish knives and forks and table and dessert knives, all with ivory handles engraved with the original owner's crest. Illustrated also is the attractive oak canteen itself, the drawers still divided and lined with baize to protect the cutlery from scratching. The presence of the original canteen will increase the value of cutlery by at least 25%.

Wine-Related Items

'Pass the port, old chap.' Blue cigar smoke rose lazily and, as the decanter circulated, the men leant further and further back in their seats. Waistcoats were unbuttoned and smiles broadened at the thought of the dinner just consumed and the tales soon to follow.

Such a Mitfordian scene may now be rare but there has been a tremendous upsurge of interest in such seemingly dated items as wine funnels, decanting cradles and 'bottle tickets' or wine labels. For a year we have held bi-monthly sales of wine relics, with perhaps the most enthusiasm coming from America. Of course, the sale does not only include silver: unusual brass corkscrews, pottery bin labels and seventeenth- and eighteenth-century glass sealed bottles are also keenly sought, and in April 1985 a whole collection of bottling equipment went under the hammer.

The silver or silver-plate mounted glass claret jug is a favourite, the more elaborate or unusual examples often making more than £1,000. The glass itself is often exquisitely cut or engraved, and this decoration is, of course, set off to best advantage when the jug is filled with rich red claret.

Massive nineteenth-century wine coolers are also extremely popular, although all too many have lost the original interior collars and fittings. The majority are made of Old Sheffield Plate and can be delightfully rococo or more sturdy and plain. They were usually made in pairs and, while a single example sells for £200–£300, an attractive pair can realize more than £1,500.

'Bottle-tickets' were first introduced in the 1740s. The earliest silver examples

1.

are of simple cartouche-shape and usually bear a maker's mark only. Later tickets became more and more fanciful and were fully hallmarked, although for many years the makers took advantage of the fact that the Government forgot to list 'tickets' when introducing the duty on silver. Consequently you may well find untaxed labels without the Monarch's head duty stamp. Some collectors look for certain makers – labels were made even by Paul Storr and Hester Bateman – while others seek unusual shapes, goblets, crescent moons, stars or vine leaves. Yet others collect unusual names engraved on the labels, 'noyau, bucellas', or the charming 'cream of the valley' – a lovely nineteenth-century name for gin. While pairs or larger sets of wine labels can command very high prices, single examples can often be found for £25–£40.

Champagne taps, toddy ladles, tantaluses – the list seems endless, and we must also include cigar-cutters and piercers, lighters and boxes, Stilton scoops, in fact anything for the 'bon viveur'. Obviously the period of graceful living is not yet over, and I am delighted that, in today's hustle and bustle, people still find time to enjoy the creature comforts of post-prandial relaxation and leisure.

Stephen Helliwell

1. *Silver mounted claret jug, the antelope's head mount by L.D., London 1884.* 13¼ in. Dec. '84, £2,000.
   All claret jugs are popular but the more unusual the better.

2. A group of typical wine related objects, all sold Dec. '84. Left to right:
   Silver spirit flask by James Dixon, Sheffield, 1881. 5 in. £260.
   An attractive and unusual oval shape with good engraving and crest.
   Silver two-handled orange strainer by John Coas, London, 1844. £210.
   A Victorian copy of a familiar Georgian punch-making utensil.
   Silver wine funnel by Edward Power, Dublin, 1818. £260.
   Note the delicately curved spigot to run wine down the side of the decanter. Irish or Scottish silver is at a premium.
   Large pair of electro-plated coasters by Elkington & Co., Birmingham, c. 1860. 9 in. diam. £350.
   These were virtually mint. They were also charming and still practical today.

3. *Case of Victorian star-cut glass decanters with engraved silver-gilt mounts by Charles Rawlings and William Summers, London, 1862.* Oct. '84, £3,900.
   The original walnut-veneered case and sound lock, and the engraved crest and motto outweighed the lack of the third label.

3   4   5

4. *Electro-plate mounted claret jug, unmarked,* c. *1860.* 12 in. £400.
An elegant shape with finely engraved floral and foliate decoration.

5. *Continental silver mounted liqueur decanter, bearing import marks for 1905.* 11½ in. Apr. '85, £450.
Probably made in Holland for the British market, the mount with attractive stamped cherub decoration.

6. *Silver-mounted glass claret jug, the mount by W.L., London, 1881.* 12¼ in. Apr. '85, £800.
Victorian novelty animal claret jugs are highly collected, this example being crudely made but still attractive enough to realize a healthy price.

7. *Silver-mounted claret jug, unmarked but probably French,* c. *1850.* 10½ in. Feb. '85, £750.
Fine example of 19th-century rococo revival, with superbly cut glass.

8. *Silver claret jug by Walker and Hall, London, 1900.* 12 in. Feb. '85, £420.
Finely-chased with acanthus leaves and vines, the latter motif repeated in the boldly scrolling handle.

9. *Victorian brass-bound Coromandel tantalus with four cut glass decanters, unmarked,* c. *1880.* 14½ in. long. Apr. '85, £950.
This tantalus was in mint condition, hence the high price.

6

7

8

9

10

11

12

13

10. *Polished onyx and gilt-brass tantalus engraved 'Betjemann's Patent 13849, London',* c. *1880.* 14½ in. long. Apr. '85, £500.
Tantaluses in oak are not rare, but this was an unusual example with applied hardstone flower decoration.

11. *French inlaid amboyna liqueur cabinet, unmarked,* c. *1890.* 12¾ in. long. Apr. '85, £650.
The fine mother-of-pearl and brass inlay and attractive gilt brass frame ensured much interest, although several of the glass fittings were badly chipped.

12. *One of a set of four green glass bottles gilt with bunches of grapes, mid-19th-century.* 12¾ in. Apr. '85, £550.
The colour contrast between the green glass and the gilt decoration made a particularly attractive combination.

13. *One of a pair of Old Sheffield Plate wine coolers, unmarked,* c. *1815.* 11¾ in. Apr. '85, £1,800.
Such pairs of wine coolers are very popular and this example, although unmarked, was in pristine condition, with finely engraved original crest.

14. *One of three silver wine labels, Peter and William Bateman, London, 1806.* Apr. '85, £140.
Wine labels are especially sought after if in sets, but individual examples can be found for £30–£40 each.

15. *Brass and mahogany decanting cradle, early 19th century.* 14½ in. long. Feb. '85, £380.
A well-constructed and unusual piece, still perfectly usable today.

14

15

Toys and Trinkets

1

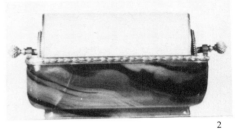

2

In the mid-eighteenth century Birmingham earned itself the rather scathing title 'The Toy Shop of Europe', as many of its 'factories' were small family units, which concentrated on the manufacture of 'toys' or amusing trifles such as snuffboxes, vinaigrettes and wine labels.

No doubt as a result of unfair criticism from London, the city of Birmingham was long associated with shoddy and inferior workmanship. When one considers the vast number of small silver items made in the late eighteenth or early nineteenth centuries which have survived after many years of almost constant use, then surely this accusation is unfounded. Certainly the original customers were more than happy with their purchases.

Today's collectors are still keen to acquire such bijouterie, all the more so perhaps, since standard snuffboxes can be bought for as little as £60–£80. Thus one can soon build up a good representative collection without spending a vast sum of money, and a whole assortment of pieces can be shown off to advantage in one display case. Many snuffboxes, vinaigrettes, vesta cases and sovereign cases can do modern duty as pill boxes or even jewellery.

While many of these pieces can be bought quite inexpensively, more unusual items invariably attract high prices. While a standard snuffbox or vinaigrette would be of plain oblong shape, relying on attractive engine-turning or bright-cut engraving for an overall decorative effect, they can also be found in other shapes including handbags, books, animals' heads, snails and even coffins. Equally sought after are those with cast and applied mounts depicting famous buildings such as Balmoral, Westminster Abbey and even Birmingham Town Hall. Visiting card cases also frequently display these cast mounts and are equally popular, especially if made by Nathaniel Mills, who was working from the mid-nineteenth century.

Many articles made for gentlemen, such as cheroot or vesta cases, were enamelled with risqué scenes. Presumably shocking and titillating in Victorian England, today they are rather amusing

and much collected. Enamelled sporting scenes and animals are also very popular, and a cigarette case decorated with a mounted huntsman leaping a fence can often realize £300–£500.

A recent sale of scent bottles again proved the popularity of novelty items, with silver-mounted porcelain examples painted to look like wild birds' eggs making £60–£80 each. These were made by one of the few London 'toy makers', Sampson Morden, whose firm specialised in pens and pencils. Once again, it is the unusual – pigs, mummies, guns and oars – which attract the attention of the modern collector.

There are many other possibilities for the collector of toys, including condiment labels, cigar cutters and piercers, needlework accessories, penknives and chatelaines, most of which would sell for less than £50. Consequently a varied and attractive group can be amassed, and such a selection would, I feel sure, prove to be a good long-term investment.

Stephen Helliwell

3

1. *A Russian silver, guilloche enamel and rose-diamond cachou box, c. 1910. 2 in. Feb. '85, £600.*

2. *A Russian vari-coloured gold, agate and guilloche enamel stamp-moistener by Carl Fabergé, c. 1910. 2¾ in. Feb. '85, £1,900.*
   Of course, not all 'toys' were made in England and many fine examples of the silversmith's and jeweller's art came from Russia. The stamp-moistener bears the all-important maker's mark of Carl Fabergé, hence the high price despite the fact that the agate water reservoir was badly split and chipped.

3. *A collection of silver-mounted glass or porcelain scent-bottles offered as separate lots in Nov. '84.*
   Scent-bottles are very collected today and when a private collection is divided into small lots for sale at auction, prices can rocket. To give some individual prices – the example top left made by the French firm Daum *c.* 1910, £180; the centre example of iridescent satin-glass painted with a chrysanthemum, £120; the two egg-shaped examples bottom centre, one with multi-coloured glass body, the other of pottery painted to resemble a magpie's egg, £100 and £80 respectively.

4. *Large Victorian silver, leather and wood letter-clip, the silver mounts by E.H.S., London, 1892. 8½ in. long. Feb. '84, £380.*
   The silversmith has introduced much life and vitality into the tiny cast figures of a terrier tormenting a spitting cat – these Victorian novelty pieces are very popular today.

4

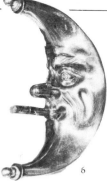

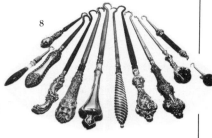

5

6

7

8

5. *Victorian enamelled silver vesta case by J. Millward Banks, Birmingham, 1892.* 2 in. wide. Feb. '84, £210.
Enamelled vesta or cigarette cases are often in rather poor condition, most being worn, badly scratched, or even chipped. This case was in mint condition with bright fresh colours and a lively scene, hence the high price.

6. *Victorian silver cigar-lighter by G.H., London, 1890.* 4¾ in. Mar. '84, £240.
Smokers' accessories such as cigar-lighters are always popular and this unusual novelty 'man-in-the-moon' could be sold equally well in a 'toy' sale or a wine-relics sale.

7. *Victorian silver auctioneer's gavel by E. Emanuel, London, 1850.* 5¼ in. long. Dec. '84, £700.
Gavels were normally made of ivory or ebony and this unusual silver example must have been commissioned as a presentation piece. Indeed it carried a charming inscription that it was given 'after an apprenticeship of great industry, integrity and care'. Finely cast and chased with flowers and foliage, it was sold with original fitted case and was in absolutely mint condition.

8. *Part of a collection of silver-mounted steel button-hooks, late 19th and early 20th centuries.*
Many of the items which fall under the category of 'toys' or 'collectables' have become totally outmoded in today's society, a good example of this being the humble button-hook, used well into this century to fasten both shoe and glove buttons. Most were made in Birmingham, and today large and decorative examples can realize £25–£35 each.

9. *Victorian silver visiting-card case, Nathaniel Mills, Birmingham, 1857.* Oct. '84, £460.

10. *Victorian silver visiting-card case, E.E., London, 1878.* Sept. '84, £140.

11. *Victorian silver visiting-card case, Hilliard and Thomason, Birmingham, 1850.* Mar. '85, £190.
Throughout the 19th century, an elaborate ritual was made of calling on friends and acquaintances to leave visiting-cards, and the cases themselves, often finely chased, are much sought after today. 'Castle tops' – examples die-stamped with buildings such as St. Paul's Cathedral (No. 9) and The Walter Scott Memorial in Edinburgh (No. 11), are particularly collected, especially if made by Nathaniel Mills, a prolific Birmingham 'toy-maker'. No. 10 is charmingly engraved with birds and flowers in the Japanese style so loved by the 'aesthetes' of the 1870s.

12. *Continental enamelled silver cigarette case, unmarked, probably German, c. 1910.* Nov. '84, £260.

13. *Continental enamelled silver cigarette-case, unmarked, probably German, c. 1910.* Oct. '84, £220.
Erotic cigarette cases, presumably rather shocking when first made but now only mildly amusing, are very popular today, as are those depicting hunting or shooting scenes. Both the tasteful nude and the pointer and setter in moorland scene (Nos. 12 and 13) are well-painted in enamels using subtle colours. Enamelled cigarette and vesta cases are both reproduced today.

14. *Edwardian enamelled silver visiting-card case by Sampson Morden, London, 1904.* Oct. '84, £210.
Novelty card-cases are very popular today and this example, finely enamelled with stamp, address and even postmark, made a good price despite much surface scratching.

9

10

11

13

12

14

Fakes and Alterations

The law is quite definite regarding alterations and additions. Perhaps the most common alteration of all is a spout added to a mug or tankard to change it to a jug. Occasionally one finds such a piece with a full hallmark on the addition, which legalizes the alteration. (To offer it for sale without re-submitting for assay is an offence.)

Other alterations include the plain entrée dish or platter that is chased and raised into a more desirable fruit basket. While 'after-chasing' was practised prolifically by the Victorian silversmiths and is not illegal in itself, the alteration in usage is a contravention of the law.

Other items to watch out for are three-prong forks that have been made out of table-spoons, and George III coffee pots made by stretching and raising plain baluster tankards. The lack of a hallmarked lid can be a good indication, although where a lidded tankard has been used, a full set of hallmarks will appear. The genuine coffee pot would normally bear the lion passant and maker's mark only.

Re-casting is another seductive trap. This often applies to tableware. For example, a cast is taken of a King's pattern fork, and any number made from it complete with hallmarks. Such a fork can be detected in several ways, the first being small pits or sand marks left by the casting. Secondly, all the hallmarks will be absolutely identical, which would not be the case if they were struck individually. Thirdly, a hand-made fork or spoon, because of the hammering in manufacture, will have a certain amount of spring when an attempt is made to bend it, whereas a cast item will have no give at all.

While any hallmark that is stamped in a place where it is likely to be polished, and consequently worn, is acceptable, such as the side of a teapot, extreme caution should be used where a hallmark is not clearly defined in area, and is not subject to wear, since this could be a soft punch used by a faker.

Another common method of faking is the inset mark. This is often seen on items such as ornate rose bowls, the disc containing the hallmark being let into the side, and the resulting patch disguised by decorating the edges with raised work or cartouche. Hallmarks on the edge of a pedestal should be viewed with suspicion, since a handle from a teaspoon can be let in and disguised. In this case the tell-tale patch should show up by breathing on the suspect area.

As stated earlier, the practice of the Victorian silversmith of 'beautifying' a piece of plain Georgian silver by ornately chasing it with such things as flowers, foliage and rustic scenes, is acceptable in the eyes of the law – but completely unacceptable to the collector. Whatever the date of the hallmark, the item can only be viewed in the light of the subsequent decoration.

Finally: so devious have some silversmiths been, that any item that appears out of keeping with its period should be viewed with suspicion.

James Collingridge

1. Quite remarkable what can be done to a massive sugar castor!

2. The alteration of an odd Georgian tablespoon to a cheese scoop probably made the item more useful to the owner. However, the change of usage is an illegal alteration and the item itself is completely out of balance.

3. This cream jug bears the soft punch marks used by the faker and close examination shows how much cruder they are than those used by the Assay Office. Generally the marks would be under the spout of this type of jug.

4. What a sad end to this pair of George III sugar tongs. One can only hope that the desecrator derived some pleasure from it.

5. This set of six spoons, supposedly made in Edinburgh c. *1690,* bears the soft punches made by the faker himself, rather than the genuine punches applied by the Hallmarking Office.

6

6a

7

7a

8

8a

6 & 6a. This castor, supposedly made in the mid-18th century, has been recast from an original. This in itself is not illegal provided that the new article is submitted for assay. However, in this instance, the original hallmarks have been reproduced. A close examination of the marks shows the small pits left by the sand casting, which, of course, cannot be polished off in the same way as the rest of the castor. Further suspicion is also aroused by the lack of a mark on the cover.

7 & 7a. One would have thought this to be quite a saleable sugar basket. However, as our photograph shows, the hallmark has been 'let in' to the base. This practice was used by the 'duty dodgers' as well as the faker when George III introduced a tax of 6*d* per oz. on silver in 1784. It was quite a saving for the devious silversmith to send a small disc weighing less than half an ounce to be hallmarked and then let it into a much heavier article. It should be said that this is an easy item to detect. Had the disc been let into the decoration of a chased item, and the edges chased over, it would have been harder to detect.

8 & 8a. This coffee pot purporting to be made by Isaac Cookson in Newcastle, 1744, shows the solder marks of the inlet plate. Even without this, one's suspicion should be aroused by the lack of a mark on the lid. This type of 'fake' was used extensively by the 'duty dodger'. A disc of silver weighing less than ½oz. would be submitted for assay supposedly as a watch back. When assayed, it would be inserted between the pedestal and the base. Whilst the silver for the item could well be up to 'standard' it allowed the dodger to get away with 3*d* duty instead of several pounds.

10

11

9. Two 18th-century sauceboats made from the bowls of punch ladles. The whalebone or turned wooden handles were removed and feet were then added to make more useful objects for the owners.

10. On the left a charming Victorian Christening mug and on the right a Georgian example, both having spouts added in the Victorian era to change them into more useful objects.

11. Two George III tankards with domed covers, which started off absolutely plain (the one on the left with body band). As with the cream jugs (No. 10) the spouts have been added. The chasing carried out in the 19th century was the Victorians' way of beautifying plain silver and is in itself legal. Were it not for the spouts, these pieces could have been offered for sale and would probably have realized about 50% of the value they would have had if left plain.

12. This bowl is an outright fake, although the method used could also be used for dodging duty. The rim of the pedestal has solder marks showing where the hallmark has been 'let in'. The hallmarks were probably taken from a piece of cutlery since they are in a straight line. A bowl of this type should have marks on the bottom or side. The piece itself is completely out of character with the marks which date it as 1794, and, for good measure, the purported makers, George Smith and William Fearn, were cutlery makers and unlikely to have made bowls.

12

Styles in Teapots

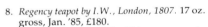

1. *Queen Anne teapot by Anthony Nelme, London, 1709, the stand and lamp by John Fawdery I, London, 1710.* 27 oz. gross. July '83, £15,660.
   The earliest teapots were of pear shape, often panelled for strength, and were very small – this reflecting the expense and rarity of tea itself.

2. *George I teapot by Samuel Wastell, London, 1723.* 19 oz. gross. July '84, £7,560.
   A plain pear-shape teapot of heavier gauge silver, it attracted such a good bid as it was in fine condition, with excellent original armorial in baroque cartouche.

3. *George I teapot by Thomas Farrer, London, 1725.* 14 oz. gross. July '83, £9,180.
   Slightly later in the 18th century, the 'bullet' teapot became fashionable. Of simple compressed shape and often with plain straight spouts, they were almost invariably undecorated, their polished surfaces serving to display the original owner's crest or armorial. This example has panelled sides as a strengthening device.

4. *George II bullet teapot by S.W. of Exeter, 1730.* 13½ oz. gross. Mar. '84, £2,200.
   By this date, spouts were frequently curved and fluted, this added shape evolving into the next.

5. *George II teapot by A.L., London, 1753.* 17½ oz. gross. Dec. '84, £480.
   In the mid-18th century, the inverted pear shape became popular, this example with contemporary rococo chasing giving a lighter more frivolous appearance. This shape is more commonly found in Scottish silver – in the 18th century Continental porcelain found its way to London and the south of England, replacing silver for teapots for several years until the customer realized that porcelain was too fragile for everyday use.

6. *George III teapot by Andrew Fogelberg, London, 1790.* 15½ oz. gross. Nov. '84, £380.
   In the third quarter of the 18th century, teapots were made from sheet silver and were usually simple in outline, relying on bright-cut engraving to enhance and lighten the sometimes solid appearance. The shape above, with its angles and corners, was probably introduced by silversmiths to compete with the makers of fused plate, who would have found tell-tale traces of copper difficult to conceal in such a design.

7. *George III teapot and stand by W.A., London, 1801.* 21¾ oz. gross. Sept. '84, £650.
   This time the teapot has moulded horizontal lines for strengthening. Notice that up till now none of the pots have had feet, hence the need for silver stands to protect the table top from heat-scorching. A teapot of this style sold without stand would probably realize £350–£450.

8. *Regency teapot by I.W., London, 1807.* 17 oz. gross. Jan. '85, £180.
   At the beginning of the 19th century styles in silver became heavier. The elongated cube-sheet became popular for tea sets and the manufacturers used as little silver as possible. Obviously the thinness of the body could lead to problems and many examples of this period show signs of later repair or thin patches when initials have been removed.

   The example illustrated below was in poor condition, hence the low price achieved. Notice, by now the teapots are raised on their own feet, so there is no need for a matching stand.

9

10

11

9. *Regency teapot by T. & J. Guest and Joseph Cradock, London, 1811.* Sold with matching sugar basin. Jan. '85, £320.
This teapot is much the same shape as the previous example and has a very similar spout, wood handle and ball feet. It differs in being chased with a frieze of rising flutes or corrugations, partly a strengthening device but also perhaps making the design somewhat lighter and more attractive. An individual teapot of this design would realize £220–£260.

10. *George IV teapot by H.H., London, 1824.* 22 oz. Jan. '84, £260.
By the 1820s a restrained and light naturalism became popular and the rounded compressed shape took over from the cube shape. This teapot is well-chased with flowers and has a finial which complements this decoration. The chaser has left a scroll cartouche for the owner's crest or initials. One must always try to press gently against this cartouche . . . if it has a slight 'give' then initials have been erased creating a weak spot. Indeed one often finds that a patch has been applied, covering such a thin spot, and this would greatly reduce the value of the piece.

12. *Victorian teapot by George Angell, London, 1855.* Sold as part of a four-piece tea and coffee service. Oct. '81, £1,700.
This heavy style is known as Victorian 'Gothic'. The large flat panels are relieved with fine engraving, the scroll design reflected in the handles and finials. Such a tea and coffee service would bring £2,500 – £3,000 today, a single teapot perhaps £400–£600.

13. *Edwardian tea and coffee service by William Hutton and Sons Ltd., London, 1908.* 35 oz. Oct. '78, £800.
Art Nouveau silver is unusual – many buyers trying to escape from the heaviness of 19th-century silver condemned the metal as well as the designs, insisting on pewter tea services like the Cymric range made by Liberty & Co. This small tea and coffee service – the coffee pot was only 6½ in. high – would bring at least £2,000 now, an individual teapot £600–£800, such is the popularity of the Art Nouveau style today. It seems odd that the latter price is almost double that which one would pay for a Georgian teapot.

14. *Art Deco teapot, unmarked but probably Danish.* Sold as part of a three-piece tea service. Oct. '84, £600.
The 1920s and 1930s saw a revival of simplicity, with plain curved or straight lines emphasizing the beauty of the metal itself and with no added engraved decoration. Here the colour of the silver contrasts well with the polished rosewood handle and finial. A single teapot in this style would realize £250–£300.

11. *Victorian teapot by R.S., London, 1842.* 19¼ oz. Jan. '85, £200.
In the Victorian period a wide variety of designs were exploited, ranging from adaptations of earlier pieces to the full extravagances of 19th-century naturalism. This teapot, made in the mid-18th-century taste, is relatively plain in outline, the octagonal spout and finial reflecting the shape of the body. Engraved with arabesques, it was in rather poor condition, hence the low price.

15

15. *Modern teapot on stand in the Queen Anne style, London, 1950.* 41½oz. gross. Mar. '85, £550.
The evolution of styles has now come full circle and this photograph illustrates a modern teapot on stand of excellent quality reproducing exactly the pear-shape of the Queen Anne example in the first photograph. This piece is even made of the higher quality Britannia Standard silver used in the early 18th century.
Although the price does not compare with that of the teapot in the first illustration, it was still a most satisfactory outcome for a 'reproduction', perhaps bought by a collector of limited means who could not afford a Queen Anne example, but who wished to display a full range of teapot styles.

12

Old Sheffield and Electro-Plate

Silver plating falls into two main categories – Old Sheffield and Electro-Plate. The former was discovered in 1742, when Thomas Boulsover found that a silver ingot could be sweated to a copper ingot and then rolled out to a thin sheet. This process lost favour in the 1860s when Elkington patented the use of electrolysis. This method completely covered the joint marks left in the making, which were formerly covered by strips of silver or embellishments. This is the main way of distinguishing between the two processes. Another distinction is that in electro-plating it is necessary to refine the silver to 99%, which gives it a much whiter appearance than the 92.5% standard normally used.

Old Sheffield in good condition can realize as much as the equivalent silver piece and the electro-plate of the 19th century is fast gaining popularity.

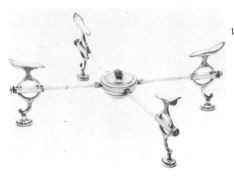

1. *Old Sheffield plate dish cross*, c. 1770. 11¾ in. across. Mar. '85, £220.
   Adjustable dish cross with central burner, sliding legs and dish supports to accommodate dishes of various sizes, and struts that also rotate so that the cross will support both circular and oval dishes. Made mainly in the last quarter of the 18th century, they are now uncommon.

2. *Old Sheffield plate lidded tankard*, c. 1770. 9¾ in. Jan. '85, £110.
   Lidded tankards in fused plate are relatively common and inexpensive. Most have a wooden base to add weight and solidity and, if in good condition, realize between £60 and £80 at auction. This quart-sized example has particularly good and elegant proportions.

3. *Old Sheffield plate coffee pot*, c. 1770. 10¾ in. Mar. '85, £110.
   The vase-shape was very popular in the late 18th century and was adapted for use in the manufacture of all sorts of objects ranging from small cream jugs to massive tea urns and wine coolers. Notice that the spout has a silver wire soldered onto its edge to disguise the tell-tale line of copper.

4. *Old Sheffield plate salver*, c. 1780. 18½ in. diam. Feb. '85, £300.
   The earliest examples of fused plate were very simple, reflecting both the fashions of the time and the techniques of the northern craftsmen, soon to develop great skill in reproducing any designs produced in silver.

5. *Old Sheffield plate cake basket*, c. 1780. 15½ in. Mar. '85, £120.
   When pierced and delicate silver became fashionable in the 1770s the fused plate makers were faced with a dilemma. If they used the traditional piercing-saw, jagged edges would result thereby exposing the copper. They developed the use of fly-punches, each punch fitted with a shaped steel stamp to cut out the desired design in one action. Each stamp had an angled blade which dragged the silver through the hole, thereby disguising the copper edge. Before long silversmiths adopted it as a quicker and cheaper method of decoration. This basket is particularly light and pretty, although not in excellent condition.

6. *Coffee-pot, mid-19th century.* 10¾ in. Feb. '85, £90.
   The coffee pot illustrated here is interesting as it combines the two techniques of fused plating and electro-plating, the body being made from silver fused on to copper, the legs, handle, spout and finial from electro-plated nickel. It must have been made in the 1850s in the transitional period from one technique to another. Its style is somewhat cumbersome and yet its interesting mode of manufacture would ensure its place in a representative collection of silver-plate.

7. *Old Sheffield plate lidded vegetable dish,* c. 1820. 14¼ in. long. Feb. '85, £120.
   Dishes and tureens made of solid silver were very expensive because of the sheer weight of metal used, and so many were made of fused plate. Crests created a problem, however, as the engraving would reveal the copper beneath the thin layer of silver. Always enterprising, the makers soon developed a technique of cutting one plate out and inserting another, first of solid silver and later of fused plate but with a much thicker coating of silver. Such vegetable dishes are popular when sold in pairs.

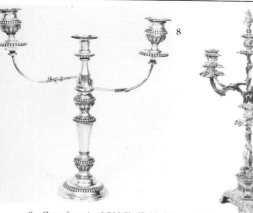

8

9

11

10

12

13

14

8. *One of a pair of Old Sheffield plate candelabra,* c. 1820. 26 in. Mar. '85, £350.
Many of the Sheffield metalworkers specialized in candlesticks and enormous quantities were made in the late 18th century and throughout the 19th. This one shows a restrained use of fluting and gadrooning. Close examination of the columns shows a seam or line of copper, betraying the fact that this was made from a flat sheet of fused plate curved and soldered. Many pieces show this soldered line, sometimes dentilled to give greater strength. Candlesticks and candelabra are at a premium today.

9. *Massive electro-plated candelabra by Frederick Elkington and Co., Birmingham.* 39 in. Feb. '85, £200.
The death knell began to toll for fused plate in the mid-19th century when customers began to demand extremely naturalistic pieces smothered in flowers and fruit. These were relatively easy and inexpensive to manufacture, using Elkington's electro-plate process.

10. *Old Sheffield plate tea kettle on stand,* c. 1830. 22 in. Feb. '85, £180.
Most examples of fused plate are large as there would have been less advantage in making smaller pieces in the new technique as they required so little silver anyway; snuff boxes and so on are relatively uncommon. This massive tea-kettle on stand, using the inverted pear-shape, much loved in the first half of the 19th century, has a bone handle.

11. *Electro-plated tea kettle on stand by Martin Hall and Co., Sheffield,* c. 1865. 16½ in. Mar. '85, £150.
The amusing tea kettle is supposedly based on gypsy design and, as you can see, the warming stand and even the handle and spout of the kettle itself have been cast to resemble twigs with a wonderfully moulded bark effect. This example is complete with original spirit lamp and would have served at many a Victorian afternoon tea party. The kettle tilts forward on the crossed twig stand to avoid risk of splashing boiling water.

12. *Old Sheffield plate tea urn,* c. 1810. 25 in. Mar. '85, £220.
Fused plate tea urns were made often and would have been used by the wealthiest families, as their sheer size would have necessitated a considerable outlay if made of solid silver. This example, with its heavy moulded oblong shape and lion's mask handles and claw feet, is typical of Regency design.

13. *An electro-plated tea urn,* c. 1880. 32 in. Mar. '85, £260.
In Victorian times the tea urn was still considered indispensable for formal 'at home' afternoons, when friends would call. This electro-plated example is a reproduction of a Georgian design of about 1770, although the original would have been much lighter in appearance and, indeed, much smaller. This example still has the interior sleeve to hold a lump of cast iron which would be heated in the oven and then dropped into the urn to keep the water at boiling point. Today, these large examples of Victorian electro-plate are much in demand as sideboard decorations.

14. *Electro-plated and cut-glass biscuit barrel, by Martin Hall and Co., Sheffield,* c. 1870. 9¾ in. Mar. '85, £140.
The Victorians loved the combination of silver or electro-plate with cut-glass as seen in this biscuit barrel. The metal mounts are deliberately restrained with simple beading and engraving to show off the lavishly star-cut clear glass barrel. Such items are popular today, combining an attractive design with a practical object which would be ideal for serving both sweet biscuits at tea or crackers at the end of a meal.

5.   *Jewellery and Watches*

Introduction
by David Lancaster

During a break in a recent game of badminton I was chatting to my doubles partner about our respective occupations. On hearing that I valued jewellery for an auction house he sighed and said he wished he had known. There followed the inevitable story of his mother helping a local charity run a car-boot sale and donating a box of Gran's old jewellery to the cause. Within seconds of the sale being open to the public all the jewellery had been snapped up by one man who paid the price asked without argument and went off whistling. After similar experiences several of the larger charities have recognized the danger of guessing the value of donated jewellery and regularly bring parcels into us for our opinion, often leaving the more valuable pieces with us for sale, before offering the remainder through their normal outlets.

No.1 shows an item which arrived in a small collection labelled gilt costume jewellery, an easy mistake to make as it has no obvious markings, is not gem set and is light in weight. However, this Bulla locket is a very nice example of Italian archaeological style jewellery popular between 1860 and 1880 and usually brought to England as a souvenir of a visit to Rome. Still in its fitted case and in perfect condition, it aroused keen competition. When one considers that this pendant only qualifies for the description antique, that is over 100 years old, by a few years, and twenty years ago would have been dismissed as Victorian nonsense, it becomes clear that Gran's trinkets can quite suddenly acquire a new status. Indeed, with the resurgence of interest in Art Nouveau and Art Deco now being followed by growing demand for 1940s and 1950s jewellery, the old date-line limitations have little meaning, and items are much better judged on style and quality.

A glance at any local paper will reveal the number of antiques fairs, markets and car-boot sales taking place on

1. *Gold Bulla pendant in Etruscan style, 19th century.* Mar.'85, £800.
2. *11th Lancers gem-set badge brooch.* Mar.'85, £240.
3. *Diamond and enamel RAF Wings brooch.* Mar.'85, £750.
4. *Ruby and diamond moth brooch.* Apr.'85, £420.
5. *Rose diamond and gold winged beetle brooch.* Apr.'85, £260.
6. *Gold, enamel, diamond and pearl snake bangle, 19th century.* Apr.'85, £1,550.

6

4

5

and stained horn, and even earlier plastic items providing they exhibit strong design. Quite often such pieces will appear at auction in a jewel box of assorted oddments, and those who have not taken the trouble carefully to assess each piece in the collection are often aghast at the prices realized by such lots. It is of course imperative that anybody contemplating buying jewellery at auction attends the preview and carefully examines the pieces under consideration. Although descriptions such as 'diamond' and '18ct. gold' may be taken at face value it must be borne in mind that the majority of items on offer are second-hand and will have been subject to some wear and tear. All joints in bracelets and necklaces need testing for free play, and brooch clasps for security, while ring shanks should not be too thin. These points can all be established by careful viewing, but setting a realistic price to pay is far more difficult. If an estimate is given in the catalogue this will be a guide, but it is still necessary to know which items are in such demand that they will frequently outstrip their estimates. One such category at present are the brooches fashioned as the badges of the various corps and regiments of the fighting forces, reproduced in diamonds and coloured gems by such jewellers as Garrards, and originally sold to the wives of serving officers. This has now become a popular collecting field embracing both the little 11th Lancers badge bar brooch, No. 2, and the more imposing diamond and enamel RAF wings brooch, No. 3.

The general brooch market has been quiet for some time but is now showing a revival, especially for those brooches depicting animals and insects, either in natural or novelty poses. The two small winged insect brooches illustrated, Nos. 4 and 5, are of the type which easily outsell similarly sized stars, crescents and flowers. The ruby and diamond moth, though smaller, is of better quality than the gold and rose diamond flying beetle which employs more metal and fewer gem-stones. The change from natural creepy-crawly to jewelled ornament certainly greatly enhances the desirability of these insects, and the same can be said of that symbol of eternity, the snake. Once he has been rendered non-slithery and transmuted to gold, enamel, diamonds and pearls he becomes far friendlier, and this nineteenth-century hinged and sprung bangle, No. 6, appealed to a wide audience.

While demand for jewellery is strong in nearly all areas, from Victorian silver items to diamond tiaras, with newly expanding fields of wrist-watches and lighters adding interest, the one demand throughout is for quality. Good design and delicate workmanship can count for more than a mass of poor-quality diamonds. A good signature is also a great asset and top prices continue to be taken by such names as Cartier, Rolex and Dunhill in their respective fields.

any given weekend, and when one considers that this is going on throughout the country it is remarkable just how much jewellery is on offer to the public. The fact that the public are responding is evidenced by the continuous and growing demand for all categories, and it is interesting to note that more and more members of the public are trusting to their own judgement and competing directly with the traders at auctions. Thus the attendance at a typical jewellery sale is now a remarkable mixture of private buyers, part-time traders running stalls at occasional markets, the regulars from Portobello Road, and representatives of the high-class jewellery shops, all competing with Continental and American buyers on shopping trips in this country. Despite the weak pound the Americans have not had it entirely their own way, for although they could buy at a discount, the high interest rates available in their own country meant that more money went directly for guaranteed interest rather than the long-term investment represented by jewellery.

The diversity of buyers is well matched by the mixture of jewellery, wrist-watches, timepieces, coins and medallions normally on offer. Here again a trip around the fairs soon confirms the rapidly growing popularity of some of the less valuable materials such as marcasite set in silver, carved

Necklaces

Perhaps weathered fish vertebrae are not your idea of exciting personal adornment, but 27,000 years ago one of our ancestors found them desirable enough to string together and wear around the neck, thus starting a fashion which has survived all of the dramatic alterations in mankind's lifestyle.

The range of necklaces popular today is extremely wide and embraces most of the styles of the last two centuries. Always in demand are the long muff and guard chains from the second half of the nineteenth century, and provided these are still their original length of around 60 inches they fetch from £200 upwards, depending on the carat of the gold and the style of linkage. Earlier gold chains are scarce as the wear between links limits their lifespan, but the occasional well-preserved example, perhaps with typical gloved and jewelled hand clasp, can easily clear £1,000.

While older neckchains are broken up because they have worn out, necklaces set with precious stones suffer the same fate so that the stones may be reset in the latest fashion. In consequence the period necklaces that most regularly appear on the market are those set with stones of small value or decorated only with enamel. Early in the nineteenth century rich red garnets were much appreciated. In No. 1 the colour of the stones is enhanced and matched by the insertion of coloured foil between the garnets and settings. In France, Napoleon encouraged the setting of cameos as jewellery rather than as static displays in collector's cabinets, and the graduated shell cameo necklace with festoon chain connections was high fashion in 1820 (No. 2). By the middle of the century Italian goldwork inspired by Etruscan antiquities was the popular souvenir of foreign travel, and the fringe necklace No. 3 demonstrates the workmanship without glitter which was taken to its ultimate by Castellani and the Giulianos. English goldsmiths were also producing fine although more traditional work such as the long chain No. 4. This has been broken up into short lengths, but these have fortunately remained together. The hollow gold links are light yet give an appearance of strength, reinforced by the black enamel scrollwork. The matching garnet-set padlock clasp is hinged to reveal a hair locket with sentimental inscription.

The early twentieth century saw a reaction against Victorianism leading through the whiplash curves of Art Nouveau, and elegance of the Edwardian style, to the angularity of Art Deco. No. 5 is a delightful example with a combination of classical scrolls and chains with a foretaste of Deco in the geometric drops.

We have travelled through the changing fashions of 200 years, and yet each of the necklaces discussed could be worn today without appearing strange or dated. Because of their simplicity, elegance and wearability they have proved excellent investments, both financially and for pleasure.

David Lancaster

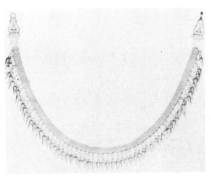

3. *Hellenistic gold woven collar necklace with continuous fringe of drops, c. 1850. Mar. '84, £1,500.*

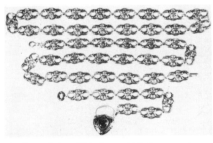

4. *Long chain with hollow gold links, enamel scrolling and garnet-set padlock clasp, c. 1880. July '84, £1,900.*

1. *Floral garnet necklace with gold mounts, c. 1840. Nov. '83, £680.*

2. *Necklace of ten graduated shell cameos connected by festoon chains, c. 1820. Aug. '84, £950.*

5. *Edwardian festoon necklace of pearls and diamanté scrolls and drops, c. 1910. Apr. '84, £800.*

Brooches

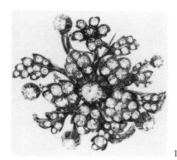

1

2

3

4

5

8

1. *Silver and brilliant cut lead glass paste flower spray, late 19th century.* Mar. '85, £100.
Made with all the care and skill appropriate to more expensive materials. The stones are cut as brilliants and set in cut down collets in the same manner as diamonds of the period. The brooch would have been a fairly expensive piece of fashion jewellery when new and its quality continues to attract admirers.

2. *Gold, rose diamond and cultured pearl flower brooch, c. 1900.* Apr. '85, £100.
In many ways the opposite of No. 1, this brooch is made to an impressive description but disappoints upon inspection. The diamonds are thin slices facetted only on the upper surface and spread as far apart as possible over the heavy gold leaves. An example of the importance of inspecting the actual piece rather than relying upon a catalogue description.

3. *Victorian diamond, rose diamond and pearl flower head brooch.* Mar. '85, £780.
A good example of traditional Victorian flower jewellery, the flower head well packed with brilliant and rose-cut diamonds in individual settings. This brooch has a detachable pin and would originally have had an alternative hair slide fitting. It might well also have formed part of a tiara.

4. *Edwardian diamond openwork brooch/pendant.* Mar. '85, £1,100.
Edwardian jewellery is typified by the use of knife-edge open-work platinum settings, and this large but delicate snowflake pendant captures the style of the period excellently. A good demonstration that the quality of diamonds used is not the only factor, for style and wearability are important influences on the value of diamond-set jewellery.

5. *Sapphire and rose diamond openwork brooch/pendant with central cabochon sapphire, Edwardian.* Mar. '85, £1,500.
Another Edwardian pendant but one which attempts to keep a foot in both markets by combining the new light open style with the floral swags which were so much a part of Victorian decoration. The central cabochon sapphire adds a touch of colour to an attractive and well-made piece.

6. *Diamond circle brooch in case stamped Tiffany, Paris, Edwardian.* Apr. '85, £1,000.
A lovely simple early 20th-century diamond brooch of superior quality and excellent design. Although the brooch is not signed the case is stamped Tiffany, Paris, and the quality of the brooch certainly supports such an attribution.

7. *Diamond and grey blister pearl twin hearts brooch, Victorian.* Apr. '85, £1,400.
Victorian sentimentality reigns supreme with two hearts joined by a ribbon bow, and still commands a considerable following in our brave new world. A carefully assembled brooch based on the two similarly shaped grey pearls displaying the best of Victorian workmanship in a pleasing and wearable format.

8. *Diamond star brooch, late 19th century.* Mar. '85, £700.
One of the staple designs of the Victorian era was the star, to be seen in graduated lines on tiaras, applied to the front of lockets, as hair ornaments and of course as brooches. Such large numbers of very stiff standardized stars were made that a considerable quantity have survived and are assessed simply on their diamond content. As in many collecting fields, the item which was the most popular in its own day is now the least desired – but it will certainly return.

Earrings & Pendants

1

2

3

5

7

1. *Pair of gold enamel and pearl Etruscan style drop earrings, signed C.G. for Carlo Giuliano, 19th century. Apr. '85, £1,400.*
   Signed pieces of jewellery by the famous firm of Giuliano are always eagerly sought after, and this very pretty pair of enamel earrings in the revived Etruscan style was no exception. The family used various names, as sons joined the firm, but in this case the C.G. in a plain applied oval plate may be dated between 1870 and 1896. The excellent original condition of this pair resulted in a high price.

2. *Pair of Continental vari-coloured enamel on gold multi-drop earrings, late 19th century. Apr. '85, £350.*
   A pair of flamboyant and colourful earrings, probably Austro–Hungarian, which despite the lightweight, hollow construction give an impression of mass. Desirable for their ornamental qualities rather than any special workmanship, the price reflects the general strength of the earring market.

3. *Pair of gold and pearl drop earrings, mid-Victorian. Apr. '85, £220.*
   A pretty pair of earrings, their greatest asset being the original condition and freedom from the dents and bruises so easily made on hollow gold stampings. When compared to similar style and period brooches, it can be seen that earrings command a very considerable premium.

4. *Pair of 18 ct. gold and diamond drop earrings, signed Cartier, London. Apr. '85, £950.*
   Signatures are important on jewellery and the name of Cartier will always attract attention. Despite being rather cumbersome, the quality of manufacture and good name ensured a strong price for these earrings.

5. *Art Nouveau diamond and fancy cut peridot pendant. Apr. '85, £420.*
   Art Nouveau pendants were produced in vast numbers, the mass market being catered for by very light 9 ct. gold stampings set with garnets and pearls. However, this example is of far better workmanship: 15 ct. gold, with the specially selected central peridot and diamonds used to highlight the clear tendril design. This quality was recognized by the buyers, the price paid being many times the value of the materials involved.

6. *Gold, enamel and carved hardstone stickpin, 19th century. Mar. '85, £480.*
   A charming pin of excellent quality. The detailed carving and enamelling ensured that the numerous collectors of stickpins would be hot on the trail, as the eventual price proved.

7. *Cannetille gold and topaz cross pendant, on a neckchain, first half 19th century. Mar. '85, £240.*
   A delicate piece of jewellery from the late 1820s. Despite beautiful workmanship in the delicate filigree gold style known as Cannetille and the use of precious topaz, little enthusiasm could be generated because of the basic shape. Crosses in various materials and styles represent excellent value for the buyer at present.

8. *Painted oval miniature mounted in gold as a pendant with half pearl border, Edwardian. Apr. '85, £240.*
   An Edwardian trinket, no doubt painted from a photograph and given as a minor gift, but having immediate appeal. Children and animals are always good subjects in jewellery, and the high price reflects the demand for this type of sentimental ornament.

Bracelets

1

1. *Florentine mosaic panel bracelet with gold mounts in the Etruscan style, 19th century.* Mar. '85, £820.
   During the mid-19th century the Florentine mosaic industry enjoyed a strong revival, and this bracelet is an excellent example of the pietra-dura work of the period. The stone mosaics in a background of Belgian black marble are notable for their naturalism and delicate shading, admirably complemented by the gold settings. A piece with excellent investment potential.

2. *Diamond 19 stone line bangle, late Victorian.* Apr. '85, £850.
   A simple pretty diamond bangle incorporating typically deep-cut mediocre quality stones, reflecting the Victorian interest in jewellery as ornament rather than investment. Although not easy to wear these bangles are always popular and fetch strong prices.

3. *Diamond and ruby line bangle, late Victorian.* Apr. '85, £320.
   Another similar bangle using gold wirework to emphasize the rather small gems. When compared with No. 4 it will be seen that one pays for lightness and delicacy.

4. *Gold, rose diamond and calibré turquoise bangle, Victorian.* Mar. '85, £850.
   An excellent example of Victorian jewellery, with turquoise carefully cut to shape and highlighted with rose diamonds. Compared with Nos. 2 and 3 it is far more representative of Victorian workmanship but its sheer mass held the price to a fairly modest level.

5. *Gold and turquoise light-weight link bracelet, Victorian.* Mar. '85, £200.
   An impressive looking bracelet but of flimsy construction in hollow gold pressings. However, worn with care it gives an appearance of far greater opulence than the actual price would suggest.

6. *Diamond-set bracelet watch mounted in platinum on an expanding link backchain, c. 1940.* Mar. '85, £1,400.
   Enjoying a return to fashion after many years in the doldrums are ladies' diamond-set bracelet watches. A few years ago this watch would have been just so many carats of rather poor diamonds, but having escaped the breakers its value has increased rapidly to the present level and will probably continue to rise.

7. *Woven hair bracelet with repoussé gold locket clasp, c. 1830.* Apr. '85, £220.
   A piece for the collector rather than for wear; reactions to woven hair jewellery vary from admiration to revulsion. This bracelet, with its clasp incorporating a locket for yet more hair, is a standard item of 1830s jewellery, when it would have been part of a suite.

2

3

4

5

6

7

Mourning Jewellery

1. *Gold mourning bangle enamelled in black and white with bright cut engraved decoration, the navette-shaped miniature painted in sepia with a lady beside a tomb, c. 1785. King Street, Dec. '84, £800.*

Death was a constant companion to the people of earlier centuries in a manner which we with our health service, ambulances and sanitation find difficult to comprehend. One method they used to remind themselves to live each day to its full was the *memento mori* jewellery adorned with enamelled skulls and skeletons as well as symbols of passing time and the reaper which became popular in the sixteenth century. These beautifully made but rather grim reminders of human frailty gradually gave way to more restrained woven hair lockets and rings with hair-set bezels, often distributed in accordance with the requirements of a will. By the second half of the eighteenth century death was viewed in a more poetic manner, and the skull and scythe had been replaced by the weeping willow and urn. No. 1 shows a fine

2. *Gold ring enamelled in red and black with a crown, c. 1817. King Street, Mar. '84, £1,150.*

3. *Gold and white enamel mourning band ring, sold together with another similar ring, c. 1818. King Street, Mar. '84, £140.*

mourning bangle, the miniature with inscription 'Forgive the wish that would have kept thee here'. The surrounding enamel also bears an inscription commemorating Charles Petley Rayley d.1785. This is an excellent example with intact enamelwork and a crisp clear miniature. Apart from condition another factor which will add greatly to the price of mourning jewellery is association with important personages, and No. 2 certainly qualifies in this respect. It is inscribed outside 'Meliori ornata corona', and inside 'Illust. Princ. Carlotta Augusta Plorant Gentes Ob. 6 Nov. 1817, aet.22'. Princess Charlotte Augusta (1796–1817) was the only child of the Prince Regent and Caroline of Brunswick. More typical of the rings regularly available is No. 3. Interestingly the enamel is white, symbolizing the virginal unmarried state, and this ring commemorated a young man of 24 who died in 1818. Both of these would have been from a series made for distribution to friends and relatives of the deceased.

The Victorians with their large families and high infant mortality often needed jewels capable of commemorating more than one person, and one sometimes sees large oval lockets with several divided compartments each containing a lock of hair and neatly engraved with initials and date. No. 4 is an alternative answer to the problem, a gold bangle with three spherical memorial hair compartments, each glazed back bearing a name or initials.

The greatest influence on the fashion for mourning jewellery in the nineteenth century was of course Queen Victoria, who had always strictly supported the conventions, and on the death of Prince Albert in 1861 indulged in an orgy of mourning. She no doubt left detailed instructions for the distribution of suitable momentos upon her own death, and No. 5 is one of these pieces. The reverse is engraved 'Queen Victoria's hair given by H.M. to M.A.Cust'. With the death of Queen Victoria the country was glad to shrug off all the trappings of mourning leaving behind a fascinating collecting field where each piece is engraved with details which open up a vast field for research.

David Lancaster

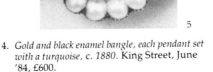

4. *Gold and black enamel bangle, each pendant set with a turquoise, c. 1880. King Street, June '84, £600.*

5. *Gold circular brooch containing hair surmounted by the letter V with a diamond crown above. King Street, June '84, £350.*

Victorian Design

1. *Suite of silver brooch and earrings with applied gold floral decoration, and a silver floral brooch.* Apr. '85, £120.

   In the second half of the 19th century Birmingham was firmly established as an industrial centre and the jewellery trade flourished on the ability to produce economical pressings in quantity. These silver brooches are typical light-weight mass-produced items, but given character and charm by the addition of hand-chased gold floral decoration. Owing to the increase in mechanization there were large numbers of skilled craftsmen and engravers willing to accept any work, and thus the decoration of these pieces is often of a quality far in excess of the materials used.

4. *Gold coral-set locket pendant on a neckchain.* Oct. '84, £380.

   A very pretty oval locket pendant set with cabochon pink corals between applied wirework. It is an impressive size and in excellent condition, representing an eagerly sought type of jewellery.

3. *Gilt brooch set with an enamel of the Deposition.* Apr. '85, £140.

   The delight in large brooches is again evident here with the added problem of a deeply religious scene depicted by the enamelled central plaque. The mount is gilt metal and the enamelling is on porcelain, an economical construction which probably indicates that turnover in such brooches was always expected to be fairly slow.

2. *Gold citrine three-stone brooch.* Apr. '85, £170.

   A Victorian brooch of far less desirable design. The heavy and clumsy scroll-work centres on three yellow citrines, which with the yellow gold create a massive plaque with little appeal.

5. *Carved hardstone cameo mounted as a brooch.* Nov. '84, £600.

   During the 19th century there was a major revival of interest in cameos, and this vari-coloured agate example is of a popular style. It is based on earlier seductive and abandoned Bacchantes, but Victorian morality insisted on a respectable profile with just a small vine in the hair. The stone-carver has made clever use of the various layers of colour within the stone to give detail to the cameo, and this work of art is complemented by the simple gold brooch mount.

6. *Carved red coral pendant of a cherub and vine.* Mar. '85, £300.

   In the middle of the last century Italian red coral rose to the height of fashion, to the point where by weight it was worth more than gold. This popularity was further increased by a magnificent display at the Great Exhibition in 1851. The pendant is formed from a part of a larger carving and has a modern mount, but the quality of the work and fine red colour are not to be denied.

Art Nouveau, Art Deco, Cameos

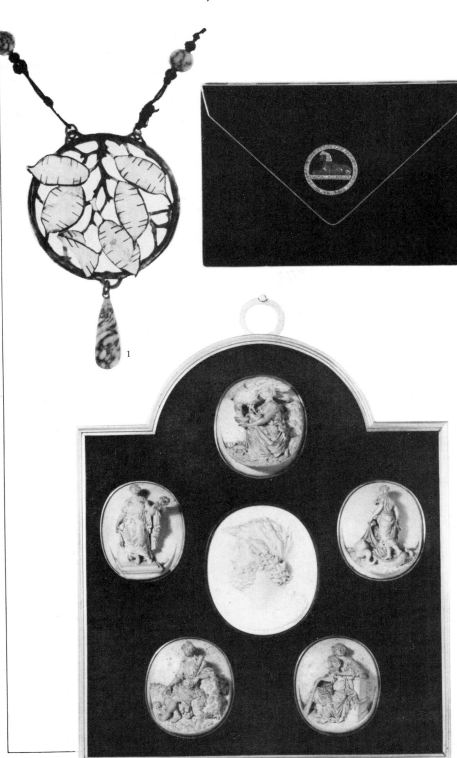

1

2

3

1. *Art Nouveau stained horn pendant with glass bead drop.* Apr. '85, £90.

   Horn was a popular Art Nouveau material with its light translucent colours which could be readily enhanced by staining and often coupled with softly coloured gems such as moonstones. It can be carved in fine detail, accepts a good polish and can be shaped for hair combs by careful heating. Many pieces are signed by artists of varying ability up to the highest standard of René Lalique. Our example, whilst typical of the period, lacks delicacy and is unsigned thus keeping the price in only two figures.

2. *Art Deco black enamel and silver gilt envelope-form minuadière (compact), the flap with an applied rose diamond lapis lazuli and aventurine quartz sphinx motif, signed Ghiso.* Apr. '85, £400.

   The first requirement with any enamelled item is that it should be in good condition as repairs to enamel are difficult and expensive. This minuadière has been well looked after and is complete with its internal fittings including lip-stick holder and eye liner pencil case. The sphinx motif became popular with the surge of Egyptian revival jewellery inspired by the discovery of Tutankhamun's tomb in 1923 and the use of blue lapis and green aventurine are dictated by these discoveries.

   The compact has a strong clear period design and is signed by a known, if not famous, maker resulting in strong competition to secure this piece.

3. *A group of six very fine Italian 'lava' cameos carved in extremely high relief depicting various classical scenes, 19th century.* Mar. '85, £620.

   The material used is actually a fine-grained sandstone found near Mount Vesuvius. These highly detailed mini-sculptures would be impractical for jewellery as the many protruding details would be easily damaged, but they make a fine display set in the contemporary gilt brass frame. This is an interesting example of a grand tour souvenir piece probably purchased at Pompeii and unusual in being so well preserved.

Wristwatches: A Growing Market

To wear a slim rectangular 1930 wrist-watch has become fashionable in recent months among people who want something of strong design that sets them apart from the quartz brigade.

Rolex is the name that the wearing collector is particularly looking for, especially from the 1930s. Rolex led the way in technique, quality and design, and the model which combines these best is the Prince (No. 4). This was made in large numbers in stainless steel, silver, 9ct gold, 18ct gold and even striped gold, and the case is curved for the wrist. The movement is made of nickel silver and is usually engraved 'Rolex Extra Prima, timed six positions observatory quality', but there are variations on this.

Condition is particularly important, as the cases tend to wear at each end and have often been badly repaired by adding an extra plate of gold. Prices range from about £600 to £3,000. If one looks at No. 3, there is very little apparent difference to the Prince, but this one can be bought for around £250 to £350 in 9ct gold. This model is slightly smaller than the Prince and the movement is engraved 'Rolex, 15 Rubies'.

The Rolex Oyster first appeared in 1927 and was the first model to be waterproof and able to withstand changes in climate. Technically this watch was way ahead of its rivals, and for sheer reliability has earned its place as one of the most sought after by collectors.

Although any Oyster-cased wristwatch is collectable at the moment, the Lady's Oyster wristwatches realize about half the price of the Gentleman's models, which start in the region of £100 to £150 for stainless steel, £150 to £200 for silver, £400 to £600 for 9 ct. gold and over £1,000 for an automatic (No. 2).

In the same way, while a gold Prince will make more than £1,000, a Princess can be bought at around £200. This discrimination is purely a matter of fashion. However, Lady's Art Deco diamond-set watches are very much in demand, especially those with a strong design (Nos. 7 and 8; see also p. 105, No. 6).

Rolex is not the only sought after make, and those made by Patek Philippe are just as keenly pursued. No. 5 shows a plain, slim and very wearable example.

1

2

3

4

5   6

Patek Philippe are as good technically and as stylish as Rolex but fewer appear on the market these days.

No. 6 shows a complicated gold Swiss stop watch, with a case that is 18 ct. gold but very thin and thus very easy to dent. This watch lacks strong design and quality and would cost up to £100. It must be borne in mind when considering purchasing such an item that the more complicated the watch, the more expensive to repair.

In general the more recent the design, the less sought after (No. 9).

To conclude, the names Rolex, Patek Philippe and Vacheron & Constantin, Art Deco designs and Oyster cases and technical quality are all features to look out for.

Ian Stanley

1. *Gentleman's 18 ct. gold perpetual chronometer, the case thick with an unusual square dial by Rolex, c. 1950. Oct. '84, £1,000.*

2. *Gold Oyster perpetual, black enamelled dial, officially certified chronometer by Rolex, c. 1940. Oct. '84, £1,450.*

3. *9 ct. gold Rolex, c. 1935. Oct. '84, £300.*

4. *9 ct. gold Prince watch, movement marked 'timed six positions by Rolex', c. 1930. Oct. '84, £1,300.*

5. *18 ct. gold watch dial, signed 'Patek Philippe, Genève', c. 1950. Oct. '84, £600.*

6. *Gold stop chronograph, no mark on movement, dial signed 'Chronograph, Suisse', c. 1950. Value under £100.*

7. *Lady's platinum diamond and synthetic sapphire watch, c. 1930. Oct. '84, £400.*

8. *Lady's gold cocktail diamond set bracelet watch, c. 1945. Oct. '84, £450.*

9. *Lady's modern white gold integral bracelet watch by Patek Philippe, c. 1970. Oct. '84, £500.*

7   8   9

6.   Clocks

Introduction
By Santiago de Barry

You may have read or seen through the media that fantastic prices have been realized in clocks, the most recent being the Mostyn Tompion, which was sold to the nation for an undisclosed figure in excess of £500,000. Here at South Kensington we concentrate on the 'lower end' of the market, dealing especially in nineteenth-century and some eighteenth-century clocks; probably the highest price realized in recent years has been £5,500 for a late nineteenth-century French green onyx and champlevé enamelled grandmother clock with side plinths (No. 1). On this level the market has been quite stable, apart from the middle range which includes gilt spelter and Edwardian mantel timepieces and late German examples where prices have been lower.

Towards the beginning of 1984, mantel clocks embellished in champlevé enamel (and not the cloisonné which it is so often confused with) realized exceptional prices, especially in the four-glass form, and sold mostly to the Middle Eastern market for figures in excess of £1,000. They have now settled in the upper £100s. High quality and unusual examples have remained high in price and are continuing to rise.

Black marble, spelter and late nineteenth-century German mantel clocks have remained in the low price range (£30–£100), and, although not that desirable at present they are bound to go up in price as the higher-price-range clocks become less and less affordable. It seems to me that the French Empire ormulu clocks are still very much underpriced: one can buy a reasonable one for as little as £300. Although many are to be found at the moment, I feel that they will be the first to increase in price. The same applies to gilt spelter clocks mounted with porcelain plaques. A single clock may only make £200 or £300, but a garniture (with side pieces) can realize as much as £800, with the better quality examples realizing over £1,000.

Longcase clocks have followed a less troubled path and are a more settled market; good mahogany and Edwardian (chiming) longcases realize the highest prices (around £1,000–£3,000), whereas the oak and pine 30-hour long-cases at present remaining in the lower £100s are surely the expensive antiques of the future. They are affordable to most home owners and are becoming popular with the interior design market, as a longcase clock seems to add a touch of homeliness to a room.

In conclusion, the clock market has remained fairly stable, with a few exceptions as already mentioned. Market supply and demand are the key factors, and this market with a 'fixed' supply and an increasing demand cannot fail but to expand, so that investments now may prove wise ones for the future.

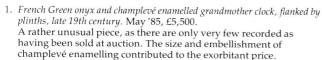

1. *French Green onyx and champlevé enamelled grandmother clock, flanked by plinths, late 19th century.* May '85, £5,500.
   A rather unusual piece, as there are only very few recorded as having been sold at auction. The size and embellishment of champlevé enamelling contributed to the exorbitant price.

2. *Georgian black lacquered Act of Parliament wall clock signed 'AYNSth. THWAITS LONDON'.* 41 in. Apr. '85, £3,200.
   A quality piece in all respects: of good age, relatively good condition and well-executed Chinoiserie decoration on the trunk door; and of course a well-known maker.

3. *French alarm skeleton time piece.* 7 in. Sept. '84, £140.
   A good price. These small French alarm clocks are quite interesting. They were introduced into this country at the Great Exhibition of 1851 by their maker Victor Athanase Pierret, and their price at that date was 25s. Very much a collector's item.

4. *George III mahogany longcase clock signed 'JNo. Manley, Chatham'.* 81 in. June '85, £1,300.

5. *French gilt brass and champlevé enamelled strut timepiece in the manner of Thomas Cole.* 11½ in. June '85, £580.

Longcase Clocks

Longcase clocks, or grandfather clocks as they have been popularly known since about 1878, are a mid-seventeenth-century invention brought about by the introduction of the long pendulum which allowed greater precision in time-keeping. To enclose the driving weight and pendulum, a case was built, which over the years developed to a very high standard of craftsmanship compared to the furniture of the same period.

The earlier examples are to be found in walnut, laburnum and olive wood veneers, either plain or with intricate floral marquetry. By the second half of the eighteenth century mahogany was introduced, and it has since remained as the predominant wood. The majority of country-made clocks have oak or pine cases.

When buying a longcase clock many factors have to be taken into account, as we must not forget that it is a combination of engineering and cabinet making in one.

To the collector it is important to know whether the movement and the case are original and made to complement each other or whether they are a 'marriage' of a case and movement of different ages. A few points to look out for are the following. First the case: check whether the top of the hood matches the top of the trunk door (No. 1), as many clocks have had additions to give them height and elegance. The plinth and the base are very often 'doctored' as they usually stood on slab floors, and with continual washing the feet rotted away. For example, No. 2 would have most likely had bun feet. The dial should fit snugly into the surround of the hood, and on opening the door one should be able to determine if this is so; also with the introduction of the arched dial in the early eighteenth-century, many square dials were amended to fit with the arched hoods of the new fashion. These are easy to spot as normally there will be a distinguishable line separating the new arch from the dial; if this is not discernible from the front, look at the back of the dial, and the soldering marks will give it away. Also the movement rests on a 'seat-board', and slots cut on either side of the supports should be looked at suspiciously as the dial may have been lowered so that it can best fit the case.

The duration and capabilities of the movement are important: if the movement runs for 8 days at one winding, it will be worth more than one which only lasts 30 hours. A simple but not absolute guide is to look at the dial; if it has no winding holes it is probably a 30-hour clock, if two winding holes it is an 8-day, and if it has three it has a chiming mechanism (No. 3), and the respective price ranges rise dramatically from around £300 to £1,000 and £3,000.

The wood used for the case is just as important, with walnut and marquetry cases realizing the highest prices at £4,000 plus, followed by mahogany at £1,000 plus and then oak and pine at £200 plus.

You must assess a clock case in the same manner as you would judge any piece of furniture. It should be on the slim side, with well-proportioned plinth and hood, and with good patina and figuring to the wood. North Country longcases, which are usually 'fat' and heavy looking, will make as little as £400 even if they are in mahogany, whereas a well-proportioned case will realize in excess of £1,000 (No. 4).

Anything which is out of the ordinary and unusual will always sell well at auction; for example, the grandmother (No. 5) in shagreen case with silver dial by Dunhill realized £3,500. 'Grandmother', by the way, merely means a clock less than 6 feet high.

Santiago de Barry

1. *Mahogany longcase clock signed John Land, London, late 18th-century.* 81 in. Sept. '83, £1,500.
   A realistic price. Notice the good figuring of the mahogany on the trunk door, also the broken arched hood matching with the trunk door. Originally it would have had finials on top to balance the composition.

2. *Walnut seaweed marquetry longcase clock signed Hen. Elliott, London, early 18th-century.* 98 in. Sept. '83, £2,400.
   A good price considering the base is later, as is also probably the caddy top. It would originally have had a flat top.

3. *Edwardian mahogany chiming longcase clock.* 110 in. Feb. '79, £2,900.
   A 'monstrous' price for a 'monster' of a clock. Although far too large for most households nowadays, they still continue to realize these sorts of prices. Notice the tubular bells visible through the glazed trunk door, a feature which always enhances the price.

4. *George III mahogany longcase clock in the Chippendale style signed Sam. Fish, London.* 106 in. Sept. '83, £2,200.
   An exquisite clock, well balanced and combining the use of good figuring on the wood with quality carving on the caddy top. Notice the moon-face aperture in the arch.

5. *Shagreen and ivory grandmother clock, with silver eagle finial, dial, chapter ring, spandrells and boss, labelled Alfred Dunhill Ltd., c. 1926.* 72 in. Apr. '84, £3,500.
   Although age is lacking compared to the rest of the clocks mentioned here, this unusual grandmother combines the use of shagreen and silver to make a very appealing clock. Of course, the fact that it derived from the workshop of Alfred Dunhill Ltd. gave an added zest to the bidding in the auction room.

6. *Mahogany timepiece longcase clock in balloon-shaped case.* 81½ in. June '83, £750.
   A good price for this longcase clock with an added feature of an unusually shaped case.

7. *Mahogany longcase clock with arched painted dial, mid-19th century.* 93 in. June '85, £600.

8. *Edwardian mahogany chiming longcase clock,* 91 in. Apr. '85, £1,900.
   A good price. Although similar in age to No. 3, it is smaller and of plainer design.

9. *George III mahogany and boxwood inlaid longcase clock.* 91 in. Apr. '85, £1,400.
   A good quality clock, with attractive 'sunset-effect' inlay and well-painted dial with face and age of moon dial in arch.

7

8

9

Mantel Clocks

When buying a clock, you may be looking for an example of fine craftsmanship in the horological field, in which a precision instrument has been encased in a 'shell' to protect it from the dust and other elements; or you may be interested in a furnishing piece to be used as part of the decoration of a room. With luck you may find a clock which combines the two in one.

There are many factors dictating the prices of clocks, but the main ones to consider are as follows: How decorative is the case? Is it carved, inlaid or embellished with porcelain panels or enamelling? What is its type of movement – French, English or German? What are its duration and capabilities – 8-day or 30-hour? Does it chime or strike on the quarters? Is it signed, and if so is the maker of any importance? Strangely enough, condition does not matter that much, unless it is seriously damaged, or if it has a rare type of movement for which spare parts do not exist any longer and would have to be made specially.

1. *French gilt spelter and turquoise ground Sèvres pattern porcelain mounted mantel clock, late 19th century.* 19 in. Feb. '83, £380.
   A reasonable price for a clock of this quality and age, this being one of the better examples of a spelter clock.

2. *Fine French ormolu and blue ground Sèvres pattern porcelain mounted mantel clock, late 19th century.* 24 in. Nov. '84, £1,900.
   The quality of this clock is discernible from the putti flanking the dial, the exquisite casting and attention to detail; the porcelain panels were equally impressive.

3. *French mahogany and brass mounted bracket clock of Regency design.* 14 in. Apr. '85, £240.
   A little high in price, but the Regency design is always popular.

4. *Regency style mahogany bracket clock signed Maple & Co., London.* 15 in. Feb. '83, £420.
   An average price for this type of clock. Notice how much better the dial and base are in proportion to the case than in No. 3.

5. *Brass mantel clock, the case shaped in the form of a ship's stern with automaton man, ship's wheel and mast, late Victorian.* 11½ in. Oct. '83, £1,200.
   A good price for this clock, which was much sought after by private bidders.

6. *French ormolu and white marble lyre swinging bezel and movement mantel clock, signed 'Roque A Paris'.* 19½ in. June '85, £2,200.
   A respectable price for this elegant and competently made clock.

7

9

8

10

You may wonder why two apparently similar clocks should differ so much in price, for instance, Nos. 1 and 2. Both are French, they have almost the same type of movement, and are of the same date. They are quite similar in design, but in fact No. 2 is overall of finer quality. The embellishments of the case are made of ormolu, i.e. gilt bronze. The casting, attention to detail and the porcelain panels are of superior quality. No. 1, on the other hand, has embellishments made of gilt spelter, i.e. gilt metal, which is a poor and brittle substitute for ormolu.

But cases are not the only things to affect the price. Take Nos. 3 and 4, which are both copies of an 1830s bracket clock and seemingly identical. The reasons for the disparity are quite different here. No. 3 dates from the early 1900s, has a standard French 8-day movement and is not the work of a particularly notable maker, whereas No. 4 is earlier by 20 or 30 years, and it is inscribed on the dial 'Maple & Co., London', a most reputable retailer. (The name on the dial is not always the maker, but sometimes the retailer.) The movement is an English fusee, which is a higher quality movement than the French one, and therefore the clock is a more desirable item.

Finally, rarity is always important, and therefore anything which is unusual will make a surprising amount of money at auction as, for example, No. 5. This late Victorian mantel clock is both amusing and at the same time very collectable.

Santiago de Barry.

7. _French Empire black and sienna marble and ormolu mounted mantel clock in tempietto case._ 20 in. June '85, £550.

8. _French gilt brass four-glass mantel clock in rectangular shaped case._ June 85, £550. The elegant lines and well painted pendulum bob affected the price considerably as one is more used to seeing this type of clock in a plain rectangular case realizing £150 to £300.

9. _French ormolu and white marble perpetual calendar mantel clock._ 22 in. June '85, £1,400. A good price for a good quality clock, the addition of perpetual calendar dial encouraging high bidding.

10. _Brass two-train skeleton mantel clock._ 19½ in. June '85, £850.

11. _French ormolu and blue ground Sèvres pattern porcelain mounted mantel clock._ 20 in. June '85, £1,300. A very good price for this exceptionally high quality clock of its type; many similar examples are to be found in gilt spelter.

12. _French ormolu clock garniture, the mantel clock signed on dial 'E. Sevenier and G. Gobe, Bronzeurs a Paris, Rue Vielle du Temple 110', early 19th century._ 30½ in. (clock) and 32 in. (candelabra). Feb. '85, £1,800.

11

13. _French ormolu and champlevé enamelled mantel clock, late 19th century._ 17 in. Jan. '85, £800. A realistic price. These clocks embellished with champlevé enamelling (and not cloisonné) have always been popular.

12

13

Mantel Clocks (cont.)

14

15

16

17

14. *English Regency ormolu and bronze mantel timepiece, late 19th century.* 17 in. Jan. '85, £1,700.

15. *English Regency ormolu and bronze mantel timepiece, signed 'F. Baetens, 23 Garrard St., London'.* 14 in. Mar. '85, £1,300.
    Nos. 14 and 15 both fetched good prices, but it is amusing to compare the difference in price paid for virtually identical clocks in the space of two months.

16. *French Empire bronze and ormolu mantel timepiece.* 8½ in. Mar. '85, £420.

17. *Massive French ormolu mantel clock, signed 'Miroy, Frères a Paris'.* 42 in. Mar. '85, £3,800.
    A massive price for a massive clock, of a type very popular with the Middle Eastern market.

18

19

20

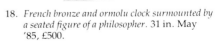

18. *French bronze and ormolu clock surmounted by a seated figure of a philosopher.* 31 in. May '85, £500.

19. *French gilt metal mantel clock shaped as a windmill with rotating arms.* Apr. '85, £450.

20. *French silvered and ormolu mounted clock modelled as a cathedral by Richond, Paris.* 21 in. Apr. '85, £400.

21. *French ormolu mounted clock cast with agricultural motifs.* 16 in. Apr. '85, £800.

Bracket Clocks

Bracket clocks are free-standing clocks normally displayed on tables or mantelpieces, but acquired their name because some of them were supplied with brackets. They are normally housed in wooden cases, sometimes with gilt metal mounts for decoration, and occasionally they have metal cases. The movements and dials are of brass. Before 1800, they were usually fitted with a verge escapement, but from about then new ones were mounted with anchor escapements, and many of the older ones were refitted.

Care must be taken to see whether an existing escapement is an original or a conversion. Bracket clocks normally date from 1660–1845, with a short revival in the late Victorian and Edwardian periods.

1. *Regency mahogany and ebony strung bracket clock, signed 'Parkinson and Frodsham, Change Alley, London',* 15 in. Mar. '85, £700.
A good price considering this is quite a plain-looking bracket clock, but the importance of the maker obviously created greater interest. A similar clock by a lesser-known maker might only make £300-£500.

3. *Regency rosewood timepiece bracket clock by G. Monti, Sandwich.* 12½ in. Mar. '85, £850.

2. *Mahogany and brass mounted bracket clock by Vulliamy, London, c. 1810.* 10½ in. Mar. '85, £1,400.
Vulliamy was one of the leading Regency makers, and this is reflected in the price for his clock. It is elegant and restrained by comparison to the more provincial No. 3, which may be noted is only a timepiece, i.e. non-striking.

4. *Late Victorian carved oak chiming bracket clock, signed 'S. Smith & Sons, 9 Strand, London, W.C.'* 29 in. with bracket. Apr. '85, £800.
Very popular of its type, usually with 'massive' three-train movements chiming on both bells and gongs.

Carriage Clocks

Carriage clocks were made in large numbers in the nineteenth century and, of course, quantities are still produced today. The majority came from France. The retailer's name appears on the dial and the maker's trade mark is stamped on the back plate on the better clocks. Two stamps to look out for in particular are a parrot on a stand with the initials 'H.J.' (which stands for Henri Jacot) and a beehive between the letters 'A.M.' (for Margaine).

A standard carriage clock (No. 1) is plain, made of brass with a white enamel dial and stands approximately 5 inches high, with platform or lever cylinder escapement (No. 2). Size is an important factor: the smaller the better. A miniature (3 inches) or smaller can triple the price and, if enamelled, the price can increase by a factor of 10. The same applies to giant carriage clocks (10–12 inches or more). Carriage clocks of this size are comparatively unusual and prices can stretch to £1,000 or more.

Decoration can add greatly to the price, particularly a porcelain front and side panels; pierced fretwork panels, pillars and engraving all contribute. Enamelling of any form (champlevé, cloisonné and guilloché) is a bonus. Shape plays an important role in determining desirability; oval cases are particularly sought after, as are caryatid cases (each corner of the column depicting the top half of a female figure).

A standard timepiece will just tell the time, but many extra features may be added, such as an alarm or a secondary ring on the dial (No. 4); striking for the hours, half hours and even minutes (for these gongs are attached to the backplate); and lastly repeating mechanisms which have a small button on the top of the case. Each extra feature will add to the price.   *Ian Stanley*

1. *Plain brass carriage clock, white enamel dial, platform cylinder escapement. 5 in. Oct. '84, £80.*

2. *Ornate pillared carriage clock with pierced fretwork front panel decoration, platform lever escapement, and strikes on the gongs every hour and half hour 6½ in. Oct. '84, £300.*

3. *Miniature brass clock, vertical cylinder escapement, circular white dial. 2¼ in. Mar. '85, £260.*

4. *Brass combination carriage clock/barometer, inset with compass, platform lever escapement. 6 in. Mar. '85, £300.*
   Note small third dial for alarm.
   Nos. 1–4 all late 19th century.

5. *Edwardian silver timepiece, vertical lever escapement, case engine-turned, on four bun feet. 1½ in. Mar. '85, £260.*

Miscellany

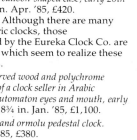

1. *Mahogany and rosewood cross-banded Eureka electric clock in balloon-shaped case, early 20th century.* 14¼ in. Apr. '85, £420.
   A good price. Although there are many types of electric clocks, those manufactured by the Eureka Clock Co. are the only ones which seem to realize these sorts of prices.

2. *Black Forest carved wood and polychrome painted figure of a clock seller in Arabic costume with automaton eyes and mouth, early 19th century.* 18¾ in. Jan. '85, £1,100.

3. *French walnut and ormolu pedestal clock.* 63½ in. June '85, £380.

4. *Patent 'Coronation Clock'.* 13½ in. June '85, £300.
   A good price for a clock that is of relatively low quality in the craftsmanship and materials used, but it is an interesting example for the collector.

5. *Regency mahogany wall regulator by Wassell & Halford, London.* 30 in. May '85, £1,800.
   A good price for a high quality clock.

6. *Late Georgian mahogany circular wall clock by Recordan, late Emerys, London.* 14 in. diam. Mar. '85, £800.
   There are many English wall dials to be found, which are mainly timepieces. Mostly they can be bought for about £150, but this has a striking mechanism and is overall of high quality.

7. *Walnut Vienna wall regulator by M. Schonberger, Vienna.* 45 in. Apr. '85, £900.
   Again quite a few Vienna regulators are found at auction, realizing between £200 and £400, but this one's case and movement are of higher quality than usual and of course it is signed, an unusual feature in these clocks.

8. *Stained walnut Davidson's patent memorandum clock.* 12 in. May '85, £140.
   The quality of the casing may not be very high, but the unusual construction and the addition of a memorandum dispenser make it a very collectable item. One has to be very careful with this type of movement, as if it is in need of repair it can be very costly to restore.

9. *Brass repeating striking clock, platform lever escapement, bamboo pillars, vari-coloured front and side panels, in the Oriental style.* 7 in. Mar. '85, £520.

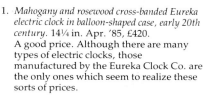

7. *Decorative Objects and Sculpture*

Introduction
by Christopher Proudfoot

Of all categories 'Objects of Art' is the hardest to define. 'Objects' are the sort of things that might be found ornamenting a well-kept furniture dealer's shop – items too small to be included in the term furniture itself, but essential ingredients in the furnishing of any house nonetheless.

Apart from specialist sub-sections like clocks, sculpture, musical instruments and carpets, the main groups can be classified as follows:

Boxes: Tea caddies, writing boxes, workboxes, games boxes.

Lighting: Brass and ormolu candlesticks, chandeliers, electroliers, standard lamps, oil lamps.

Fireplace equipment: Coal scuttles, fire-irons, andirons, fenders, grates, fireguards, fire-screens, pole-screens, and even complete fire surrounds.

Papier mâché and Tole Ware (painted tin): Especiaiiy trays, in addition to boxes, coal scuttles, small tables and other items covered by other headings.

Treen: Domestic wood objects, often turned, and extending to such elaborate artefacts as spinning-wheels.

Objects of vertu: Small pieces artistically worked in ivory, enamels, mosaic and the like, although those based on precious metals or stones are included in silver sales.

Pewter and brass-ware: Anything from Communion plates to jelly moulds, from samovars to warming pans.

Garden furniture and statuary: Stone, terracotta, cast-iron and lead urns and statues, sundials, garden seats and tables.

Boxes come in mahogany, rosewood, oak, satinwood, walnut, macassar ebony, lacquer, fruitwood, ivory and mother-of-pearl. Porcupine quills and paper scroll work are

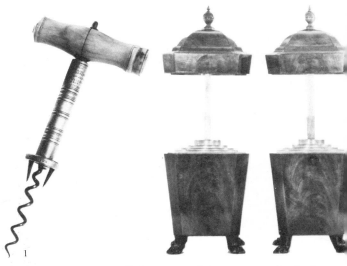

1

sometimes applied. All these materials were popular in the eighteenth and nineteenth centuries. Tea caddies, belonging as they do to the Georgian period, are found mainly in mahogany, sometimes inlaid, with late examples often in rosewood. Prices range from £30 for a plain mahogany caddy to £200 for a good example of a sarcophagus-shaped Regency caddy in rosewood, complete with its glass mixing bowl.

Writing boxes, often known as lap desks, open to provide a sloping leather-lined writing surface, with compartments for pens, pencils and ink and powder bottles, and space for stationery below. They are really a portable version of the Davenport desk, and remain very saleable despite the seemingly endless supply. Most are William IV or Victorian, and prices are in the £30–£40 range for average examples, with the better types going up to £400 or so. Plus factors are brass or mother-of-pearl inlay, exotic wood such as macassar ebony, and a complete interior – the leather devoid of marks and both ink bottles present with their lids.

3

4

5

Dressing cases are comparable, covering the same period and similar styles, with internal fittings still more important. The same can be said of games boxes, where it is obviously particularly important that all pieces are present. Unfortunately the chess boom seems to have declined over the last year or so, and now only the best chess sets attract good prices (up to £300).

Lighting equipment forms one of the most important elements of the interior decorator's art, and brass or ormolu wall brackets are in constant demand. Even reproductions of eighteenth- and nineteenth-century styles sell well, which is fortunate as they form the majority of those offered for sale. There is now also considerable interest in early purpose-made electrical lights – that is, fittings designed specifically for electricity as distinct from those originally made for candles, or in imitation of traditional candle holders. In the nature of things such fittings (including the charmingly named electroliers) tend to be of the Art Nouveau period and style. Even these are now reproduced, and can be seen in every High Street lighting shop and revamped pub, but that only augments interest in originals. Large chandeliers have always been notoriously difficult to sell at auction, but while those only suitable for use in a ballroom may have a limited market, Regency gilt brass chandeliers of practical size for a drawing room regularly sell in the £1,000–£3,000 range, and even the much simpler hall lanterns of the same period can go into four figures.

Victorian oil lamps have long been popular, and the better quality designs, such as brass Corinthian columns, can bring £100–£200. Even the mass-produced lamps, in which a cut-glass reservoir sits atop a cast-iron or stamped brass and black earthenware base, can make up to £60 or so, despite their lack of any obvious quality or rarity.

A society that has blocked up so many fireplaces in the last forty years seems to have an amazing appetite for the

1. *Early Victorian brass cork-screw with bone handle stamped 'Robert Jones & Son, Maker, 105 Cheapside, Birmingham, Reg. No. 423, 8th Oct. 1840'. 17½ in. Jan. '85, £450.*
A good price for this unusual example of a corkscrew.

2. *Pair of Regency mahogany cutlery urns. 21 in. June '85, £2,500.*
A very good price, the fine quality and good condition playing a large part in the price realized. Although there are numerous types of cutlery boxes to be bought at auction, this design, with the lids rising on a central support, is the most popular.

3. *Pair of French Empire bronze and ormolu twin-light candelabra, early 19th century. 21 in. June '85, £1,000.*
A realistic price for these fine quality and elegant light fittings, of which larger and more monumental examples are fetching exorbitant prices at auctions.

4. *French ormolu hanging lantern, early 19th century. 33 in. June '84, £600.*

5. *One of a pair of ormolu four-light wall lights, the backs inset with porcelain plates. 24½ in. May '85, £650.*

6. *English violin, unlabelled, c. 1780, in case.* 14⅛ in. long. Mar. '84, £140.
   Many violins can be bought for much less than this, some for as little as £20.

7. *Six-key boxwood clarinet, with ivory collars, stamped 'Wainwright', London'.* 25¾ in. Mar. '84, £85.

8. *English lignum vitae wassail bowl, 17th century.* Aug. '83, £2,600.

9. *George III mahogany and brass-bound peat bucket.* 14¼ in. Sept. '84, £850.

10. *Pair of French Louis XVI style veined rouge marble and ormolu mounted ornamental urns, early 19th century.* 19 in. Aug. '84, £750.
    Numerous pairs of ornamental urns can be found at auction, rouge and green marble being the most popular.

accoutrements of the fireplace. Sets of old-fashioned, long-handled fire-irons (comprising poker, tongs and shovel), in steel or brass regularly sell in the £50–£100 bracket – the fact that designs which first appeared in the eighteenth century were still being produced in the early part of the twentieth may have something to do with this. The same applies to pierced steel and brass fenders: although these normally fitted between the jambs in the eighteenth century, the same style was used for many of the nineteenth-century fenders which enclosed the whole hearth, and these too could still be bought in the early twentieth century, long after the rococo elaborations in cast iron of the mid-Victorian period had faded from the scene. All are very saleable, although it is still possible to find pierced fenders of simple design for less than £50. Also very saleable are cast-iron firebacks (ideal for inglenook fireplaces, but much copied) and eighteenth-century basket grates. Typically, these are adorned with Adamesque oval paterae and urns, normally with a pierced skirt echoing the fenders described above, and examples with any pretensions to age now regularly sell in the £300–£400 bracket.

Victorian cast-iron register grates, which fill the whole fireplace opening, are still around in fairly abundant quantities, and tend to sell from £50 down to £10 for small, late examples. The small ones survive in large numbers because they were fitted in bedrooms and were not replaced when downstairs grates were modernized in the 1920s–1950s, but the larger sizes are now being sought by owners of Victorian houses wishing to restore the original fittings, and it cannot be long before they begin to make more at auction.

Sculpture consists predominantly of nineteenth-century bronzes, often cast after the antique or the work of contemporaries such as Barrye and P.J. Mene. Value obviously

depends on the quality of the cast as well as the appeal of the subject, but in general terms decorative bronzes of this nature can often be bought in the £200–£500 range, or for even less if they are of the cheaper (and lighter) spelter. Earlier pieces tend to be in wood, and predominantly of Continental origin in the form of painted and carved religious figures most of whose English counterparts did not survive the Reformation. Age and condition are obviously important factors here, while the subject-matter is less popular than that of nineteenth-century animalier bronzes. English medieval oak and stone carvings do occasionally appear, usually in the form of corbels, gargoyles and similar architectural embellishments. In spite of their age, their limited adaptability for display out of context tends to keep prices well down in the lower £100s for all but the most outstanding examples.

Papier mâché ware has been selling particularly well in

11

11. *Set of three French groups of frogs, depicting 'The Billiard Players', 'The Drunkard' and 'The Pipe Smoker'. Sept. '81, £210.*
Although not a very recent example, it shows the variety sold within this section.

recent months. This surprisingly durable substance was popular from the early nineteenth century to the High Victorian period. It was usually coated in thick lacquer which was decorated by painting, often in the Chinese manner, and even with mother-of-pearl inlay. The article which most obviously lent itself to being made of papier-mâché was the domestic tray, and while some of the simplest examples can be had for under £100, the more elaborate versions – provided that they are in good original condition – can make £500–£1000. An oval tray with poly-foiled border and gilt scrollwork decoration, 31 inches wide, realized £600 in October 1984 – helped, no doubt, by having the stamp of Jennens and Bettridge, probably the most famous papier-mâché maker. Wine coasters were another popular application, and a Regency pair of these realized £650 in the same sale. Pieces of furniture, for which the material is less obviously suited, are less common, but for once rarity does not equal desirability. A Victorian bedroom chair made £60 in October, and an elaborate music stand at £260 seems inexpensive against the £200–£400 commonly fetched by trays.

A notable development this year has been the launching of sales devoted exclusively to Garden Furniture. There is now widespread interest in period furnishing for outdoors, not only chairs and tables for drinks on the terrace or tea on the lawn, but fountains, sundials, urns and statuary. The quantity of modern reproductions (usually aluminium) of Victorian cast-iron furniture on the market is evidence enough of this, and inevitably the originals from which such reproductions are cast are widely sought after. A single armchair in the well-known fern leaf pattern, well rusted and lacking its wooden seat, together with an attractive but similarly decrepit wrought-iron rocking chair brought £260 in November 1984. In little better condition was a large (6 ft. 6 in.) Regency wrought-iron bench seat which sold in September for £650. Wrought iron seats, plainer and more elegant than their florid counterparts, were nevertheless more expensive to make, and are, incidentally, impossible to reproduce convincingly today at a worthwhile price.

Objects of Vertu

Perhaps in no other field had a craftsman such scope for his talents, and such a wealth of materials in which to work. The most common, mundane item was not beneath the notice of imaginative craftsmen, and the ordinary in their hands quickly become a work of art, a beautiful object.

The ordinary chatelaine, from which the mistress of the house would hang her keys, scissors, nutmeg grater and so on, was lovingly chased and decorated. The walrus ivory shoe horn shown here was carved as a gift to the maker's wife. The quality of the workmanship is exquisite, with Tudor roses and a touching legend around the edge. It is dated 1613 (No. 1).

The lovely enamelled necessaire was made to keep sewing implements. An ordinary box would have housed them just as well. But that wasn't good enough for the woman who could afford such items, or for the craftsman who could delight his patron by the ingenuity of his workmanship. No. 3 is formed as a book; one side opens to reveal a useful extra compartment, the other, containing bodkin holder, scissors and so on, is cleverly concealed – and further demonstrated the skill of the maker.

Snuff taking was common in the eighteenth century, and containers come in a great variety. The Scottish horn snuff mull would be beautifully pressed, carefully decorated and mounted with a Cairngorm to form the cover. No. 4 seems just the normal circular papier mâché type – until one studies the cover. It is a hunting scene and the painting is magnificent.

Instead of a run-of-the-mill table seal with an ordinary turned wood handle, No. 6 is a work of art. True, the base is agate and this is common enough, but the grip is formed as a gilt bronze figure of a warrior stringing his bow, and the chasing is superb, which is all the more remarkable on such a small object.

Walking sticks were another playground for the craftsman. Some were hollowed out and fitted with a stem-like decanter and glass, others with swords, horse-measuring sticks, or even made to conceal a gun for poachers and others. Perhaps the most sought after

1. *A good James I walrus ivory shoe horn finely engraved with Tudor rose and the legend 'Robart Mindum made this shooing horn for Jane his wife Anno Domini 1613'. Apr. '85, £450.*

2. *Samson Staffordshire-style yellow enamel tea caddy, painted with a seascape and flower reserves. 3½ in. wide. Apr. '85, £190.*

3. *Enamel and metal combined necessaire and snuff box formed as a book, the pink ground in gilt and painted with panels of figures in landscapes. 3½ in. Apr. '85, £350.*

4. *Circular lacquer snuff box, well painted with a huntsman and dog in a woodland glade, c. 1830. 3¾ in. diam. Apr. '85, £240.*

5. *Burr wood circular snuff box, amusingly painted with young ladies, be-wigged men and yokels in an affray. 3½ in. diam. Apr. '85, £370.*

6

are those with beautifully carved ivory grips, or the animal's head type with moveable mouths (see illustration page 211).

The medallist's skill in No. 7 is complemented by that of the person who could fashion and form tortoiseshell to make the octagonal frame.

Other skills and materials produced the micromosaic, an Italian variation on the art of the ancients. Minute pieces of painted marble would come together like jigsaw puzzles to form a picture (No. 8).

From the rich lover of beauty of the past have come down to us the humble tea caddy, walking cane, snuff box, etui, chatelaine, necessaire, patch box, toothpick holder, all given over to the skilful craftsman to make the humdrum lovely, the common yet prized object, a work of art to be enjoyed today by the fastidious collector.

James Dick

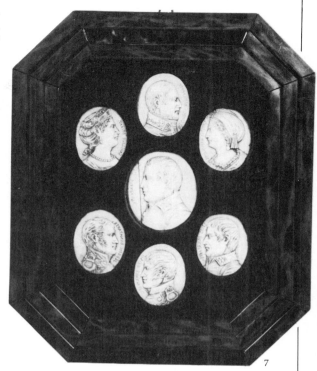

7

8

9

6. *Gilt bronze and agate seal in the form of a warrior stringing his bow. 4 in. Apr. '85, £140.*

7. *Tortoiseshell framed set of seven ivory medallions of the Bonaparte Family. Apr. '85, £420.*

8. *Italian micromosaic panel of the Colisseum. 6½ × 8¾ in. Apr. '85, £1,700.*

9. *Ivory rectangular purse, carved with the hunt, figures and game in a wooded glade. Apr. '85, £200.*

10. *French rectangular fruitwood snuff box, probably by Bagard of Nancy. Apr. '85, £240.*

11. *French mother of pearl and silver inlaid necessaire, with partly fitted interior. Apr. '85, £180.*

10

11

Tea Caddies

To a nation that thinks nothing of drinking six cups a day, it comes as no surprise to discover our ancestors' high regard for tea, and the craftsmanship displayed in the creation of containers to store it. The skill of cabinetmakers and silversmiths is clearly displayed in some of the fine examples of tea caddies passed down to us.

A discerning collector of the tea caddy will not go wrong if he or she judges any purchase on condition, on quality and on original state. Obeying these rules may lead to paying top prices, but it is exactly those buys that are likely to increase in price more rapidly than the shabby compromise at the other end of the scale.

It is still possible to buy perfectly good attractive Georgian tea caddies for around £60, and at the other end of the scale, a caddy in the form of a piece of fruit for £1,500. No. 1, made appropriately of fruitwood, was in good condition except for the replacement of a stalk finial with a ball, and was sold in December 1983 for £700. This was considered a good price at the time, but later examples on the market have seen a giddy rise.

The most common type of caddy is mahogany and rectangular, often boxwood lined. No. 5 also has an ivory escutcheon plate. The interior is fitted for two compartments, and it would date to about 1820. It was in good original condition and not expensive, but then it

is lacking any great expertise of craftsmanship. The George III bombe shaped caddy on bracket feet (No. 3) stands out for the figured flame mahogany and beautiful line. This sold for £220 in the same sale, despite the fact the ivory escutcheon plate is a later replacement; it originally would have had a brass escutcheon plate to go with the brass swing carrying handle. The rarity of finding a caddy with such shape would be the determining factor in the price.

The figured mahogany caddy with the 'Sheraton' oval inlays (No. 4) was like No. 5 in being of plain rectangular shape, but had the advantage of a central glass mixing bowl and beautiful inlaid roundels to the side and lid. There are many Sheraton period caddies to be found of smaller size for just one container, hence taller than wide, and these sell on average for £100.

The two tortoiseshell caddies illustrated both date from the early part of the nineteenth century. Both have two compartments. No. 2 realized £320,

1. *Fruitwood caddy in the form of a melon.* c. 1800. Dec. '83, £700.
   The best examples of such caddies formed as apples, pears and so on can now sell for up to £1,500.
2. *Tortoiseshell caddy, early 19th century.* Oct. '84, £320.
   The excellent condition explains this price by comparison with No. 6.

while No. 6 with the gabled lid brought £260. The line and shape of the latter are of importance but the good colour and perfect condition helped the less interesting shape of the former to the better price.

Caddies come in ivory, silver, rolled paper and a variety of woods as well as the tortoiseshell and mahogany ones discussed. The rarer the type the higher the price.   *Mark Stephen*

3. *George III bombe caddy in flame mahogany veneer, late 18th century.* Oct. '84, £220. Here it was the attractiveness of the lines and the finely figured veneer which produced a strong price – even though the original brass escutcheon had been replaced by one in ivory. Tea being a valuable commodity in the 18th century, caddies were fitted with locks.

4. *George III three-compartment figured mahogany caddy with Sheraton style inlay, late 18th century.* Oct. '84, £350. The central compartment should contain a glass mixing bowl, as here. If this has survived it will increase the price. The inlay also added to the appeal.

5. *Mahogany caddy with two compartments. c. 1820.* One of a pair, Oct. '84, £85. The comparative lateness of this piece, together with the plain design, accounted for the low price, despite good condition.

6. *Two-compartment tortoiseshell caddy, early 19th century.* Oct. '84, £260. Although the shape of this example was more interesting than that of No. 2, the condition was not as good.

7. *George III rosewood and crossbanded cut corner tea caddy, inlaid with flower paterae.* 7 in. wide. Mar. '85, £400.

8. *George III mahogany rectangular tea caddy, inlaid in harewood with shell paterae.* 4½ in. wide. Mar. '85, £150.

9. *George III satinwood rectangular tea caddy, inlaid with harewood and shell paterae.* 7 in. wide. Mar. '85, £280.

10. *George III satinwood and crossbanded cut corner tea caddy with simulated fluting, inlaid in harewood with shell and foliate paterae.* 7 in. wide. Mar. '85, £260.

11. *Early Victorian and mother of pearl inlaid tea caddy.* 9 in. wide. Jan. '83, £190.

12. *George III paper scroll tea caddy, with mahogany protective case.* 8½ in. wide. June '83, £380.

13. *A Regency tortoiseshell tea caddy in sarcophagus shaped case.* 9 in. wide. Sept. '84, £320.

Treen

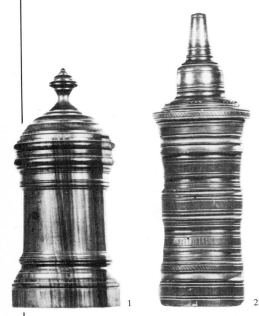

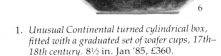

Treen has only recently been recognized as a serious branch of the antique market. Previous generations discarded it as valueless, preferring to collect precious metal and porcelain, and today the scarcity of early treen has resulted in high prices for the better survivors. The appeal is the recognition that peasant art, provincial in origin and largely practical in purpose, can have a charm that outweighs the traditional demand of collecting.

It is rare to find sixteenth-century treen, such as standing cups and mazers, outside museums, but the occasional seventeenth-century example can be encountered at auction (No. 1). Cups and other vessels are found in hardwoods such as sycamore and holly, but lignum vitae, the most desirable, had to be imported and its rarity led to turners using it only for their most important pieces (No. 2).

The three snuff boxes (Nos. 3–5) are all affordable. Although the shoe, made of rosewood, is Victorian, it is possible to find eighteenth-century examples. At auction one would expect to pay £100 for the man and between £80 and £120 for the later pieces.

Love tokens are one of the more desirable types of treen: a shoe snuff box inlaid with studs to form a heart, a Welsh love spoon intricately pierced and carved as a gift to a loved one, or even a Welsh chip carved box in the shape of a heart are all keenly sought at auction.

Scandinavian treen is one of the most expensive to buy, but also one of the most charming. A natural abundance of wood and scant daylight led Scandinavians to carve and decorate their handicrafts. The eighteenth-century birchwood kasa illustrated (No. 6), a vessel for beer, with its bold horse head handles and original paint, realized £550, but larger examples have been known to fetch over £1,000. A collector should not, however, confuse this type with the later undecorated Russian kasas, for they only fetch around £30.

Most treen is domestic and practical. Bowls, ladles, scoops, gingerbread moulds, salts, condiments, spice boxes and a host of other humdrum items are to be found. Collections of interest and character can be made for little money. For example, a nineteenth-century beachwood dairy bowl might cost around £40, whereas a purist would be happy to spend more for a sycamore bowl (No. 7), a better quality wood with more desirable colour. The majority of spoons and ladles are only a few pounds each, and one purchase is often the start of a treen collection.   *Mark Stephen*

1. *Unusual Continental turned cylindrical box, fitted with a graduated set of wafer cups, 17th–18th century. 8½ in. Jan '85, £360.*
2. *Lignum vitae jar and cover, 18th century. 7½ in. Jan. '85, £150.*
3. *Oval coquilla nut snuff box carved with a cavalier and a lady, late 18th century. 2½ in. Oct. '84, £85.*
4. *Coquilla nut snuff box carved as a figure of a man with grotesque mask, mid-19th century. 2½ in. Oct. '84, £110.*
5. *Victorian rosewood and pique work boot snuff box, with sliding cover. 3¼ in. Feb. '85, £120.*
6. *Scandinavian birchwood kasa painted with bright foliate and floral scrolls. 9½ in. Nov. '84, £550.*
7. *Circular sycamore butter dish, 19th century. 12½ in. diam. May '84, £80.*
8. *Elm straining ladle, 19th century. May '84, £35.*

Meerschaum Pipes

All the pipes on this page were sold in May 1985.

1. *Cheroot holder modelled with a child at prayer. £110.*
2. *Pipe formed as a bird. £140.*
3. *Pipe formed as a woman wearing a plumed bonnet. £80.*
4. *Pipe formed as a bewigged man's head. £140.*

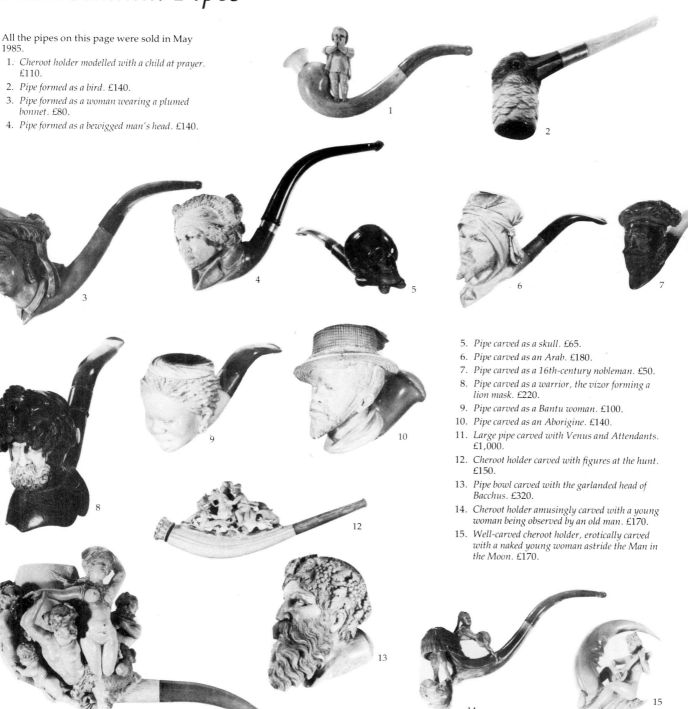

5. *Pipe carved as a skull. £65.*
6. *Pipe carved as an Arab. £180.*
7. *Pipe carved as a 16th-century nobleman. £50.*
8. *Pipe carved as a warrior, the vizor forming a lion mask. £220.*
9. *Pipe carved as a Bantu woman. £100.*
10. *Pipe carved as an Aborigine. £140.*
11. *Large pipe carved with Venus and Attendants. £1,000.*
12. *Cheroot holder carved with figures at the hunt. £150.*
13. *Pipe bowl carved with the garlanded head of Bacchus. £320.*
14. *Cheroot holder amusingly carved with a young woman being observed by an old man. £170.*
15. *Well-carved cheroot holder, erotically carved with a naked young woman astride the Man in the Moon. £170.*

Papier Mâché

1. *Pair of Victorian letter racks painted with hunting scenes after Landseer. 8¼ in. Jan. '85, £320.*
2. *Victorian inkstand inlaid with mother of pearl, stamped Jennens and Bettridge, Makers to the Queen. 9¼ in. Jan. '85, £180.*
3. *William IV tray with scalloped border. 32 in. wide. Aug. '84, £750.*

The first half of the Victorian period marked the heyday of English papier mâché. It was not a Victorian innovation as is widely assumed: the earliest substance of this kind is thought to have originated in Persia and the East, reaching England in the seventeenth century from France, mostly in the form of picture frames. The ingredients for making it vary from maker to maker but basically it is a mixture of pulped paper, glue, chalk and occasionally sand, which after being pressed, moulded and backed, formed a very hard surface that could be sawn and polished like wood.

Because of the great adaptability and economic advantages of the product, it soon developed into quite an industry, concentrated mostly around Birmingham and Wolverhampton, with Henry Clay, Jennens and Bettridge, and Benjamin Walton being the most notable contributors to an enormous output, which consisted of almost every piece of household furnishing imaginable – trays, tables, chairs, cabinets, screens, snuff boxes, etc.

The surface also lent itself very well to painting (No. 1) and inlay (No. 2), and most examples one sees will be embellished with flower sprays or copies of famous paintings (especially Landseer's) depicting romantic or moral themes, or, after 1825, with mother of pearl inlay. Both techniques were mostly applied to black grounds, but you may find the use of rouge, green and other colours. These, however, are not so common, and therefore are more desirable to the collector.

Owing to the great output and the variety of manufacturers, the factors affecting the price of such pieces must inevitably start with quality; as with paintings, a well-painted and attractive subject will enhance the value.

Let us take illustrations No. 3 and No. 4, which realized £750 and £320 respectively. Although they may appear quite similar, No. 3 is about 30 years the earlier, and the quality and condition are far superior.

Condition also has a profound effect on price; on many examples the varnish has become discoloured or, as on a painting, craquelure has formed on the painted surface. Another common problem is chipped and worn edges. Restored pieces are to be found in large quantities and it is important to check for this; on a tray, for example, it is advisable to look at the underneath and inspect the surface carefully. If you come across any bright black shiny patches be wary (No. 8). On the painted surface the gilding is a good give-away. Since most pieces are to be found decorated with gilt borders, any restoration should be obvious even to the untrained eye.

With any items that make money and become desirable, fakes are bound to appear. Papier mâché is no exception – take Nos. 5 and 6. At first sight they are two quite similar pairs of wine coasters, but No. 6 is a fake pair. Although it is quite difficult to tell from the photograph, handling the items would firstly reveal that No. 6 are lighter than No. 5, the walls are probably thinner, and when you tapped them with your finger it would make a plastic sound. In fact the fake pair are made of fibreglass. Although I have not seen many, the few that I have seen have been much of a kind: all have been on a black ground, and the decoration is usually a gilt trailing grapevine or Greek-key pattern border, with signs of over wear. The surprising thing is that No. 6 still fetched a healthy price!

As one can see, there are many things to look out for when buying papier mâché, but if you buy good quality, unrestored items, they should prove a good investment for the future. Already some outstanding prices have been realized. In March 1985 a pair of red lacquered graduated trays made £2,200 (No. 7), a previously unthought of price level. *Santiago de Barry*

4. *A mid-Victorian tray with scalloped border painted with a parrot.* 31½ in. long. Jan. '85, £320.

5. *Pair of Regency wine coasters with stencilled foliate decorated borders.* 5½ in. diam. Aug. '84, £320.

6. *Pair of simulated papier mâché wine coasters.* 5½ in. diam. Jan. '85, £100.

7. *Set of two Victorian graduated red lacquered trays.* 23½ in. and 27¾ in. long. Mar. '85, £2,200.

8. *Detail of restoration on the border of a tray.*

9. *Pair of Regency wine coasters decorated with gilt insects and flowers on rouge ground.* 6¾ in. diam. Oct. '84, £650.

10. *Regency red lacquered rectangular tray with cut corners.* 28 in. long. Mar. '85, £800.

11. *Early Regency oval galleried tray stamped Clay, London.* 23 in. wide. Jan. '85, £550.

12. *Double-waisted wine trolley stamped Leeson & Sons, Papier Machie.* 11½ in. long. Jan. '85, £480.

13. *Victorian writing slope.* 14 in. wide. Aug. '84, £200.

Papier Mâché (cont.)

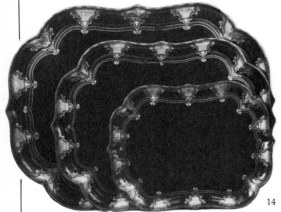

14

15

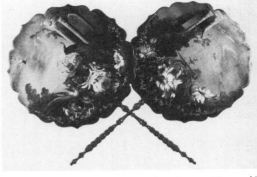

16

14. *A set of three Victorian graduated trays with scalloped borders. 19¼ in., 25¾ in. and 31 in. long. Mar. '85, £1,700.*

15. *Victorian tea-poy. 28½ in. Oct. '84, estimate £150.*

16. *Pair of Victorian hand screens painted with birds of paradise. Aug. '84, £260.*

Miscellany

1. *Victorian burr walnut games compendium, fitted with a variety of games in ivory. 13½ in. May '85, £1,200.*
   This is an exceptional example combining the skills of the cabinetmaker and the turner. The box itself is superbly made. The cabinetmaker has chosen a walnut veneer with fine figuring, and the brass mounts are finely engraved. The interior is fully fitted, which is quite unusual as in most cases they are incomplete.

2. *French green marble and ormolu-mounted three-tier letter rack. 10 in. May '85, £160.*

3. *Victorian miniature lavatory, inscribed Frederick S. Davidson, Portsmouth 1894 26½ in. May '85, £650.*
   An amusing and interesting article for the collector and historian, as the manufacturers have paid a lot of attention to detail, the wall paper, the tiles on floor, and even a roll of 'loo' paper – to make it look as close as possible to the real thing.

4. *Large parrot's cage. 36 in. Apr. '85, £280.*
   Bird cages are not unusual at auction, but when of this size and quality they tend to be more and more difficult to find.

1

2

3

5

6

7

5. *Domed leather seaman's trunk, painted all over with naval engagements, maritime scenes, and coats of arms.* 30 in. Apr. '85, £150.

6. *Pair of French ormolu two-tier six-light candelabras hung with faceted glass lusters.* 32 in. Apr. '85, £2,000.

7. *Gilt brass inkstand, shaped as a suitcase.* 7 in. Feb. '84, £260.
   Again, an amusing item, the interior is fully fitted, even with a candle nozzle.

8. *Cast-iron and brass Adam style fire grate.* 34 in. May '85, £1,300.
   An exceptional price for a fire grate, its size and quality influencing the price considerably; a similar but smaller one might make £400–£600.

9. *French burr yew, ormolu and guilloche enamelled circular jewellery box with polyfoil rim.* 11 in. diam. May '84, £800.
   The exceptional quality of the enamelling and the ormolu encouraged exceptionally high bidding for this item.

9

10. *Pair of brass door stops formed as swans.* 15 in. May '85, £300.

11. *Three brass door-stops formed as a handbell, a figure of Punch and a fly.* May '85, £180.

12. *Pair of brass door stops formed as heraldic lions.* 13½ in. May '85, £220.

The prices of Nos. 10–12 were quite high, mainly due to the fact that they were in a house sale, at The Weir, near Hereford, and not an ordinary auction. Also the good selection encouraged competition. Competition at house sales always tends to be keen anyhow, partly because of large number of private buyers, many of them local residents and sightseers looking for souvenirs, and partly because of competition between local and London dealers.

8

11

12

10

Sculpture

There was a time when one could reckon that a bronze figure, group or whatever would be worth ten times a similar example in spelter. However, the worrying thing is that bronze prices have hardly 'moved' in a decade (some, in real terms, are actually worth a lot less, such as animaliers), and the gap is closing dramatically.

In February 1985, a pair of spelter figures of warriors, admittedly some 30 inches high, fetched £360. This trend of rising spelter prices and falling, or static, bronze prices is somewhat alarming. Formerly, somebody would buy a white metal object simply because he or she could not afford a genuine bronze. So deeply does this seem to be ingrained that the prices now being paid for spelter could easily be spent to procure an item in bronze. Oh, what an irony!

Of course there are exceptions, but few. We sold a pair of greyhounds (No. 2) in July 1984 for £2,200, against an estimate of £600 to £800. The reason was that they were casts after the model by Sir William Reid Dick, one of the foremost bronze artists of this century.

Russian bronzes are popular: an Arab warrior after Lanceray (No. 3) fetched £750 in February 1985 but, again, it would have fetched this kind of price ten years ago.

Nineteenth-century marbles are also undervalued, in my opinion, with busts and groups even of good subjects, like pretty girls, fetching only £300 to £500 (No. 4).

Wood carvings of this period have to be exceptionally well executed to sell. Nineteenth-century religious subjects carved in wood are almost unsaleable.

Recently, an exquisitely carved nineteenth-century ivory panel of Christ as the Good Shepherd failed to sell at £60. Too religious, or is it that sculpture generally is not in vogue? It would be wonderful if fashion were ignored, and an eye for, and an appreciation of, quality were developed regardless. There is no reason, for instance, why a pair of spelter warriors should fetch £360 while the pair in bronze (No. 1) brings only £1,000. They are the same height but here the similarity ends.   *James Dick.*

1. *Pair of well-cast bronze figures of warriors, one loading powder into his musket. Mar. '85, £1,000.*
   A month earlier, a comparable pair, but in spelter, or white metal, fetched £360.

2. *Pair of bronze figures of Greyhounds, cast after the model by Sir William Reid Dick. July '84, £2,200.*

3. *Russian bronze equestrian group of an Arab on horseback, cast after the model by Lanceray and so signed in Cyrillic, 19th century. Feb. '85, £750.*

4. *Sculpted white marble group of Cupid and Psyche. Feb. '85, £340.*

Garden Furniture and Statuary

Garden furniture and statuary are proving a very popular attraction. For obvious reasons it is very much a seasonal matter and most sales are held between the months of May and September when more people are thinking of furnishing their gardens. Prices range from £60 for what is commonly known as a 'pub' table, with a cast iron underframe and circular wood or marble top (No. 1), to £1,300 for a pair of bronze garden urns supported by putti (No. 2). Although not everyone can afford to pay such a high price just for a pair of urns, these were of exceptional quality, and there are many which are affordable to the private buyer in the £200–£400 range.

Most of the furniture is made of wrought or cast iron. It was produced during the early part of the nineteenth century but mostly during the Victorian era. A lot of this furniture is very popular at auction, the earlier pieces arousing the most interest, like the Regency wrought iron settee (No. 3) which realized £650. The fashion of recent years has brought about an increase in demand, and therefore many copies are to be found; some of them are exceptionally good, but the majority make no effort to hide what they are. These are mostly in aluminium and are easy to spot by the difference in weight of the materials. It is much more expensive for a manufacturer today to reproduce the furniture in cast iron, and uneconomic to do so in wrought iron, as distinct from welded steel.

Although age is quite important it does not seem to be essential, and it is decorative appeal and size that seem to play a greater part in determining the price; for example, No. 4 realized £450: from the photograph it would appear to have been made of white marble but in fact it is composition stone, not dissimilar to a fine cement, and probably only about 50 years old; the buyer of this piece must have been attracted by its size and the fact that it was a nude (an infallible combination at auction).

Although furniture is to be mostly found in wrought or cast iron, the other items under this heading come in a wide range of materials such as lead, marble and stone. Garden urns, being the most popular, come in all materials and a variety of shapes, sizes and designs, and accordingly they vary enormously in price. Once again age does not play a definitive role. A pair of Victorian cast-iron campana-shaped urns 30½ inches

1. *View of part of the July 1984 Garden Furniture sale. In the left foreground are a cast-iron chair (£80 for a pair) and a 'pub' table (£130 for a pair). To the right are two Victorian white-painted cast-iron fern-leaf armchairs (£420 the pair).*

2. *Pair of bronze urns and each supported on three putti, early 19th century.* Feb. '84, £1,300.
   An outstanding price, although the fact that they were bronze and the quality of the casting was of high quality encouraged high bidding.

3. *Regency wrought iron garden bench.* 79 in. long. Sept. '84, £650.
   A reasonable price, as it is not so common to get pieces of wrought-iron furniture of that age through the auction rooms. The fact that there was some damage might have prevented it from realizing a higher price.

4. *Reconstituted stone figure of Venus, 20th century.* 51 in. on 23 in. plinth. Sept. '84, £450.
   At first sight it appears to be a low price, but it becomes reasonable if you take into account that the figure is not marble but just reconstituted stone and lacks age.

Garden Furniture and Statuary (cont.)

high (No. 5), painted in white, realized £650 in March '83, whereas a set in modern (maybe 50 years old) composition stone similar in design (No. 6) but with the addition of plinths realized £850. Obviously the buyer, undeterred by age or quality, was attracted by the fact that here was a set of four which in a garden setting would look remarkably like the real thing.

In conclusion it seems that this area of the market has no set guide lines – but buying quality always proves a good investment for the future. If you are fortunate enough to be able to buy a combination of quality and decorative appeal you can't go wrong.

Santiago de Barry

5. *Pair of Victorian cast-iron garden urns.* 30½ in. Mar. '83, £650.
   A good price for a pair of urns considering that originally they would probably have stood on plinths.

6. *One of a set of four composition stone campana-shaped garden urns on square plinths, 20th century.* 41 in. Sept. '84, £850.
   An exceptional price, but reinforcing the point that sets are a determining factor in pricing these items, regardless of age.

7. *Pair of lead two-handled urns, the bodies cast with cherubs and foliate scrolls, 18th century.* 22 in. Sept. '84, £1,600.
   A good price. Obviously the fact that they were 18th-century played a considerable part in the hammer price.

8. *Bronze bust of Neptune, early 19th century.* 36 in. Nov. '84, £2,600.
   An exceptional price for an exceptional piece.

9. *Classical bronze ornamental urn, early 19th century.* 31 in. Sept. '84, £380.

10

11

12

12. *Pair of Regency terracotta garden urns, the campana-shaped bodies cast with trailing grape vine, standing on plinths.* 46½ in. May '85, £1,100.

The high price was expected, since it is unusual to find pieces of this age in terracotta in reasonable condition.

13. *Pair of weathered carved stone garden urns, the ovoid bodies carved with acanthus leaf scrolls, mid-19th century.* 28 in. May '85, £500.

14. *Pair of bronze cranes, of Japanese design, 20th century.* 56½ in. and 47½ in. May '85, £2,600.

An exceptionally high price considering their age.

15. *Pair of Victorian cast-iron fern-pattern armchairs.* May '85, £800.

Once again, as with No. 8, an exceptional price. The chairs were of exceptional quality, and what is fondly known as 'virginal', i.e. unrestored. It is interesting to compare the price for a similar pair sold in July '84, which had been restored. They realized £420.

16. *Reconstructed stone figure of David after Michelangelo, 20th century.* 52 in. May '85, £300.

10. *Georgian lead fountain group of a swan and putto.* 47 in. Sept. '84, £4,200.

11. *One of a set of four stone garden urns on square plinths in the manner of Piranesi, early 19th century.* 90 in. Sept. '84, £3,000.

The high prices obtained for Nos. 10 and 11 are probably due to the fact that they were sold in their garden setting. Needless to say they were monumental pieces, and it seems in this field that 'big' is 'beautiful'.

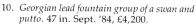

13

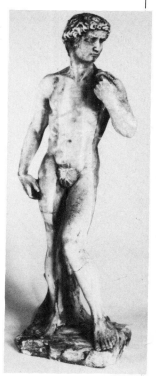

14

16

8.   *Art Nouveau to Modern Design*

Introduction
by Neil Froggatt

The category covered by Art Nouveau, Art Deco and Modern Design is a wide and varied one. In essence it deals with all aspects of twentieth-century decorative arts, but the period covered starts as early as the 1880s when forward-looking designers such as Christopher Dresser and E.W. Godwin were pointing the way forward. The last twenty years of the nineteenth century were rich in design both in Great Britain and Europe generally. The avant-garde designers of the 1870s were mainly Scottish and their influence was felt strongly in Germany and Austria with the Darmstadt School and the Vienna Secessionists. Art Nouveau followed the late nineteenth-century Arts and Crafts movement and was a style that flourished in France. It covered all aspects of the decorative arts, glass, pottery, furniture, jewellery and metalwork. It had its heyday at the very turn of the century, and continued to be popular until around 1910. Art Deco began to take shape as early as before the First World War when the arrival of Diaghilev's Ballets Russes in Paris upset the whole spectrum of colour and design. It lost momentum with the outbreak of war in 1914 but the aftermath of the war brought a renewed enthusiasm for living expressed in the decorative arts throughout the 1920s. The 1930s saw new directions and, once again, a World War interfered with these. Unlike the period after 1918, the period after the Second World War was a revolutionary one in design. All links with the past seemed to disappear and the look of the late '40s and the '50s was in every way a 'New Look'.

The 1984/1985 auction year has, yet again, shown that twentieth-century decorative arts are enjoying ever increasing popularity, at both the lower and the upper ends of the market. There have been sharp price increases in all sorts of areas, notably Lalique, Clarice Cliff, Shelley and Carlton Ware. But, in general, all twentieth-century studio pottery and studio glass have enjoyed a boom period. It was surprising and unexpected when a Clarice Cliff vase, expected to fetch far less, reached a record price of £3,600 at auction. A Lalique decanter with silver stopper made an encouraging £1,600. The Doulton market, which many felt must have reached its peak, has peaked again and expectations are still high (see pp. 58–60).

The continuing upward trend has been give a boost by new areas, and all categories of postwar design from glass to furniture have begun appearing at auction and selling to an enthusiastic new clientele, who, on the whole, are a younger crowd than has been seen recently at auction. There is still a lot of sorting out to do and it is perhaps a somewhat speculative market at the moment. But this very uncertainty also makes it one of the most exciting areas at auction, with new records being set almost every time something appears.

1. *One of a pair of Thebes stools with concave leather seats,* c. 1900. 14 in. Feb. '85, £550.

1

Art Nouveau

The 1900 Paris Exhibition of Decorative Arts heralded the commercialized beginnings of the 'Art Nouveau' period and also marked a break with a long tradition of historicism. Art Nouveau swept the whole field of design from architecture to furniture, from glass to metalwork. It was distinctive for its sinuous plant forms and maidens with flowing hair, and there was always an underlying sense of movement incorporated into object design.

The extravagant fantasy of Art Nouveau was embodied in the metalwork of the period, and a good example can be seen in No. 10 (overleaf). This mirror of white metal with its interlacing scrolls was typical of the imaginative use of whiplash motifs which completely transformed the look of everyday objects such as mirrors, vanity sets or ordinary household articles like bowls and vases. Sculpture was also transformed, and nude maidens and stylized dancing figures by artists such as Raoul Larche or Agathon Leonard (see p. 144) have enjoyed a profitable revival at auction over the past decade.

The Art Nouveau movement was closely associated both in England and the rest of Europe with the Arts and Crafts Movement, a distinctive feature of which was its forward-looking Studio Pottery. The products of such factories as Moorcroft, William de Morgan and Martin Bros. have shown a steady rise in price.

With glass the two main centres of production were Austria and France. In Austria the leading glass firm of this period was Loetz, maker of fine iridescent glass, which was copied extensively. In France there was a revival of the art of cameo glass with such brilliant masters of the art as Emile Gallé and Antoine Daum. There was also renewed enthusiasm for *Pâté de Verre*, a form of reconstituted crushed glass made by Argy Rousseau and Almeric Walter. In America the revival of Studio Glass was due almost exclusively to the brilliance of fort Tiffany, whose Favrile Glass and leaded glass lamps have been making auction history recently.

Neil Froggatt

1. *Liberty & Co. Cymric silver and enamel belt,* c. 1900. 26 in. long. Apr. '85, £580.
2. *William De Morgan covered vase by F. Passenger,* c. 1900. 10½ in. Jan. '85, £1,500.
3. *Moorcroft Florian vase, baluster in shape, in the Lilac pattern.* 10½ in. Jan. '85, £420.
4. *A pair of Moorcroft Florian ware tapering candlesticks in the Lilac pattern,* inscribed W.M.D.E.S. 10½ in. Jan. '85, £350.
5. *'The Gypsies', a Charles Vyse earthenware group,* c. 1925. 10½ in. Mar. '84, £650.
6. *'The Greek Dancer', a bronze figure after G. Bayes, inscribed Gilbert Bayes.* 15½ in. Feb. '85, £550.

Art Nouveau (cont.)

7. *Liberty & Co. pewter clock with enamelled face, designed by Archibald Knox, 1903.* Apr. '85, £1,100.
8. *Tiffany iridescent glass vase.* 12¼ in. Mar. '85, £500.
9. *Martin Brothers stoneware face jug, 1896.* 8½ in. Sept. '84, £1,600.
10. *W.M.F. white metal mirror.* 20 in. Jan. '84, £450.

7

8

9

10

Art Deco

Art Deco is the blanket term used to refer to the decorative arts between the wars. It covers many aspects of design from the starkness of the Bauhaus and modern movement to the sheer extravagance of French art, in particular the work of designers such as Jacques Emile Ruhlmann with his furniture in rare and precious woods inlaid with mother-of-pearl and ivory and Jean Dunand with his masterpieces in lacquer and crushed eggshell. Apart from these, there was mass production to cater for what fast became a popular taste among the middle classes, partly in emulation of their richer peers.

René Lalique, whose ever popular vase decorated with budgerigars is seen in No. 4, was both a designer and businessman who typified the ideal of art in industry during the period between the wars. He started life as an artist/jeweller during the Art Nouveau period but was seduced by the commercial lure offered by mass production, striving at the same time to maintain artistic standards. His designs were always sophisticated but at the same time universally popular. His example was followed everywhere in the commercial Western world, but he enjoyed complete supremacy.

Metalwork during the Art Deco period adopted the stylistic symbols used in other areas of the decorative arts. In France, silversmiths like Puiforcart and workers in wrought iron like Edgar Brandt were the height of fashion. In Scandinavia, Georg Jensen, with his flatware and other work, forged a style of his own, distinct from that of the French but very much in the Art Deco tradition.

In the field of ceramics, although the French were at the time considered the leaders, a curious pattern has emerged since the revival of Art Deco in the 1960s. Perhaps the most successful ceramics at auction have been the angular shapes of the British potter Clarice Cliff (Nos. 5–8), whose work was produced in large quantities but, because of her inspired variety of design, the variations are endless and her work has proved to be

among the most collectable Art Deco. There were other British designers such as Susie Cooper and Charlotte Rhead, and recently there has been a growing demand for Shelley, Carltonware and Foley Intarsio Ware. For Doulton figures, see p. 55.

Perhaps the most collectable items of the Art Deco period are the bronzed or bronze and ivory dancing figures by Chiparus, Preiss and Lorenzl (Nos. 2, 11 and p. 144, Nos. 2, 3, 4, 8). These have had a dramatic auction history and their light-hearted elegance remains ever popular among collectors.

Neil Froggatt

1. *Danish white metal and ivory tea and coffee service by F. Hingelberg, c. 1940. 7 in. May '84, £1,000.*
2. *'The Stile', a bronze and ivory figure by Ferdinand Preiss. 9¾ in. Nov. 83' £2,600.*
3. *Large Goldscheider pottery figure, c. 1920. 18 in. Apr. '85, £1,700.*
4. *'Ceylan', a Lalique opalescent glass vase. 9¾ in. Jan. '85, £800.*
5. *Clarice Cliff jug, 1515, in the 'Lucerne' pattern. 10½ in. Apr. '85, £1,600.*
6. *Clarice Cliff Inspirational vase in the 'Cloure' pattern. 7½ in. Apr. '85, £750.*
7. *Clarice Cliff Inspirational 'Lotus' vase with three russet and mauve posies. 11 in. Apr. '85, £2,000.*
8. *Clarice Cliff Inspirational vase in the 'Persian' pattern. 8 in. Apr. '85, £600.*
9. *'Ceylan', a Lalique opalescent amber glass figure, c. 1930. 9 in. June '85, £3,600.*
10. *Maurice Dufrene semi-lune desk, signed, 1935. 30 in. Apr. '85, £2,800.*
11. *'Pierrot', a patinated bronze and ivory figure, inscribed D.H. Chiparus. 12 in. Feb. '85, £1,250.*

2

3

4

5   6   7   8

9

10

11

Ceramics

1. *Rozenburg eggshell pottery vase*, c. 1900. June. '85, £720.

2. *Foley 'Intarsio' pottery stick stand*, c. 1910. 27½ in. July '85, £950.

3. *Gallé faience pottery cat*, c.1910. 13¼ in. Mar. '84, £1,500.

4. *Moorcroft three-handled loving cup*, c. 1920. 5¼ in. Mar. '85, £350.

5. *Clarice Cliff Fantasque Bizarre teaset for 2, painted in the 'Summer House' pattern,* c. 1930. Feb. '84, £850.
   An identical set for 6 persons made £2,200 in Feb. '85

6. *Two Foley 'Intarsio' pottery teapots, modelled as President Kruger (left) and Joseph chamberlain,* c. 1920. July '85, £550 (left) and £500 (right).

7. *Moorcroft studio pottery vase*, c. 1920. 12¼ in. Mar. 85, £550.

8. *Martin Bros. stoneware bird, c.* 1902. July '85, £1,600.
   Grotesque birds by the Martin brothers have increased dramatically in price in the past 2 years, an unusually large owl selling at Sotheby's in 1985 for £54,000.

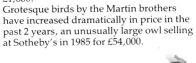

Glass

1

2

3

4

6

7

1. *'Rampillon', a Lalique opalescent glass vase,* c. *1930. 5 in. Apr. '85, £350.*
2. *A pair of Gallé enamelled glass vases,* c. *1900. 5 in. Apr. '85, £200.*
3. *Muller Frères cameo glass vase,* c. *1910. 11 in. Feb. '85, £480.*
4. *Daum etched green glass vase* c. *1920. 14½ in. Feb. '85, £420.*
5. *Art Deco leaded glass window,* c. *1920. 67 in. × 76 in. wide. Jan. '84, £1,600.*
6. *Lalique opalescent bowl,* c. *1920. 9¼ in. diam. Feb. '84, £700.* An identical bowl was sold at Christie's King Street in April 1985 for £1,700.
7. *'Naiades', a Lalique glass clock,* c. *1930. 4½ in. square. Mar. '84, £400.*
8. *Orresfors 'Graal' glass vase by Edward Hald,* c. *1920. 5½ in. Mar. '84, £150.*
9. *Daum cameo glass lamp,* c. *1910. 13 in. Apr. '85, £1,300.*

5

8

9

Sculpture and Metalwork

1. *Bronze figure cast from a model by Charles Sykes, c. 1920. 14¼ in. Feb. '84, £600.*
2 & 3. *Two ivory figures by Ferdinand Preiss, c. 1920. 6¾ in. Feb. '84, £1,100.*
4. *Lorenzl bronze and ivory figure, c. 1920. 8¾ in. May '84, £350.*
5. *'W.M.F. liqueur set, c. 1900. 15½ in. May '84, £240.*
6. *Tiffany studio silver vase, c. 1900. 15 in. Apr. '85, £500.*
7. *'Cruel Love,' a bronze and ivory cast from a model by Agathon Leonard, c. 1910. 9½ in. Mar. '84, £350.*
8. *'Girl on Wall', a bronze and ivory figure by Ferdinand Preiss, c. 1920. 9 in. Mar. '84, £1,900.*
9. *'Radha', a gilt bronze and ivory figure by Paul Philippe, c. 1910. 15¼ in. Jan. '84, £1,100.*
10. *'Hi There', a gilt bronze and ivory by D. Alonzo, c. 1910. 10¼ in. Jan. '84, £280.*
11. *Carved ivory nude figure by L. Rousseau, c. 1910. 7½ in. Jan. '84, £380.*

1

2   3

4   5

6

7   8

9   10   11

Postwar Design

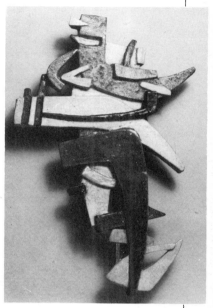

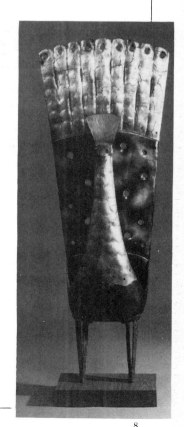

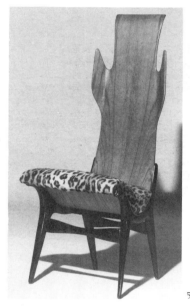

1. *Barovier and Toso 'patchwork' glass vase,* c. 1950. 9½ in. Feb. '85, £400.

2. *Cenedese glass vase,* c. 1960. 13 in. Apr. '85, £800.

3. *Abstract ceramic wall plaque by Giovan Battista Mitra,* c. 1950. 25 in. Christie's King Street, Apr. '84, £540.

4. *Brass and metal floor lamp by Arteluce,* c. 1950. 78 in. Christie's King Street, Apr. '84, £388.

5. *Plywood side chair designed by Dante la Torre, manufactured by Pozzie Verge,* c. 1960. 62 in. Christie's King Street, Apr. '84, £1,188.

6. *'Egg' armchair designed by Arne Jacobsen and manufactured by Fritz Hansens,* 1957. Christie's King Street, Apr. '84, £280.

7. *'Macchina per caffé expresso' by Gaggia.* 14½ in. Christie's King Street, Apr. '84, £216.

8. *'Il Grande Pavone', enamelled copper sculpture by Palo de Poli.* 6½ in. Christie's King Street, Apr. '84, £7,020.

9. Costume and Textiles

Introduction
by Susan Mayor

In the 1984–5 season there has been a marked increase in interest across the board but particularly in decorative needlework and fine costume. There have been signposts over the years: Lord Trevor's set of 12 early eighteenth-century needlework hangings, 96 × 25 in., £40,000 in 1983; a Renaissance bed tester appliqué with yellow satin grotesques, French, mid-sixteenth-century, now in the Victoria and Albert Museum, £28,000 in 1980; and the Marquis of Lansdowne's suite of 11 Chinese silk panels embroidered with birds and trees, £19,000 in 1982; and in the costume line the embroidered nightcap thought to have been worn by Charles I when he was beheaded in 1649, £13,000 in 1983; the suit worn by Prince Rupert, Count Palatine of the Rhine and Duke of Cumberland (1606–87), £11,000 in 1983 (now in the V & A); closely followed by a fine gentleman's dressing-gown or banyan, 1710, £8,200 in 1983 (also now in the V & A).

As of May 1985, the top price for the season stands at £16,000 for two large late decorative carpets, one of them over 31 feet long, (see p. 154). They were sold in August, when most London salerooms are closed. Then came a set of four decorative nineteenth-century tapestries woven with medieval scenes which fetched £12,000, a fine set of late seventeenth- or early eighteenth-century crewelwork at £11,000 (No.1) and a rare seventeenth-century Mughal velvet floor-spread at £10,000. In July 1984 we sold an important collection of late medieval vestments that had belonged to the Duke of Norfolk in the early nineteenth-century, the highest price fetched being £8,000 for an English late fifteenth-century chasuble, sold to the V & A. The Roman Catholic diocese of Shrewsbury sold a rare needlework altar frontal worked by the Nuns of Sion in exile in Flanders in 1587. This was bought by the V & A for £8,500.

1. *A fine set of late 17th/early 18th century crewelwork.* May. '85, £11,000.
   A remarkable price, considering that it had been cut.
2. *A dress of ivory silk woven with mauve, orange and olive green flowers,* c. *1830.* May '85, £1,400.
   Even though this was damaged under the arms it was most attractive.
3. *A dress of white organdie printed with blue and red flowers by Chanel,* c. *1930.* May '85, £2,200.

1

2

4. *A fine gentleman's suit of deep blue satin, the borders embroidered in chain stitch with garlands of pink roses; with waistcoat and breeches. French, Lyons, c. 1770. May '85, £3,000.*

5. *A needlework picture worked in raised or stumpwork with a lady and gentleman, her clothes trimmed with seed pearls, the palace with mica windows, English, c. 1660. 16 × 20½ in. Feb. '85, £4,200.*

6. *A textile printing block for a border worked in carved wood and strips of brass with an Egyptian frieze, early 19th century. 3¼ × 8 in. From the Cantrol Collection. Nov. 1984, £160.*

7. *A reclining nude on a length of artificial linen designed by Henry Moore for Ascher Ltd., c. 1940. 36 in. × 4 yards long. Nov. '84, £400.*

8. *One of a pair of needlework pictures of an elegant couple by a ruined temple with a country house in the distance, English, early 18th century, framed and glazed. Each 25 × 20 in. Oct. '84, £4,400.*

So far this season the highest price for costume was £5,500 for a pair of mid-seventeenth-century ladies' slippers, or mules, and the same price for a lovely pink and white striped open robe and petticoat, worn by an ancestress of the vendor in Peru in the eighteenth century, both sold in February 1985.

These sales of fine early costume also include important costume right through to the present century by the most famous designers: Chanel, Madeleine Vionnet, Balenciaga and Fortuny are among the most sought after. Condition, of course, is paramount, but even an altered 1930s black lace dress by Vionnet fetched £850 in February 1985. Then there were three very fine Chanels of the early 1930s in

May. One, of white organdie printed with blue and red flowers, is so fresh and enchanting that it brings back memories of Cecil Beaton's photographs. It fetched £2,200 and was bought by Chanel (No. 3).

Men's clothes tend to be much rarer than women's, and a gentleman's woollen coat of the 1740s made £5,000 in October 1984. A complete suit of royal blue satin of a less rare date, 1770, fetched £3,000 in May (No. 4).

At the lower end of the market sales have contained many decorative 1920s sequinned dresses ranging from about £100 to £400 in price, accessories such as crocodile suitcases and handbags, Louis Vuitton luggage at prices ranging from £200 to £900, and Paisley shawls averaging about £150 (the finest Kashmiri shawls tend to be included in special Oriental and Islamic sales). In the linen and lace section there are normally damask tablecloths (even early seventeenth- and eighteenth-century damask, recently a rare dated example of 1643 made £500), and lace tablecloths – large circular examples are in great demand and can fetch as much as £300. Here it is worth looking for multiple lots with tablecloths averaging sometimes under £10 each. Double linen sheets with fine embroidered turnovers can now fetch up to £150 each, quality and condition being paramount, and there is much in this line to be had for less.

English embroidered pictures are now much more eagerly collected. Those fine seventeenth-century ones can easily fetch over £4,000 if in fresh condition. Raised work or 'stumpwork' is very rare and this greatly adds to the value (No. 5). Though the golden age of English embroidery was the thirteenth century, even in the nineteenth few other countries produced decorative embroidery to compare with the finest English work.

One new departure this season was a sale of a selection from the Cantrol Collection of nineteenth- and twentieth-century textile printing blocks from David Evans & Co. in November 1984. This realized £15,235 (No.6). Recently too there have been some interesting wallpapers. French collectors have been buying eighteenth- and nineteenth-century papers in sales in Paris and Monte Carlo for some years. Now their English counterparts seem ready to follow. Thirteen panels dating from the 1840s to the 1870s, some in the style of Bruce Talbert, realized £1,800 in May. I have also noticed a demand for twentieth-century textiles designed by artists such as Henry Moore (No. 7).

There is now an international clientele which includes interior decorators, local ladies, dress designers and theatrical costumiers, as well as the standard collectors and dealers.

Historically speaking, the wealth of England has been based as much on wool, on cotton spinning and on the silk trade, as on the sea, coal, pig iron and railways, so there is a certain appropriateness – given the present enthusiasm for 'heritage' – in the current revival of interest in textiles, costume and embroidery.

And what of the future? Needlework is perhaps the field to watch. Even the rarest pieces are still cheaper than comparable items of woven tapestry (No.8).

Lace

Lace is not a new collectors' field but one beginning to show signs of revival after a fallow period. In the heady 1890s many collectors were women, but some were men such as Professor McLeod of Belgium whose collection was sold in 1980, and Mr Whitehead, whose collection was sold in February 1985. This last was beautifully mounted in an album with pink silk leaves and realized £3,000. Most collections were stored in lace boxes and tissue paper, or even in metal document boxes which still turn up in bank vaults or solicitors' offices. This is a survival from the days when lace was as valued as jewellery. In sales of the 1880s fine flounces of lace would fetch some 500 guineas. The fashion died out after the First World War and collections were tucked away and half forgotten. It was not until the early 1980s that collecting revived. Several factors contributed. In 1981 the collection of Mrs Walter Burns of North Mimms, a sister of J. Pierpont Morgan, was sold, and several lots fetched thousands. Many museums bought, there were international exhibitions, and Santina Levey of the Victoria and Albert Museum brought out a scholarly book.

Almost simultaneously, there was a new revival for wearing lace, and leading designers used it. The idea of wearing old lace was not new, it was done in the 1890s and Edwardian days. This is why many fine flounces were unfortunately altered into collars and cuffs.

Nowadays lace buyers fall into two groups: collectors of fine early lace, and buyers of lace to wear or use in decoration. As many early pieces were altered to suit Victorian and Edwardian whims, complete late seventeenth- to mid-nineteenth-century specimens are the most sought after (No.1). Seventeenth-century collars are very rare: one that perhaps belonged to King Charles I made £1,300 in 1982. It would have cost a fortune new. Fine unaltered flounces of *gros point de Venise* are prized, as they have so often been rearranged. I have seen a fine set that had been applied to bed hangings in the eighteenth century. Fine deep flounces of *point de France* to drape dressing tables are the third

seventeenth-century rarity, and these realize about £2,000.

From the eighteenth century come lappets and cap backs for fashionable women indoors (Nos.2 and 4); matching sets complete with frill are very rare. Pairs of fine Flemish bobbin lace lappets fetch from about £100 to £500, as do cap backs. Then there are dress robings, shaped borders to fit inside dress necklines, with matching sleeve ruffles. They too are very rare. So are decorative mid-eighteenth-century lace aprons. A torn one sold for £200 in 1984.

From the first half of the nineteenth century fine lace was produced in Honiton: bonnet veils, fichus, shawls, collars and handkerchiefs. Collectors should also look at fan sales for fans with lace mounts and in the costume sections of sales for parasols with lace mounts.

Collectors of lace to wear look for fine, long, deep flounces of Brussels and Honiton of the mid- to late nineteenth century, and wedding veils, some fine examples of which make £200–£250 each. Also desirable are Irish crochet collars and jackets, and striking lace such as Carrickmacross and Maltese.

Susan Mayor

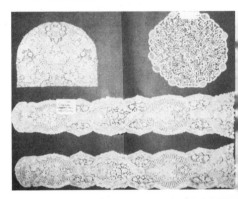

1. *A fine length of Italian needlelace, 1620–40. Oct. '84, £1,100.*
2. *A lady's cap back with matching pair of lappets, Flemish, mid-18th-century, with on the right a baby's cap back or crown of Honiton lace, early 19th-century.*
These and No.4 are from the collection of Mr Whitehead.

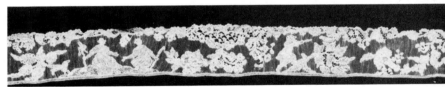

3. *A border of Brussels lace worked with sportsmen and shepherds and shepherdesses, mid-18th-century. Feb. '85, £300.*
Amusing subjects realize more than just flowers: another lot in the same sale was worked with fountains and dolphins and realized £450.
4. *A joined pair of 18th-century lappets.* From the collection of Mr Whitehead.
5. *A detail of a 19th-century Brussels lace shawl.*

Chinese Embroidery

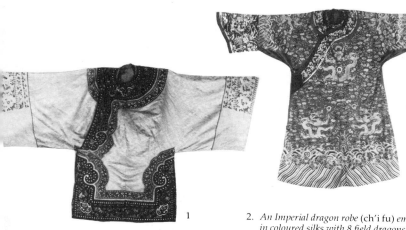

3. *An embroidered silk shawl finely worked in brightly coloured silks on a black ground with exotic peacocks and other birds among peonies, carnations, scrolling blossom and butterflies, with deep knotted fringe. For export, Ch'ing dynasty, second half of the 19th century.* Apr. '85, £260.

1. *A Chinese jacket of fine sky-blue silk damask with appliqué blue and black silk satin borders and sleeve bands embroidered in bright colours with butterflies (symbolizing great age), peonies (symbol of spring and wealth), lotus flowers (symbol of purity and summer), and other motifs. Ch'ing Dynasty, 19th century.* Apr. '85, £70.

2. *An Imperial dragon robe (ch'i fu) embroidered in coloured silks with 8 field dragons and a 9th dragon out of sight on the inner flap (number 8 was associated with Buddhism and Taoism and number 9 in ancient Taoist mythology was considered most symbolic of man). Ch'ing dynasty, second half of the 19th century.* Apr. '85, £280.

Chinese embroidery is inseparable really from Chinese costume, since the Chinese embroidered almost everything from skirts and shoes to bedspreads and wall hangings. So, for specialist collector or idle wanderer through the salerooms, there is much to choose from. However, the subject can be narrowed by date if not by classification – the vast majority of Chinese embroidery sold at auction dates from around the second quarter of the last century to about the mid-1920s.

After looking at several pieces – either fragments such as sleeve-bands (pretty decorative cuffs attached to the sleeves of a coat or jacket), or an item of dress, a jacket, say (No. 1) – it soon becomes apparent, even to the complete amateur, that motifs are used again and again: the same birds, flowers, trees, pagodas, bridges and landscapes, not to mention the numerous Buddhist and Taoist symbols scattered over any remaining space. Probably the best-known Chinese symbol is the Dragon, and the best-known representation of it in embroidered costume, the Dragon Robe (*Ch'i-fu*). In No. 2

we can see the traditional design of the dragon (symbol of Imperial authority chasing the flaming pearl, sacred symbol of the heavens) among bats, clouds, thunder lines and other motifs symbolizing good fortune and long life, over a deep border of waves and the sea (*li'shui*) symbolizing the Earth, and the mountain representing the world.

Chinese embroidery was thus not just decoration, but embodied a whole philosophy of life. A notion, however vague, of Taoism (the celebration of nature and the universe, and man's living in spiritual harmony with that universe), Buddhism and Confucianism, with their complex mythologies and sets of symbols, is helpful. Of course, one can enjoy it on a purely decorative level – and few decorative hangings can compete with a colourful Chinese silk embroidery of exotic birds among flowering trees – but a sense of the religion is important really to understand the whole feeling behind these extraordinary designs, where highly stylized representations of nature mix freely with symbols without any

regard for proportion or depth, but rather for balance, symmetry and harmony of pattern, reflecting man's harmony with the universe.

Many examples survive, and often in remarkable condition too. In the last century, with European ladies demanding more and more exotic oriental accessories, much was made for export. Probably the most common dress accessory was the shawl, usually embroidered in bright colours on a cream or black silk ground (No. 3); they can make from as little as £30 to as much as £300, depending on decorative quality, fineness and condition. Specialized Oriental and Islamic sales offer a very wide range of Chinese embroidery: from large hangings where the prices go into the thousands, to small panels, for instance 'rank badges' (decorative squares worked with birds or beasts, and applied to robes to indicate civil or military rank) which can make under £20 each. So enthusiasts can pick up a fragment of a civilization for as little as £15.

Emma Clark

Costume

1. *An open robe and petticoat of brown silk figured with leaves and sprigs of blue flowers, with sack back, the cuffs with whitework ruffles inscribed 'Ruffles work of Cath J Capper', English, c. 1760. Feb. '85, £2,800.*
   It is rare for the original ruffles to remain.

2. *An open robe of cotton, printed overall with red and blue convolvulus with red stems against a grey ground, English, c. 1785. May '85, £2,200.*
   Printed cotton dresses are rarer than silk. This dress of course lacks a petticoat, but it may well have been worn with one of a different material.

3 & 3A. *A dress of yellow striped lawn printed with sprays of blue flowers, with 'gigot' sleeves, English, c. 1829, with a length of the same material stamped with manufacturer's name and date. Oct. '84, £600.*
   All documentation such as this adds greatly to the value of costume.

1

2

3a

4. *A dress of ivory satin printed in vertical bands of grey fleck design and in larger pink and grey chiné design, the sleeves striped with pink silk, c. 1934. May '85, £1,200.*

5. *Paul Poiret label from a black velvet dress. c. 1918. Oct. '84, £850.*
   Poiret dresses are much sought after. 20th-century couturier labels are sometimes very imaginative. Madeleine Vionnet used her fingerprint.

6. *One from a collection of designs by Revill & Rossiter for HRH Princess Patricia, daughter of the Duke of Connaught, third son of Queen Victoria. Feb. '85, £140.*

7. *A wedding dress and coat of white panné velvet, trimmed with raised-work flowers embroidered with glass bugle beads, paste and artificial pearls, the cuffs trimmed with fur, labelled Modéle Molyneux, 5 Rue Royale, No. 35713, c. 1922. Sold by Lady Alexandra Metcalfe, daughter of Lord Curzon. Feb. '85, £700.*
   The coat was made out of the train to the wedding dress.

4

6

5

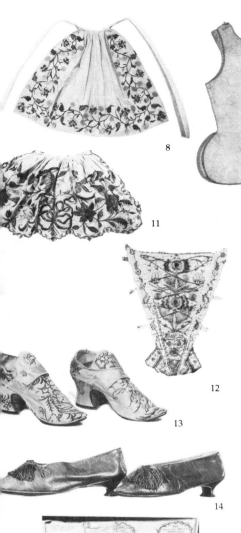

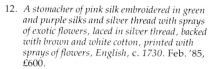

8. *A short apron of ivory silk embroidered with brightly coloured flowers and yellow and orange fruit, c. 1730.* May '85, £290.
This was slightly split but the colours were very bright and fresh. It fetched more than aprons usually do, but not as much as No.6, which was very elaborate.

9. *A rare lady's waistcoat of linen finely quilted in yellow silk with flowerheads and ferns, bound in citron yellow silk braid and piped at the shoulders and down the front with similar ribbon, English, c. 1730.* May '85, £2,500.

10. *A gentleman's waistcoat of dark green striped silk woven à disposition (to shape) with a trellis containing peacock feathers and with a border of lilies of the valley, the lower border with allegories of love, French, c. 1785.* Oct. '84, £150.

11. *A short apron of ivory silk embroidered with carnations and peonies, worked in coloured silks and raised gold thread enhanced with sequins, English, professional needlework, c. 1730.* Feb. '85, £750.
These aprons formed part of fashionable dress in the 1730s. They were even worn at Court, and this was an exceptionally fine example.

12. *A stomacher of pink silk embroidered in green and purple silks and silver thread with sprays of exotic flowers, laced in silver thread, backed with brown and white cotton, printed with sprays of flowers, English, c. 1730.* Feb. '85, £600.
Strangely, the following lot in the same sale, almost identical but for colour (it was white embroidered in blue and green), fetched much more, £1,100.

13. *A fine pair of ladies' shoes of ivory silk brocaded with sprays of pale green and yellow flowers with white level rands and high heels, English, c. 1750.* May '85, £600.

14. *A pair of shoes of bottle-green morocco with low heels, the upper trimmed with a tassled silk fringe trimmed with a rosette of silver thread, c. 1790.* Feb. '85, £700.
These were a rare colour and in very good condition. All interesting shoes are much sought after. At about this period one begins to find decorative labels inside the shoes – had this pair been labelled they would have fetched even more.

15. *'The Traveller's new guide through the principal direct roads of England and Wales', printed in rose madder on cotton, late 18th/early 19th century. 24 × 26½in.* Feb. '85, £160.
We find there is great interest in printed and commemorative handkerchiefs. A silk one with a map of Paris recently fetched £1,000.

16. *'The funeral procession of Lord Viscount Nelson to St. Paul's Cathedral, January 1806', printed in sepia and rose madder on cotton. 22 × 26in.* Feb. '85, £300.

17. *A pair of boys' dress wellington or opera boots stamped with the Prince of Wales's feathers in gold on the heels, the leggings also embroidered thus, c. 1846. 5½in. long, 8in. high, in fitted case.* Oct. '85, £2,200.
Almost certainly made as a presentation to the Prince of Wales as a child, an association which largely accounts for the exceptional price.

18. & 18A. *A black satin coat by Worth, embroidered in black beads with stylized roses with Worth label and model number 25630 and owner's name, c. 1905–8. Made for the American heiress Mrs Bramley Martin, whose daughter married the fourth Earl of Craven.* Oct. '84. £750.
Labels on costume came in by the 1860s, and if of a known dressmaker they greatly enhance the value.

Fans

Some great collections of fans were built up a hundred years ago, most notably that of Lady Charlotte Schreiber, who gave the greater part of hers to the British Museum in 1891. The other well-known collection of that period was formed by Robert Walker, who in turn had bought some of his collection from Sir Augustus Wollaston Franks of the British Museum. Sir Matthew Digby-Wyatt formed yet another splendid collection which forms the basis of the Victoria & Albert Museum's collection. But fans are such small objects that important yet previously unknown, or little known, collections have appeared for sale over the last ten years. In particular, the collection formed by Mrs Baldwin of Milwaukee and sold by her daughter Mrs Pabst in 1978, and the collection of the Duquesa de Marchena, sold in 1977. There are now two fan societies, the Fan Circle International in London, and the Fan Association of North America.

Most fans on the market date from the eighteenth and nineteenth centuries. There are also a few rare late seventeenth-century examples, a number of very decorative 1920s advertising fans and pretty ostrich feather fans.

Eighteenth-century fans are mainly painted. Fans were an international market, both leaves and sticks being exported and made up in most countries. There are also interesting printed commemorative fans from the eighteenth century.

From the beginning of the nineteenth century the large majority tend to be printed – at first in stipple engraving – then from the middle of the century in lithography. From this period there also survive many fine lace fans, and in the 1860s there was a revival of fine painting. The best of these were produced by two Parisian makers, Duvelleroy and Alexandre, who commissioned fashionable decorative artists of the period such as Antonio Soldi. The finest of this type are now reaching £3,000.

Many Englishmen travelled in China in the nineteenth century and brought back Cantonese fans as presents, which supplemented the sticks and leaves that had already been exported. There are also some very fine Japanese fans to be found, and one fine example, an ivory brisé fan with elaborate *shubyama* work, or mosaic inlay, of about 1880, made £2,400 in 1983.

It was only in 1978 that prices for fans started to spiral and reach once again the heady levels of the 1880s.

Susan Mayor

1. *Fan, the leaf drawn in black and sepia ink with elegant figures and a court dwarf departing for a hunt, the reverse similarly drawn with picnickers by a river, after Vernet, the mother-of-pearl sticks etched with Chinese figures in European dress and silvered, probably Flemish, c. 1750, the sticks Chinese for the European market.* 11¼in. Mar. '85, £300.

2. *Fan, the chickenskin leaf painted with a trompe l'oeil of prints signed and dated Albonesi Romanus 1760, the mother-of-pearl sticks painted with figures, silvered and gilt – Italian, 1760, the sticks possibly French.* 11½in. Mar. '85, £620.

The artist is presumably Angelico Albonesi, who was working as an engraver in England and Italy during the second half of the 18th century, producing among other things Roman views. Few 18th-century fans are signed but it is not uncommon to find Italian decorative artists signing fans – the subject-matter of these fans was often classical ruins to sell to tourists.

3. *Fan, the leaf a hand-coloured etching of the Three Kings, with bone sticks, English, c. 1750.* 11in. Mar. '85, £180.
   There is no example of this printed fan in the Schreiber Collection, which makes it rare, although it is a Biblical subject, which is normally less saleable.

4. *Fan, the leaf printed with a hunting scene signed O. de Penne, 1885, the tortoiseshell sticks semé with rose diamonds, the reverse printed with the monogram of the recipient, Princess Marie d'Orléans who married Prince Valdemar of Denmark in 1885.* Sept. '84, £950.
   Olivier de Penne was a well-known artist, but we find that Second Empire fans of the 1860s in 18th-century style sell even better.

5. *An ivory brisé fan carved to resemble a sheaf of corn when closed, French c. 1860.* Feb. '84, £210.

6. *A pair of Canton ivory parasol fans, each with hanging box, and all carved with initials, c. 1800.* Dec. '84, £1,100.
   Although they were damaged they made a strong price, as it is rare to find a pair with boxes.

Samplers

Several hundred samplers a year are sold at South Kensington. They vary from the dreary (high-minded moral or religious verse) to charming and decorative pictures skilfully embroidered in many colours and stitches. Prices vary accordingly, from about £40 to as much as £2,000 (No. 1).

Samplers started life as a record of embroidery patterns which could then be copied. The word itself comes from the old French 'exzamplaire' translated in 1530 as 'exampler for a woman to work by'. The earliest dated sampler is English, 1598, and is in the Victoria & Albert Museum. The role of the sampler changed a good deal over the centuries. In the seventeenth century, because of the increasing number of printed patterns in book form, its original function became obsolete. It became a means of instructing young girls in the embroidery techniques of the day – preparing them for their roles in later life as housewife, maid or lady of leisure.

Typical of an early seventeenth-century sampler is the 'spot motif' (No. 1), so called because the various motifs are embroidered at random and bear no relation to each other in design or proportion. However, by the middle of the century we can see much more concern with overall design (No. 2). The horizontal border patterns of geometric floral motifs are typical of samplers worked from c. 1650 until c. 1720. Then until around the end of the eighteenth century, it became less a means of practising techniques and more a decorative picture. It was still useful for learning, but it also served as a record of a child's name, age, home (houses, gardens, animals and plants are common features c. 1750–1850), family, school and teacher. Samples were used in teaching religious knowledge, hymns, popular verses, and simple arithmetic. Geography too was a popular subject: many map samplers survive from the late eighteenth and early nineteenth centuries varying from complicated Globe maps to less ambitious maps of England and Wales. During this period the shape of the sampler changed too, from long and narrow to rectangular or square – more appropriate for the picture it had become.

Most surviving samplers date from the late eighteenth and early nineteenth centuries. The prettiest, I think, are often Regency. One of my favourites is by Mary Bye (No. 3), in which the verse, mercifully, is not too overpoweringly moral. The horizontal bands that once formed the whole are now border only, a frame for picture and verse. The picture itself is now worked more simply in a limited variety of stitches.

The life of the sampler as a decorative picture and record of a child's achievement, to be kept and handed down, really ended around the middle of the last century. Although it continued to be worked by young girls to the end of the nineteenth century (particularly 'darning' samplers) and beyond (my mother embroidered a boring cross stitch one in 1934), the combination of Berlin woolwork patterns and the sewing machine was too much for the sampler. Alas, too late for the poor girl who inscribed her sampler, 'Harriet Smith, who worked this in the Ninth Year of her Age . . . and hated every stitch'!

Emma Clark

1. *Spot motif sampler worked in coloured silks and silver metal thread on a linen ground, with some raised work in many types of stitch including double-running, long-armed cross, eyehole, rococo, satin and tent stitches, c. 1610–40. 10½ × 6½in. Apr. '84, £1,000.*

2. *A sampler by MH dated 1650, worked in coloured silks on linen, with horizontal borders of formalized flowers including Tudor Roses, Honeysuckle and Acorns, with some raised work, in various stitches including double running, Montenegrin cross, cross, satin and Algerian eye stitches. 20 × 8¼in. Feb. '85, £2,000.*

3. *A sampler by Mary Bye finely worked in bright colours, mostly in cross stitch with a girl picking flowers in a blue 'Empire' dress, and a boy picking fruit from a tree, with trailing strawberry border on two sides, early 19th century. 12½ × 16½in. Nov. '84, £550.*

4. *A sampler by Mary Bird, aged 12 years in 1805, finely worked in coloured silks in a variety of stitches.*
Sold at Christies South Kensington for £400 on 9 Oct. 1984. Six months later, on 4 April 1985, this same sampler was sold at Phillips for £460. To make a substantial difference in price it would probably have been better to wait at least a year, as £400 was a high price to pay in the first place.

1

2

3

4

Nineteenth-Century Needlework Carpets

1

2

3

4

5

6

Needlework carpets have really taken off in the last year. The first staggering result was for two long runners (No. 1). Although not of an unusual design – it is of 'squares' each with a spray of flowers – they were in mint condition and very large, and could have been cut up to make smaller carpets or even cushions.

No. 2, although not in such good condition and far smaller than No. 1, is a much more unusual pattern. Worked in pastel colours it is earlier than No. 1 and the design is far gentler, more sophisticated and elegant than the somewhat harsh squares of the runners.

No. 3 shows a corner of a large carpet worked with a highly decorative and unusual lobed medallion pattern mostly in dark blue and crimson. Although larger than No. 2, it is worn, and its chunky pattern probably does not have quite such a wide appeal as the more delicate flowery pattern of No. 2.

Nos. 4 and 5 show two needlework panels rather than carpets. Even so their lush floral patterns, good colouring and condition make them highly decorative pieces.

No. 6 is the corner of an unusual embroidered carpet shaped to fit around a four-poster bed. Again, it is the decorative qualities that determine the price. Its curvilinear lattice pattern enclosing leafy sprays is worked on a delicate deep rose coloured ground and the curling ribbon border is also in deep rose against a pale green ground.

Emma Clark

1. *A detail from one of two long embroidered wool runners worked in coloured wools in gros point on a cream ground, probably late 19th/early 20th century. 31ft. 5in. × 5ft 5in., and 13ft. × 5ft 5in. Aug. '84, £16,000.*

2. *Needlework carpet worked in gros point, probably second quarter of the 19th century. 12ft. 8in. × 11ft. 8in. Nov. '84, £8,500.*

3. *Large needlework carpet densely embroidered in cross-stitch in wool, probably third quarter 19th century. 15ft. × 12ft. Mar. '85, £4,600.*

4. & 5. *Two embroidered wool panels, one embellished with beads, both worked densely in cross stitch, mid-19th-century. 4ft. 7in. × 2ft. 1in., and 2ft. 3in. × 1ft. 6in. Mar. '85, £850*

6. *Shaped needlework carpet embroidered in wools in cross-stitch, originally made to fit around a four-poster bed in an Elizabethan farmhouse in Westmorland, c. 1860–70. Apr. '85, £3,500.*

Patchwork Quilts

All of these were offered on the same day, so the prices are for intrinsic merit, rather than because of trends. No. 1 sold well because although relatively modern, the quilting is fairly traditional and the piece is in mint condition. No. 2 demonstrates the technique of appliqué at its best – it is also elaborately quilted.

No. 3 sold very well as it combines an unusual, simple design with rare, vibrant cottons, some of which date from the 18th century. No. 4 shows a popular design and here is composed of particularly cheerful cottons – its small size may have kept the price down.

Tessa Charlton

1. *Early 20th-century 'Durham' quilt. 84 × 96in. Apr. '85, £380.*
2. *19th-century 'Kentucky Oakleaf and Acorn' appliqué quilt. 82 × 64in. Apr. '85, £320.*
3. *Patchwork quilt, early 19th-century, some of the cottons probably earlier, possibly Continental. 88 × 90in. Apr. '85, £500.*
4. *'Log Cabin' patchwork cover, most of the cottons 19th-century. 72 × 62in. Apr. '85, £90.*

1

2

3   4

10. Photographs

Introduction
by Lindsey Stewart

The last year has seen a steady and encouraging improvement in the market for both nineteenth and twentieth-century photographs. Regular buyers seem to have shown more enthusiasm, new bidders have been noticeable in the salerooms, and several collectors who have not been seen for some time have reappeared with renewed interest. While prices have risen to some extent across the whole range of material on offer, there has been an increased demand for quality. As a result, a few items of special interest have attracted considerable attention, and examples of rare early works in good, complete condition have frequently sold for amounts well over their upper estimates: Fox Talbot's influential book *Pencil of Nature*, 1844, for £30,000 against an estimate of £12,000–£15,000 (see p. 162); a portrait by J.M. Cameron for £4,000 with estimate of £1,500–£2,500; and a group of four stereoscopic daguerreotypes by Antoine Claudet for £12,000 against an estimate of £3,500–£5,000.

Several identifiable factors have contributed to this upsurge in the market, and most have their origins across the Atlantic. The world of photographic collecting in the United States is longer established and more sophisticated than that in Britain, with a greater accent on long-term investment. This to some extent explains the interest in quality material with a well-documented background and sound provenance, those items in any field of collecting which are most likely to increase in value regardless of fashionable trends. As a majority of photographic lots tend to make their way to North America, the strength of the dollar against the pound has been responsible for enthusiasm from American bidders. Similarly, the low pound has proved an additional incentive to Continental buyers.

A rather more unusual factor, but one which has certainly affected the market, has been the decision by the J. Paul

1. *William Henry Fox Talbot, The Pencil of Nature, Plate IV, 'Articles of Glass', 1843–4.* Calotype, 5 × 6in.

Getty Centre to establish a permanent collection of photographs. In such a relatively young field, there remains room for an element of authority to be added by the participation of a body with such wealth and influence. This tends to boost morale amongst other collectors and dealers which is reflected in stronger bidding and higher prices.

Daguerreotypes and Ambrotypes

Daguerreotypes and ambrotypes are small photographs, usually cased, in which the image is on a surface of silvered metal or glass rather than paper. They were most popular during the 1850s, and many survive today. Their prices vary enormously, with individual images selling from two or three pounds to several thousand.

The daguerreotype was invented in France in 1839 and the ambrotype was introduced in Britain *c.* 1852. The daguerreotype process was complicated and slow. By comparison, the production of ambrotypes was relatively inexpensive and simple, and was quickly seized upon as a money-spinner by all kinds of people with no previous experience in either photography or art. Several skilled daguerreotypists operated in Britain during the 1840s and 1850s, but the process quickly faded from popularity with the proliferation of the ambrotype during the later 1850s. Given a daguerreotype and an ambrotype of similar subject and quality, the former is likely to have more commercial value.

Naturally price increases if the work is by a well-respected photographer, and names include Antoine Claudet, William Edward Kilburn, T.R. Williams, Richard Beard, John Benjamin Dancer and John Mayall. An advertising label was often fixed to the reverse, or stamped onto mounts or cases.

Both types were used predominantly for portraiture, especially half-figure studio portraits. The use of elaborate props and embellishments such as hand-tinting or gilding add interest, and some photographers can be identified by particular studio backgrounds. This is most noticeable with Antoine Claudet, whose long draped window with landscape view beyond is often recognizable.

If sitters are unidentified, the price is rarely very high, although larger whole-plate portraits (approx 6½ × 8½ inches), nudes or studies including unusual items, especially of photographic interest, do better.

A fine full-length daguerreotype of a young lady and a dog (half plate) sold for £420 (No. 1), while a whole-plate of two Argentine sisters made £600, and a stereoscopic daguerreotype of a reclining female nude fetched £1,500, all in October '84. A quarter-plate ambrotype of a young man with a stereoscopic viewer then made £130 in March 1985.

If the sitter is of some historical importance, a portrait may be worth a considerable amount (see p. 158, No. 1). A portrait of Wellington, by Claudet made £10,000 at Sotheby's in October 1984.

The earliest daguerreotypes were mainly outdoor subjects, especially architecture and topographical views, as the exposures were usually too long for even the most patient individual. The few that have survived are mostly now in museum collections. However, it is possible to find later outdoor scenes, which are very much rarer than portraits. Good architectural and landscape views are in much demand, as are subjects of historical and documentary interest. Still-lifes were popular with stereoscopic photographers, and they are desirable now. While an ambrotype portrait may be worth under £5, an outdoor subject can have considerably more appeal. A good quarter-plate of a village scene recently sold for £130 (No. 3) as did a view of a clothier's shop with the proprietor and his wife in the doorway.

Lindsey Stewart

1. *Daguerreotype portrait, half-plate, 1850s. Oct. '84, £420.*
2. *Daguerreotype family portrait, 1850s. June '84, £600.*
3. *Rural scene, quarter plate, ambrotype, 1850s. Mar. '85, £130.*
4. *Port of Bastia, Corsica, pair of circular (3¼in. diameter) daguerreotypes forming panoramic view, 1850s. Oct. '82, £2,000.*

2

3

1

4

Victorian Stereos

From humble beginnings 3-D stereographs have become an important feature of photograph sales. A staggering £12,000 was paid in June 1984 for an important stereoscopic daguerreotype of the pioneer stereographer Antoine Claudet. Admittedly Claudet was a photographic legend in his own life time, but this price represents a very serious commitment to the field, which in the more affordable areas offers enormous potential for the collector.

Stereo daguerreotypes are generally the best sellers. Prices range from £50 to £80 for an unattributed study to £300 or more for a good studio portrait or still-life. Photographers' credits can be found printed on the reverse or below the glass overmatt. Nude studies are at a premium (No. 2). Hand-tinting can enhance the value but if crudely applied steer clear. A fracture of the airtight paper seal will cause oxidation of the image, a costly fault to put right.

By far the most common form of stereo is the stereo card. 1850s and '60s studies are the most desirable with the images fixed separately to pale coloured card mounts. Prices vary dramatically, depending on earliness of subject, or the numbers produced by large-scale view publishers. Tableau vivant themes are eagerly sought today. Good groups of hand-tinted cards by Elliott (No. 3), Silvester, Phiz, Goodman, Lake Price, Toby and others range between £100 and £300. A series of 27 sold in March 1985 for £420.

Documentary sets are worth searching out, especially exhibitions. In 1862 William England was commissioned to record the International Exhibition. This is an interesting set concentrating on the stands and with detailed annotations and series numbers on the mount (No. 4). Other series worth noting: 'The Great Eastern Steamship' published by the London Stereoscopic Co. and including the immortal portrait of Brunel seated before the launching chains sold singly at Sotheby's for £450 in 1982; Alpine views by England and Braun about £2 a card; scenes in London Zoo by Frank Haes £5 a card; and American railways – a group of thirty-two 1870s cards of the Central Pacific Railroad selling for £1,100 in March 1985.

Topographical and town views survive in great quantities but pre 1880s American and British subjects are worth acquiring, particularly 'Instantaneous' views by Anthony and Wilson at around £3 a card. European subjects and the late nineteenth-century published sets in book-form cartons have not as yet moved beyond the £50-a-hundred mark.

Other types of stereo include transparencies on tissue or glass. Tissues, due to their fragility, are generally in poor condition; good unpunctured tissues by Elliott, Silvester etc. can, however, change hands at up to £50 a piece. Glass transparencies are normally of limited appeal unless executed by The Lumière Bros. using their Autochrome colour process – fine examples will make £300 or £400 each.   *David Allison*

1

2

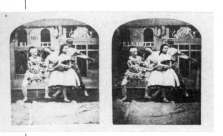

3   4

1. *Stereoscopic daguerreotype self-portrait of Antoine Claudet posed with his son and grandson beside some of his own photographic inventions, late 1850s.* Sold with 3 other family stereo daguerreotypes, June '84, £12,000.

2. *Stereoscopic daguerreotype, reclining nude with basket of flowers, mid 1850s.* Oct. '84, £1,500.
   This one is probably French; any daguerreotype of life models, curiosa, etc. is at a premium. This was a high quality, finely hand-coloured example.

3. *Stereo card by J. Elliott, one from a group of 33 tableau scenes, late 1850s.* Mar. '85, £160.
   Hand-coloured cards with images mounted separately and with photographer's credits on pale-coloured mounts are in great demand – especially theatrically-staged scenes of this type.

4. *Stereo card, International Exhibition of 1862 from a group of 100.* June '84, £240.
   An especially interesting card showing the interior of an early photographic gallery.

Photograph Albums

A large section of any sale comprises bound albums of photographs. Mixed albums of travel and architecture predominate, the majority from between 1870 and 1900. The photographs, taken by professionals, were stocked in bookshops and print shops in popular tourist centres, and could be purchased either individually or bound in albums. They often have captions or credits along the lower edge, and names commonly found include 'G.W.W.', 'J.V.', 'Frith's Series', Alinari, Sommer, Scowen, Skeen, Bonfils, Zangaki, A. Beato, Taber and Burton Bros. Prices vary according to countries – Britain, the Continent and Scandinavia are the most common, the Middle and Far East, Africa, Australasia, and the Americas rarer. Typical examples from March 1985 show eight mixed European albums going in one lot for £45, while a single album of Jamaica and South America made £320.

Earlier travel albums, from the 1850s or 1860s, are rarer – compare Nos. 1 and 2. Early work by named photographers is in much demand including that by Samuel Bourne (India) and Francis Frith or Francis Bedford (Egypt). Individual photographers attract interest for their quality work – John Thomson (Far East), Carlton Watkins and Timothy H. O'Sullivan (North America, No. 3).

Portrait albums appear regularly, and family or military albums from the 1850s compiled by aristocratic amateurs are popular. These usually sell between £100 and £300, although a good one, such as No. 4 by the talented amateur C.S.S. Dickins, will make much more. Cartes-de-visite albums from this early period are in demand. Such leading portraitists as Silvy, Mayall, Disderi, Rejlander, Carrick and Nadar are especially desirable, as are notable sitters – writers, artists, scientists, statesmen, Civil War heroes and freaks! An album containing 192 such portraits by important photographers made £500 in March. Later nineteenth-century anonymous family albums are abundant and rarely attract interest – one lot of 17 albums sold for £150.

Albums documenting a particular subject or event can attract keen bidding. Recent examples include 'Forth Bridge Construction 1885' for £260 and 'Studies of Prison Life' (No. 5). Another interesting category exists – albums compiled by or relating to a 'great' photographer. In March we sold a mixed one on Ceylon, combining three portraits by Julia Margaret Cameron with watercolours and diary entries. This made £1,400. Another lot in the same sale comprised two part-albums dating from the 1850s with a wide range of subjects by photographers including Roger Fenton. This was the last remnant of two large portfolio albums thought to have been originally compiled by or with Fenton, and including many superb examples of his work. The lot sold for £10,000 bringing the total over several years for the two albums to approximately £200,000! *Lindsey Stewart*

3. *T.H. O'Sullivan, 'Cañon de Chelle', Plate 12 from the 25-plate Wheeler Expedition Survey in Arizona and Utah, 1872.* Mar. '85, £12,000.

4. *'Chimney Sweep', from a mixed portrait and country house album by C.S.S. Dickins.* May. '85, £800.

5. *Plate from an 1890s album, 'Studies of Prison Life', photographer unknown.* Oct. '84, £900.

1. *Typical late 19th-century view from a lacquer-bound Japanese album of 50 photographs with caption and reference number printed in the negative.* Mar. '85, £95.

2. *Group portrait by Felice Beato from a Japanese album, 1860s.* Oct. '84, £4,000.
Beato was the first and possibly most important photographer to work in Japan, and the inclusion of several photographs by him, as well as the early date, explains the exceptional price.

Julia Margaret Cameron

Julia Margaret Cameron (1815–79), is one photographer whose work is widely known outside the often esoteric world of photographic collectors. Publicity over the retention of fine examples of her work for museums in Britain has meant that for many people Cameron is synonymous with expensive.

Prices do, however, vary considerably, and sales of photographs over the last year show this, in some cases even for prints from the same negative. In March and October 1984 we offered two separate prints from one negative made by Mrs Cameron – a portrait of the poet, Sir Henry Taylor, 'A Rembrandt'. This is one of the best-known portraits of one of her closest friends. Each of them was an albumen print, mounted on card, with the printseller Colnaghi's blindstamp and typical ink inscriptions by Mrs Cameron. The first sold for £420, while the second fetched £2,400 (No. 1).

The fact that two different copies of the same image should appear in the space of seven months indicates that they are not particularly rare. Mrs Cameron was prolific, and this was one of her most popular photographs. The difference in price was due to differing quality. The first was the familiar mid-brown colour with yellowish highlights, the second an unusually rich print with deep purplish brown tones. The latter had been printed and toned in such a way as to accentuate the dramatic effect of the image. To find such a rich quality and colour in a Cameron print is extremely rare.

In October 1984 there were two portraits by Mrs Cameron of the great Hungarian violinist Joseph Joachim (Nos. 2 and 3). In the first, the sitter is posed, draped in black velvet, while in the second he is clearly identified as Joachim by the inclusion of his violin. The former is an albumen print with Colnaghi's blindstamp on the mount, along with the photographer's inscription, and it sold for £1,900. The latter, which had been torn and repaired, is a photogravure print probably by J.B. Obernetter of Munich with facsimile inscription on the mount, and it sold for just £22. In this case the difference of condition is an obvious element, but this is not the only

1

2

3

4

factor. Had the second print been in perfect condition it would still have made no more than £100. An albumen print is one made from the negative probably by the photographer herself, and even she could not have produced two identical prints. Photogravure printing is a photomechanical process in which a printing plate is made, and many of prints produced. From the commercial point of view they are thus of less interest. A third portrait of Joachim – a stunning albumen print in superb condition sold in March 1985 for £4,000 (No. 4).

It may be disappointing to realize that not all photographs by Julia Margaret

1. *Sir Henry Taylor, albumen print.* Oct. '84, £2,400.

2. *Joseph Joachim, albumen print.* Oct. '84, £1,900.

3. *Joseph Joachim, photogravure print.* Oct. '84, £22.

4. *Joseph Joachim, albumen print.* Mar. '85, £4,000.

Cameron are likely to fetch high prices. However, this may encourage the new collector who sees that it is possible to purchase a perfectly good photograph by her for what remains, in terms of today's art market, a very modest price.

Lindsey Stewart

Miscellany

These two pairs of photographs, Nos. 1–2 and 3–4, demonstrate plainly the difference in commercial value between platinum and photogravure prints.

1. *Life and Landscape on the Norfolk Broads, by Peter Henry Emerson, from a volume of 40 platinum prints, 1886.* Mar. '85, £13,000.
2. *Pictures of East Anglian Life, by Peter Henry Emerson, from a volume of 32 photogravure prints, 1888.* Mar. '85, £700.
3. *Wells Cathedral – A Sea of Steps, platinum print by Frederick Evans, 1903.* 9½ × 7½in. Oct. '83, £9,000.
4. *Ely Cathedral – South-west Transept to Nave, photogravure print by Frederick Evans, early 1900s.* 8 × 5in. June '84, £3,240.

Two documentary photographs of historical interest, the first a turn-of-the-century scene from Paris by Eugène Atget, the second an example from a large collection of photographs of London in the 1920s by a photographer named George Reid, previously unknown in the salerooms.

5. *À l'Homme Armé . . ., printing-out-paper print by Eugène Atget, c. 1900.* 8½ × 7in. Mar. '83, £2,100.
6. *Covent Garden, gelatin silver print by George Reid, 1920s.* 8 × 10in. June '84, £7,000 for a collection of over 1,000 prints.

Miscellany

Nos. 1–3: a comparison of prices realized for carte-de-visite portraits.

1. *Anonymous carte-de-visite portrait, late 19th-century, of small value.*

2. *Carte-de-visite portrait by Sarony from an album including others by Silvy, Disderi, Claudet and others.* Mar. '85, £110.

3. *Carte-de-visite portrait of I.K. Brunel.* Mar. '85, £85.

1

2

4

5

Nos. 4–5: examples of portraits of well-known figures autographed by the sitters.

4. *Autographed portrait of J.A. McN. Whistler, M. Menpes, and W.M. Chase, platinum print, 1880s.* 4½ × 6½in. Oct. '84, £1,500.

5. *Autographed portrait of Mark Twain by Underwood & Underwood, carbon print.* 10 × 8in. Oct. '84, £550.

Two of the earliest examples of the use of photographs to illustrate books. The first, a calotype frontispiece to a privately circulated booklet published Jan. 1844. The second, Plate VI of 24 calotypes from The Pencil of Nature, June 1844 – Apr. 1845, by William Henry Fox Talbot, the inventor of the calotype process. This was the first major publication on photography to be illustrated with photographs.

6. *'Record of the Death-Bed of C.M.W.', frontispiece plate by Nicholas Henneman.* 3¼ × 2¼in. Oct '84, £2,200.

7. *'The Open Door', W.H.F. Talbot.* 5.75 × 7½in. Oct. '84, £8,500.
   A complete copy of *The Pencil of Nature* sold for £30,000 at the same time.

7

6

Twentieth-Century Photographs

1. *Nude, by Bill Brandt, 1956 (printed 1970s).*
   13½ × 11¼in. Mar. '85, £600.
2. *Yom Kippur, New York, by Robert Frank,*
   1950s. 9 × 13½in. Mar. '85, £950.
3. *Satyric Dancer, by André Kertesz, 1926*
   (printed 1970s). 10 × 8in. Oct. '84, £550.
4. *Das Lichtrequisit, by Laszlo Moholy-Nagy,*
   c. 1922-30. 9½ × 7in. June '84, £4,800.
5. *Two Barns, Upper New York 1955, by Minor*
   White. 8 × 10in. Mar. '85, £700.
6. *Muscle Beach, Venice, California, by Max*
   Yavno, 1950, printed later. 11 × 19in. £500.

11. *Postcards and Ephemera*

Introduction

by Dominic de Beaumont

Some of the most unlikely things are classified as 'Printed Ephemera' – who would have thought that a menu from the *Titanic* would have surfaced in a London saleroom? Or that those cut-out-and-paste-down scrap albums would prove as popular with buyers as they were among compilers in the past? The holiday postcard to which we rarely give a second thought, the cigarette card which was so carelessly tossed away, all such things come under the broad heading of 'Ephemera'.

So many ephemeral items have been considered as worthless or just pieces of paper, that people are very often surprised to find out just how much their scrap or postcard albums can be worth. One would expect ephemeral items to be common; of course this is partly true, but how many postcards have you come across written by Winnie the Pooh? Such things may not be worth thousands, but if they are interesting and unusual they will be keenly sought after, and once condition and scarcity are taken into account the best will fetch hundreds of pounds.

As with other collectables, the state of the market fluctuates. At present photographs signed by royalty and film stars are enjoying a healthy boom. So next time you're sorting through grandfather's hoard, think twice before you throw anything away – it could actually be worth something. And one of the nicest things about collecting ephemera is that almost anyone can afford to put together a collection – there is always a wide variety to choose from, and prices start in single figures.

1 & 2. *Postcard of Winnie the Pooh, A.A. Milne and Christopher Robin. The reverse inscribed and signed by A.A. Milne, together with a rare signature by 'Pooh'.* Mar. '85, £700.
The same postcard without the inscription or signature is worth only £10.

3. *Photograph of Queen Victoria, signed and dated 1897.* 11½ × 7 in. July '85, £330.

4. *Signed photographic study of Sir Winston Churchill, c. 1955.* 13½ × 10¾ in. July '85, £620.

WINNIE THE POOH
WITH A.A. MILNE AND CHRISTOPHER ROBIN

1

2

3

4

Postcards

Many people now want old postcard views of the towns or areas in which they live. This type of topographical card was available in two forms, printed, or more desirable, real photographic. The real photographic cards were mainly produced by local firms and were issued in relatively small quantities. Because they are less common and generally more interesting than their printed counterparts, they are more expensive. Prices for this type can vary enormously depending on detail, animation, condition, location and scarcity. For example, a good-quality real photographic street scene card with people, trams, carriages and shop fronts, with the location and manufacturer's name printed on the front, can fetch up to £30.

Because of their range, postcards attract specialized collectors from many different areas, a good example being railway station postcards. The main factors governing prices, apart from obvious animation, clarity and the type of printing, are size of station, interior or exterior, whether the station is now closed or open, and location. For instance, a real photographic postcard of Okehampton station (closed), animated with both trains and people and a good panoramic view, makes up to £12. Prices have risen significantly over the last five years.

Postcards produced to commemorate state funerals, exhibitions, expeditions, strikes and even disasters have leaped ahead, in some cases doubling over the last year. A good real photographic card of a mining disaster would have fetched up to £8 in 1982, but in 1984 up to £15. These disaster cards include railway and automobile accidents, fires, floods, lightning damage and landslips. This is a vital record for local historians.

A different type that has steadily gained higher prices is the Art Nouveau and especially Art Deco. A card by Arpad Basch in 1975 would have fetched £20, today £75. Similarly, an early Raphael Kirchner would have fetched £8 in 1975, while today one would have to pay £30. Alponse Mucha virtually is Art Nouveau, and recently a card, No. 11 from his 'Collection des Cent', published

by E.G. of Paris, 1901, realized £120. A typical Art Deco postcard by Mela Koehler would realize in the region of £20 and one by Annie French at least £50.

Although 'Glamour' cards have always been popular, they are still relatively inexpensive, prices ranging from £1–£3. This type offers a wide range from Deshabillé, pornographic and lesbian interest to fully-clothed pretty girls. It would appear that the more erotic cards are steadily increasing in price as they are becoming scarce.

Dominic de Beaumont

Naturally cards such as these are usually sold in large lots at auction, so individual prices can only be approximate.

1. *Town Hall Luton, after the Great Riot, 19 July 1919.*
   This real photographic postcard gives you the atmosphere after the Luton Riot, located and dated, worth about £7.

2 and 3. The street scene in No. 2 shows advertising signs and people, but is hard to locate and is printed, only worth up to £1. No. 3 is real photographic, charming and located (Clock Tower, Leicester), worth £8.

4. *A flood in Southsea High Street, c. 1910.* Value up to £10.

5. Alphonse Mucha, one of the most sought after postcards from the 'Collection des Cent', c. *1901.* Jan. '85, £120.

Cigarette Cards

1

2

3

4

Whatever your views are about smoking, there is one side effect which needs no Government Health Warning – cigarette cards. First produced in America in the early 1890s, this effective form of advertising rapidly spread across the Atlantic to England. Soon many of the larger British Tobacco Companies such as Players, Ogdens and Wills were issuing coloured lithographed cigarette cards to an exceptionally high standard. One such company, Salmon and Gluckstein, produced many sets of exceptional quality including the humorous set of 'Billiard Terms' (1905). A complete set in fine condition can make in excess of £150 (Nos. 1 and 2).

The smaller firms like Taddy, Kinnear and Richmond Cavendish produced only a few thousand cigarette cards, and the demand for these cards increases each year. For instance, in 1982, a set of 50 from the popular 'Royalty Series' (1903) by Taddy could be purchased for £55, but now a set in fine condition would make £90 (cf. No. 3).

Cigarette cards up to 1910, and particularly those from the 1890s, in good condition, realize the highest prices. Single cards can fetch up to £200 and complete sets up to £2,000; though the sets that command a four-figure price are so far exceedingly rare. One later example is Taddy's 'Clowns and Circus Artistes': while these cards were in preparation the company closed down in 1920. It is thought that only 15 sets exist today.

During the 1920s and 1930s the smaller tobacco companies were taken over by the giants like Players and Wills. These firms then began producing many new sets in vast numbers. Although many are both charming and informative, the prices at present paid for them are a reflection of this fact – they are just too common. For example, a set of 50 'Railway Engines' (1924) by Wills makes a mere £9 at auction and 'Cinema Stars' (1924) by Godfrey Phillips fetches £15.

Yet all cigarette cards are increasing in popularity and thus scarcity as increasing numbers of collectors discover their potential. Time is on the side of the established collector, and those just entering the field should move fast.

Dominic de Beaumont

Cigarette cards are also usually sold as part-lots, so once again individual prices are perforce approximate.

1 & 2. *Reverse and front of a rare and attractive cigarette card from a set of 15 produced in 1905 by Salmon & Gluckstein, entitled 'Billiard Terms'. A single card from this set fetches £10 or more.*

3. *The Empress of Russia, from Gallahers 'Royal Series', a set of 50, 1902. A popular and attractive set, estimate c. £80.*

4. *Two examples of Ogden's 'Poultry', both produced in 1915, one from a set with 'Ogdens Cigarettes' and the other from a set with no brand name on front. Estimate £15–£20 at auction for the brand-name set, £20–£25 for the rarer set.*

5. *Cigarette card used for propaganda during the First World War by Wills, 1915. From a set of 12, this powerful design was taken from a poster. £15–£20 for the set.*

6

7

8

6. *One example from a set of 20 entitled 'Yachts' produced by Richmond Cavendish, 1900. This card would fetch £25 or more at auction.*

7 & 8. *Reverse and front of an 'Every Day Phrases' card by Players, a series of 25 produced in 1901, illustrated by Tom Browne. Each card fetches up to £6.*

Miscellany

1. *A 'Neverbend' stainless steel spade with an ash shaft and handle, the blade engraved 'H.M. The Queen used this spade to plant a tree in Tutbury Castle on the occasion of her visit March 28th 1957, A Truly Royal Day'.* 37 in. Estimate £60–£100.

2. *Two English stand-up cards,* c. 1890. Each worth up to £10.

3. *Three examples from a rare set of 25 Wills Miniatures, 1914. Each enamel oval measures 2½ in. high. Issued for Wills cigarette cards.* July '85, £450.

4. *Stevengraph entitled 'Are You Ready?' showing the start of the Oxford–Cambridge Boat Race.* July '85, £60.

5. *Postcard signed by Laurel and Hardy.* Estimate up to £50.

6. *Postcard showing the tramway terminus at Westbury,* c. 1910. A clear real photographic postcard worth up to £10.

7. *A tinplate biscuit tin, modelled in the shape of a champagne bottle, made by G. Willes Wain, Brighton,* c. 1910. 15 in. Estimate £50–£80.

2

3

Are you Ready?

4

5

6

7

12.   Toys

Introduction
by Timothy Matthews

'I wish I had kept them' – a sentence that is often used when people learn of the high prices dealers and collectors are paying for tinplate trains (see pp. 172–3), Victorian games, clockwork tinplate toys, rocking horses and Dinky Toys, to name only a few.

The market for tinplate toys is extremely strong. For example, in May '85 a Meccano constructor car No. 2 outfit and original box sold for £600. This car was in near mint condition. In the same sale an '0' gauge (3-rail) electric model of a Continental 4-6-2 'Pacific' class locomotive and bogie tender sold for £1,500 (for further tinplate toys, see pp. 170–1). If toys are in good working order with good paintwork and have their original boxes, then collectors will pay high prices to secure them (No. 1).

If the toy is rusted, but not broken or damaged, collectors will still be willing to pay high prices; a rare tinplate toy of a carousel with lady and gentlemen riders, in its original fine paintwork, reached £900 in January 1985 (No. 2). In May 1985 a tinplate limousine made by Tipp & Co., Nuremberg, *c.* 1928, again covered in rust, reached £480.

All lead soldiers are sought after, and soldiers made by Courtenay between 1920 and 1950 are leading the field. Mr Courtenay casted and hand-painted the English and French armies at the Battle of Agincourt, 1415. These soldiers are extremely rare, very well detailed, and almost lifelike, (No. 3). Also popular are Britains soldiers and other figures (see pp. 174–5).

Rocking horses too are selling well; a dapple grey horse, with open mouth, horsehair mane and tail, leather saddle, reins, martingale and crouper, fitted on steel bar and trestle wood supports, reached £420 in March 1985. If the horse is stripped down or battered, then it should reach a figure between £200 and £300. Repainted rocking horses depend on whether the original horse is late Victorian or Edwardian and on how good the finish is.

1

2

3

4

Early card games (No. 4) and jigsaws in their original wooden boxes are very collectable too. In order to sell, jigsaws must be complete and in good condition. An early Georgian jigsaw, 'The Ship', depicting a three-masted ship of the line and some of its equipment, by Dalton and Clarke, in London, *c.* 1789, with its original cloth scroll drawing, realized £220 in January 1985. 'The progress of wool', showing scenes from sheep shearing to cloth weaving, by J. Wallis, London, *c.* 1815, reached £110 in December 1984. Victorian building blocks in their original illustrated wooden boxes together with all six sheets gain good prices too, usually realizing between £60 and £100. No. 5 is a good example of a German wooden toy.

Diecast toys are selling very well indeed. These need to be in boxes, and the paintwork needs to be good quality in order to reach top prices. Dinky Toys tend to dominate the saleroom floor, followed by Corgi Toys, Spot On, and Matchbox. A Dinky 920 Guy Warrior Van advertising 'Heinz Tomato Sauce' and a No. 514 Guy Van advertising 'Slumberland' sold for £400 in May 1985. A group of 'Lesney Models of Yesteryear' in original boxes sold for £340 in the same sale. In the same sale a quantity of Spot On and Tenko toys in their boxes reached £340. Advertisements can help with both diecast and tinplate toys, because they add a period flavour (No. 6).

So where will the market go? Prices should continue to be strong as more collectors seek the toys they want. There can be no shortage of supply as almost every home has something, and manufacturers such as Britains and Dinky Toys release their old stock. On the buying side the surge in toy prices, especially those for toy soldiers, has been largely due to the American investors and collectors and the recent strength of the dollar. This has prompted a buying rush from the other side of the Atlantic.

5

6

1. *'Kadi', painted and lithographed toy of coolies carrying a tea-chest on poles, fitted with flywheel mechanism, by Lehmann, c. 1912. 7 in. long. July '84, £300.*

2. *Printed and painted clockwork tinplate toy of a carousel, with a simple musical movement, painted tinplate horses with lady and gentlemen riders, by Güntherman, Nuremberg. 8 in. Jan. '85, £900.*

3. *A group of Courtenay hand-painted lead soldiers of the armies at Agincourt.* Top price was £1,900 for a foot figure No. Z.17 of the wounded Gui, Sieur de Rochfort. Surprisingly, King John of France and Philip le Hardi of Burgundy were among the cheapest at £170 each. The mounted Earl of Warwick reached £1,400. All were sold to an American collector, Dec. '84.

4. *'Changeable Ladies and Changeable Gentlemen', handpainted etchings on paper cards, forming various famous characters of the late 18th and early 19th centuries, c. 1820. Two sets, Dec. '84, £550.*

5. *Schoenhut Humpty Dumpty circus, painted wood and cloth with figures and animals and catalogue in original illustrated wooden box (26 pieces in all), German, c. 1900. Sept. '84, £500.*

6. *Printed tinplate toy of an early double-decker bus with clockwork mechanism, causing the bus to advance and the ticket collector to collect fares on the upper deck, J. Distler, c. 1929. 8¼ in. long. May '84, £700.* Advertising material, as well as ingenuity, adds to appeal.

Tinplate Toys

Alfa Romeo P2's are back on the circuit! These famous Grand Prix racing cars of the mid-1920s are back, only this time on the tinplate toy circuit. A French company called C.I.J. manufactured these toy cars in the late 1920s, in the national colours of the countries competing in Grand Prix racing. Hence silver represents Germany, green Great Britain, blue France and red Italy; however, other colours such as white and even mauve and orange are also to be found. These large and impressive toys, measuring 20 inches, were sold for 24s. (£1.25) in 1926 and 35s. (£1.75) in 1929. Today in auction they are reaching between £500 and £600 for near mint examples, even higher prices if boxed (No. 2). An unboxed example fetched £600 in January 1985.

Tinplate toys made by the German manufacturers between 1900 and 1930 are today realizing between £400 and £10,000. Collectors are eagerly seeking toys made by Carette, Bing, Märklin, Lehmann and Günthermann, just to name a few. These companies were producing not only cars but trains, ships, aeroplanes, stationary steam engines, figures and many other subjects. The detail and accuracy of these toys make them collectors' pieces, and inspire collectors to pay truly remarkable prices for them (Nos. 3, 4, 8). A less distinguished but still fine three-funnel clockwork ocean liner by Bing realized £800 in March 1985. A Lehmann 'Motor Coach', c. 1925, may not have quite the cachet of a ship, but it too made its price (No. 5).

Set against these very finely made printed and painted tinplate German toys were the British manufacturers such as Wells, Brimtoy (No. 6) and Chad Valley, who began to compete with the continental market in the 1930s and 1940s, producing on a cheaper basis cars, aeroplanes and trains. Today at auction a Chad Valley four-seater hard-top car with a clockwork mechanism would realize between £40 and £60. The famous company Tri-ang began to produce small tinplate commercial vehicles with clockwork mechanisms at the same time called Minic Toys: a set of six of these in their original boxes should realize £60–£80. A Minic London Bus advertising 'Bovril' reached £55 in March 1985; with a box it would have probably sold for £65.

In the mid-1950s the Japanese produced clockwork and battery operated tinplate and plastic toys very cheaply, and began to capture the market from the German and British manufacturers. These toys are fast becoming important collectors' pieces. For example, a lot of ten, complete in their original boxes, should realize £60–£100. In certain areas, however, they have already achieved this status. Robots are currently in great demand, with up to £500 being paid in America for the rarer Japanese pieces from the 1950s.

Current trends of rising values for early tinplate (1900–30) may well continue into 1986. It is likely that this will favourably affect prices at the lower end for more recent toys.   *Timothy Matthews*

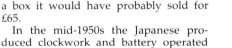

1. *Various makers' trade marks: a. GBN, b. Lehmann, c. Meccano, d. Bassett-Lowke, e. Bing, f. early Märklin and g. late Märklin, c. 1930.*
2. *P2 Alfa Romeo Racing Car by C.I.J., France, c. 1926. May '85, £800.*
3. *1911 Mercedes Voyager Limousine by Bing, in original box. May '84, £8,500.*

4

5

6

7

8

9

4. *'Victoria', a rare Dreadnought (less guns and lifeboats) by Märklin, c. 1902. May '84, £8,500.*

5. *'Motor Coach', EPL No. 420, by Lehmann, c. 1925. Mar. '85, £400.*

6. *Two printed and painted tinplate clockwork aeroplanes by Wells (left) and Brimtoy (right), c. 1935. Jan. '85, £170 (Wells) and £65 (Brimtoy).*

7. *A collection of late 1950s and 1960s Japanese toys.* These are still lotted up in sales. A group of ten could make up to £100.

8. *A very fine Bing hand-enamelled tinplate model of an early two-seater Benz racing car, German, c. 1904. 11¼ in. May '85, £9,200.*

9. *A printed and painted tinplate of Sir Malcolm Campbell's 'Bluebird', by Gunthermann, c. 1932. Jan. '85, £380.*

Tinplate Trains

1985 commemorates the 150th year of the Great Western Railway; in January a gauge 2 live-steam spirit-fired model of the G.W.R. 4-4-0 locomotive and tender No. 3410, 'County of Northampton', in original livery and box, by Bing for Bassett-Lowke, 1910, was still steaming at £450. In the March sale a gauge 00 clockwork model of the G.W.R. 2-6-0 locomotive and tender No. 4331 in original green and gold livery, by Bassett-Lowke, reached £380. A gauge 0 G.W.R. clockwork trainset by Hornby including a 4-4-4 tank locomotive, a rake of four-wheeled coaches and track in its box, 1930, realized £220.

Over recent years clockwork trains have been overtaken by the table-top layouts of 00 gauge by Hornby Dublo, Hornby, Tri-ang Hornby, Fleischmann and Trix Twin Railways. However, we are now witnessing a comeback of the large gauges. Collectors, dealers and enthusiasts are divided by their preferences, the most popular gauges being 00,0, 1, 2, 3 and 4. Railway accessories are also being bought avidly.

As long ago as 1879 there were German firms producing tinplate engines run by live steam. (When the first railways were constructed in the 1820s and 1830s such toys had been made of wood.) By the end of the nineteenth century they were producing high quality trains of all gauges. A very rare Märklin tinplate gauge 0 clockwork locomotive 'Rocket' with its original box reached £25,000 at Sotheby's in May 1984. Märklin emerged as the leading manufacturer of tinplate trains, and other small firms copied their style, especially K. Bub. Bassett-Lowke, a British company, purchased these finely detailed trains from Carette, Märklin and Bing and sold them under their own name. For example, a very fine gauge 1 (3-rail) electric model of the Great Northern Railway 4-4-2 'Atlantic' locomotive and tender No. 1442, in original livery, by Bing for Bassett-Lowke, sold for £650 in March 1985 (No. 5). A gauge 0 clockwork model of the British Railways 4-6-2 locomotive and tender No. 60103, 'Flying Scotsman', made by Bassett-Lowke, sold for £600 in September 1984.

It is not only the German tinplate trains that sell well at auction, Hornby trains are very collectable too. Frank Hornby began his company at the turn of the century producing Meccano. It was not until after the Great War that this famous name was to capture a large slice of the British Market and spread into Europe too. These trains may not make as much money as the German locomotives or those of Bassett-Lowke, but they are just as keenly collected. At the top end of the Hornby market there is a gauge 0 (3-rail) electric model of the L.M.S. 4-6-2 locomotive and tender No. 6201 'Princess Elizabeth' in original presentation box which has sold for £600. However, Hornby trains were produced to capture the lower end of the market: trains that the young schoolboy could

afford as well as a few top models for the enthusiasts. A No. 1 tank locomotive in original box and in good condition would realize between £20 and £30. Nonetheless, a few items such as a station, a couple of coaches and some coal trucks would push it to £50–£80.

As long as the locomotives and rolling stock are not damaged, rusty or repainted, they will make good prices, especially if there are original boxes. Railway track does not sell. However, lineside items such as level crossings, stations, water towers and tunnels will help to boost locomotive prices.

In the 1950s Hornby phased out their 0 gauge clockwork and electric trains in favour of 00 gauge 'table top' railways as there was a growing demand for small railway systems. A collection of 10

1

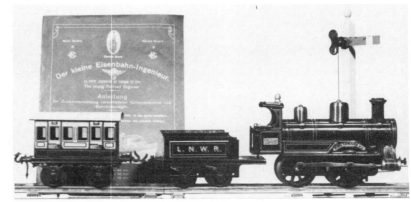

3

Hornby 'Dublo' locomotives should realize £50–£80. A rival company, Trix Twin Railway, produced 00 gauge locomotives in the 1950s, and 10 locomotives with 20 coaches and some lineside items sold for £130 in March 1985. More recent Tri-ang Hornby plastic trains of the 1960s and '70s are starting to be sought after too. These must be in very good condition and in original boxes to sell. Continental HO/00 gauge makers such as Fleischmann, Lima and Liliput are selling well. Ten boxed locomotives will sell for £120 as a lot. Even the Japanese models gain high prices, for example one 00 gauge (2-rail) electric metal model of an American type 0-8-0 locomotive and twin-bogie tender by Tenshodo realized £65 in January 1984.

However, table top railways were around long before the 1950s. It was the Germans who produced them first in 1923. The Bing table top railways began as clockwork sets and in 1925 they became electrified. By the mid-1920s sets by Bing, Märklin and K. Bub were capturing the European market. It was not until the late 1930s that F. Hornby produced the first Hornby Dublo Catalogue. A Bing No. 2 Table Top Railway set, complete with G.W.R. 2-4-0 tank locomotive, a rake of three G.W.R. four-wheeled passenger carriages, a station, signals and track sold for £140 in March 1985 (No. 7). Even without the box, two almost identical lots in the same sale sold for £130 and £140! *Timothy Matthews*

1. *A gauge 0 clockwork 4-4-0 locomotive and tender No. 2265 'Princess Elizabeth' in original paintwork by Bassett-Lowke. Mar. '85, £150.*

2. *A very fine gauge 1 clockwork 'Atlantic' 4-4-2 locomotive by Bing, c. 1935. Dec. '84, £1,300.*

3. *A very fine gauge 1 clockwork trainset by Bing, c. 1910. Mar. '85, £1,300.*

4, 4a *A very rare twin bogie plate car with an early monoplane, by Märklin, c. 1928. Sold as one lot, May '85, £420.*

5. *A Gauge 1 (3-rail) electric model of the G.N.R. 4-4-2 'Atlantic' locomotive and tender, by Bing for Basset-Lowke. Mar. '85, £650.*

6. *Two Hornby gauge 0 clockwork locomotives, of the type which realize between £80 and £120 in toy sales. Left, Mar. '85, £80; right, May '85, £95.*

7. *A very fine Bing Table Top Railway, with instruction booklet and original box, German. c. 1926. Mar. '85 £140.*

4

4a

5

6

7

Lead Soldiers and Other Figures

Attention, stand at ease, present and slope arms, lying, kneeling and standing firing, at the trail, shoulder arms, running and standing in the on guard position – these are some of the positions Britains adopted for their figures. They were made of simple casts from 1894 until the introduction of plastic soldiers in 1962. The paintwork was rough by today's high standards, but the detail was surprisingly good. Early figures were made with no identifying marks and were cast on oval bases. A box of 16 Seaforth Highlanders (1st issue) with plug hands, oval bases and running at the trail would realize £200–£300. In 1900 a copyright date was printed on the bottoms together with the date of registration, and this soon changed to being casted on.

Each year the range expanded, the bases changed from rounded to square shaped, some models were withdrawn and reintroduced with new numbers sometimes many years later. A few rich customers paid an extra sixpence to have their set painted by a more skilful painter, which shows in the fineness of the lines, and these sets particularly make high prices. Guardsmen are the most common types, and in March 1985 a set of No. 120 Coldstream Guards firing kneeling in their original box reached £70. The Scots Greys are a good standard set (No. 1).

Britains also began to produce display boxed sets which were very popular, and today collectors are paying good prices for them. A Britains set No. 2094 Open Landau, with H.M. Elizabeth II and Prince Philip in Admiral's uniform, and outriders, was sold for £160 in March 1985 (No. 2). A Britains Display set No. 73 with the R.H.A. collar harness gun team, Band of Line, Gordon Highlanders, Royal Welsh Fusiliers, 17th Lancers, Scots Greys and Life Guards, in original box with removable tray sold for £1,100 in July 1984. At Phillips in November 1984, a set of 13 khaki R.H.A. soldiers with steel helmets made £6,000. In their January 1985 sale the same set reached £7,200.

It is not only Britains' soldiers which make high prices. Collectors and dealers will pay high prices for Britains Model

1

Home Farm items. A small quantity of animals and people with some carts, trees, bushes and fences will realize £60–£100. If the collection has any original boxes then the prices will be higher. A village idiot would realize £100–£150 on his own! He is easily recognizable as he is wearing a straw hat and carrying a long blade of grass which he is sucking. A Britains set No. 168, Civilians, in original box, containing policemen, yachtsmen, two ladies in long dresses and three gentlemen, sold for £520 in December 1984. A Britains No. 158 Railway Station set sold for £600 at the same time. Britains set No. 158, Famous Football Teams, Aston Villa, Middlesborough and Portsmouth, complete in original boxes, all gained prices over £300. These sets are extremely popular and were produced in the 1920s when football became our national sport, although earlier sets had been produced (No. 4).

Britains miniature gardening sets are also gaining high prices. A quantity of various items with a catalogue sold for £600 in March 1985. A boxed set No. 23MG in its original box with a garden shelter and greenhouse in original boxes sold for £300 in January 1985. A Britains Zoo set with animals, keepers, fencing and scenery, in its original illustrated box, made £140 in the same sale.

Britains Military Equipment, such as field guns, limbers, Howitzers, ambulances, ten-wheeled army covered lorries, staff cars and motorcycles gain high prices too, as long as the pieces are in good condition (No. 5).

Generally, Britains are the most collectable of all the lead soldiers, mainly because the range was so vast. The soldiers were of good quality, realistic and

good scale (mainly 54mm) and also packed in attractive illustrated boxes. The old boxes were hand-painted with scenes by F. Whisstock, with his name on the lid, and these boxed soldiers are extremely popular. Later boxes became more formal and illustrated either a dismounted Scots Grey, a Life Guard Trooper or the traditional 'Toy Soldier' peering round a fir tree and had Britains marked in large letters on the top.

Then there are the second-grade Britains; these can be spotted by the inferior paintwork. Also Timpo and Crescent produced soldiers from the 1930s to the present day. These were of lower quality and do not reach high prices. J. Hill & Co. produced some coronation coaches, soldiers and other miscellaneous items, all of which will sell if lotted together.

The Germans, who introduced lead soldiers into this country in the 1840s, produced high quality lead soldiers, one of their makers being G. Heyde. Germany also produced flat soldiers during the nineteenth century. These are, however, not particularly valuable or sought after. The German firms Elastolin, Lineol and Schuco manufactured composition soldiers of the German

Army when the Nazis came into power in the 1930s. Today these models of various Nazi leaders and troops are reaching very good prices (No. 6); a small quantity of composition figures including Mussolini, Hindenburg, two Labour Corps R.A.D. figures and eight others, two carrying Nazi flags, reached £360 in March 1985. Other companies such as Hausser and Tipp and Co. began to make vehicles, tanks and guns to accompany these figures. A Mercedes open tourer German staff car, made in the late 1930s by Tipp and Co., realized £320.

Timothy Matthews

1. *Britains set No. 32, The 2nd Dragoons, 'The Scots Greys' at the trot, with officer, in original Whisstock box, c. 1910. Dec. '84, £50.*

2. *Britains set No. 2094, State Opening, London, with H.M. Elizabeth II, Prince Philip in Admiral's uniform, outriders and six Windsor Grey horses in original box. Mar. '85, £160.*

3. *Various Britains box lids. The originals are on the right and two reproduction ones on the left.*

4. *Britains famous football teams – Woolwich Arsenal, c. 1910 (with oval bases and stamped copyright). May '85, £320. Teams average £250–£350.*

5. *A small quantity of accessories such as are sold in mixed lots (left to right):*
   No. 1264: 4·7 in. naval gun – £5–£8.
   No. 112: No. 2 Howitzer in original box – £20–£30.
   No. 1292: Royal Artillery gun and limber – £10–£15.
   No. 1432: Army covered tender (10 wheels) in original box – £50–£80.

6. *A collection of Lineol and Elastolin composition German Army figures and two very fine vehicles by Tipp and Co., c. 1938. As a group, £500–£800.*

7. *A rare Britains set No. 434 R.A.F. monoplane in original box. Mar. '85, £1,200.*

3

4

5

6

7

13. Dolls

Introduction
by Olivia Bristol

During 1984–5 there have been twelve Doll Sales at Christie's South Kensington and many more elsewhere, so it is possible to get a fairly clear picture of the state of the market. There has been enough to suit collectors at all stages and of all depths of pocket.

Perhaps the greatest change over the year has been the rise in prices for Teddy Bears. This was first apparent in September, and in January Phillips took £1,100 for a Steiff bear. South Kensington followed in May, selling a Steiff with a leather muzzle for £1,300. Four days later Sotheby's took £1,800 for a blonde Steiff bear without its buttons. All this gives a new meaning to the bear market.

Back in June 1984 we sold a very fine quality eighteenth-century carved, turned and painted wooden doll with ball and hinge joints at shoulder and elbow, and beautifully fitting hinge joints at the knees and hips. On most eighteenth-century dolls only the faces and necks have gesso, with paint covering the arms. The legs are left with only a thin wash of white paint. The point about this doll was that her entire body was painted flesh colour. Also she still had her original dark human hair wig, and a turban with a blue silk ribbon which matched her sash and open robe. Together with all her wardrobe and a number of letters relating to her, she fetched a thoroughly justified £5,800.

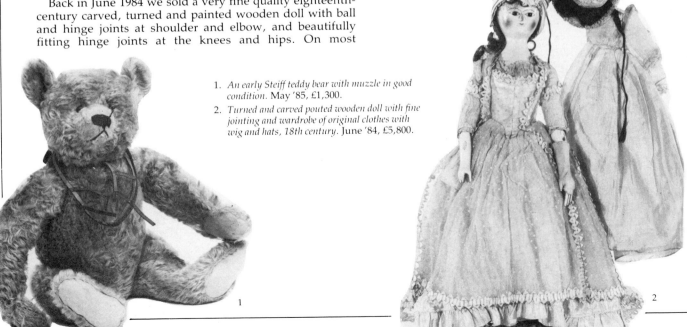

1. *An early Steiff teddy bear with muzzle in good condition.* May '85, £1,300.
2. *Turned and carved pouted wooden doll with fine jointing and wardrobe of original clothes with wig and hats, 18th century.* June '84, £5,800.

1

2

Automata

Most automata have been expensive toys for the amusement of grown-ups. In the eighteenth century makers of automata such as James Cox and Henri Maillardet often opened exhibitions to the public. Henri-Louis Jaquet-Droz made elaborate automata, notably of writers, a draughtsman and a piano player. The habit of copying, or even the same manufacturer making late versions of a model, was widespread. One of the greatest late nineteenth-century makers, G. Vichy, made a famous automaton of a pierrot playing the banjo to a sickle moon, which was copied by Leopold Lambert. Many automata by Vichy are very tall, often standing 30 inches or more in height. His Negro figures with musical instruments have exceptionally fine leather faces with expressive facial movements even to the lips. Both the mechanism and musical movement are contained in the body of the figure, or in the background props so that movement to a foot is possible. In a ballet dancer figure by Lambert, she sits on a box containing the movements so that a kicking action can be reproduced. Another dancing figure, probably by the same maker, does a pirouette by pivoting on one leg, the wires for the head and arm movements being contained in the continually based straight leg.

An attractive seated child with the movement contained inside the body was sold in January 1985 (No. 1). The fine quality bisque head was by Jumeau, and it is rare to find an automaton in such good original condition.

A very unusual figure, sadly not working, was sold in January 1985 (No. 2). This appeared to be French, being modelled as a composition-headed clown – he sat on a painted metal drum playing a metal cello. Because of his more toy-like appearance, it was good to see his original clothes still in place. Another automaton with the child mainly in mind is the Roullet et Decamps 'doll cart' (No. 3). This of course had no musical movement, the walking mechanism being contained in the body of the standing doll.

A more unusual type of automaton is the standing figure of a doll holding lorgnettes and dressed as an 18th-century man (No. 4).   *Olivia Bristol*

1. *Seated girl, the bisque head by Jumeau, c. 1914.* Jan. '85, £2,200.
2. *Composition-headed clown playing the cello, French, c. 1880.* Jan. '85, £700.
   A good price, considering that the model no longer worked.
3. *Doll cart automaton by Roullet et Decamps, c. 1892.* May '85, £1,300.
4. *Man in 18th-century dress, probably by Decamps, c. 1913.* Mar. '84, £1,700.
5. *Breathing Dancer of the Seven Veils, c. 1900.* Sept. '84, £1,500.

Technical Terms

Open-closed, pouty, water-melon, bee sting; wired, fixed, flirting, intaglio, googli.

The first four terms refer to mouths, the rest to eyes. To the non-dolly public they may sound strange, but such descriptive words can affect doll prices dramatically.

For example, most bisque-headed dolls were made with an *open* mouth, showing a row of teeth, or perhaps only two. Often these are broken, as a child can push imaginary food or hard objects through the mouth into the head. With an *open-closed* mouth this is impossible as, although the mouth appears open perhaps with moulded teeth and tongue, there is no actual hole. This much rarer method of modelling appears mainly on character dolls and is highly desirable (No. 1).

A still rarer type found on character dolls is the *pouty* mouth typified by the Kammer & Reinhardt 114, sometimes known as 'Mein Liebling', which currently enjoys enormous popularity. Prices range from £600 for an 8 inch version to £1,500 plus for one 25 inches or more (see No. 3). *Pouty* mouths are also found occasionally in character dolls made by the Société Française de Bébés et Jouets, or SFBJ, whose initials are stamped on the back of the head with the mould number.

There is only one maker of bee sting mouths – so immediately one thinks in terms of three noughts. Lèon Casimir Bru and his son worked in Paris at the end of the last century, making high quality dolls of distinctive appearance (No. 2). One would normally expect an average sized Bru to fetch £3,000–£5,000. Brus have been copied widely, both in Paris and America, so be wary if offered a 'Bru' at what appears to be an exceptionally reasonable price.

The terms which refer to dolls' eyes can also indicate not only type, but also date and potential price. The earliest form of *sleeping* eyes is found at the beginning of the nineteenth-century in dolls which have been dipped in wax and the eyes attached to wire which protrudes either between the legs or later at the waist. When the wire is pulled the doll drops her wax-covered lids. Once manufacturers had perfected eyes that closed by means of a lead weight when the doll was laid down, this was universally adopted. *Fixed* eyes, therefore, can indicate an early bisque-headed doll, and in conjunction with a *closed* mouth may double the price.

Kammer & Reinhardt's first character doll, mould 100, is modelled as a baby. The eyes are not glass but *intaglio*, modelled in the bisque, the iris being a dip in the eyeball, sometimes with a white dot to bring the face alive. Other manufacturers also adopted this price-enhancing touch (Nos. 4 and 5).   *Olivia Bristol*

1. *Armand Marseilles popular Dream Baby mould 341 with closed mouth always fetches 50% more than the open mouth mould 351.*

2. *Typical Bru bébé with bee-sting closed mouth and the favourite kid body with bisque shoulders and arms and wood and composition legs. June '84, £4,800.*
   Note the adolescent figure unique to Bru.

3. *Rare Kammer and Reinhardt character doll with closed pouting mouth, mould 109. Aug. '79, £1,000.*
   This doll would be worth twice the price now.

4. *Composition portrait doll modelled as Shirley Temple in original dress with flirting eyes. Nov. '81, £350.*

5. *Unusual composition-headed character dolls with huge googli eyes and amusing contemporary clothes. Apr. '84, £450 (left), £320 (right).*

Dolls' House Furniture

Most 19th-century dolls' house furniture comes from Germany – Nuremberg and Walterhausen in particular being major places of manufacture although there is some very pretty French furniture decorated with chromolithographic scraps of children and flowers. Miniature furniture was made out of many different materials, most of which would have been quite unsuitable for full sized pieces, for instance ivory, bone, continental silver, feathers, card, beads and porcupine quills. Metal furniture of many different types is found, tinware coloured a reddish brown from the middle of the century from Germany, and later softer pieces made of a lead alloy which bent very easily. Even Dinky produced cast metal furniture in the 1930s, each room with its own boxed set. Wire was also used, particularly for beds and cots combined with tinplate sides.

Most of the furniture was made of wood, from delicate sets of drawing room furniture upholstered in coloured silks and with turned legs, to solid kitchen dressers. Every style is reproduced and some, particularly Edwardian and later furniture, was painted cream or white while other pieces had transfer or stencilled decorations and some were covered in printed papers. Rare pieces include items such as a tapestry frame complete with embroidery and a Chesterfield desk. There are also pianos, wash stands with holes for ewer, basin and mug, needlework tables complete with scissors, cottons etc. and bureaus with writing flaps, mirrored alcove and cupboards. Another type of furniture popular with dolls' house owners is printed paper on wood. This enables all sorts of decoration to be simulated, wood graining, inlay carving and upholstery which in a larger piece would appear hideous but in a dolls' house merely amusing and charming.

Home-made furniture is quite common and generally does not fetch as much as manufactured pieces – the *Children's Encyclopedia* edited by Arthur Mee gives several directions for making dolls' house furniture. Miniature furniture made by cabinet makers can command very high prices if of sufficient quality. They are usually reproducing

earlier designs. A mahogany Georgian style kneehole desk, 4½ in. wide, fetched £260 in December 1984.

Apart from the furniture, the chattels of a dolls' house are usually interesting. The china and flatwear come in a variety of qualities. Some dinner services are transfer-printed with coloured flower sprays. Other items are of turned wood with painted line decorations; these include bedroom sets of ewers, basins and candlesticks. The kitchen often displays all sorts of obsolete equipment such as Dutch ovens, housemaids' boxes and batterie de cuisine complete with meat covers, and knife and cutlery trays, bellows and jelly moulds.

'Titania's Palace' was sold by Christie's in 1968 and again in 1978 when it fetched a world record price for a dolls' house, £135,000. This price reflected the quality of the contents, many of which were *objets de vertu*. A lot of the furniture was made by Fred Early and other fine Dublin cabinet makers.   *Olivia Bristol*

1. *Group of Austrian and Czechoslovakian wooden furniture, c. 1929. Dec. '84, £100.*
2. *George II style American silver tea and coffee set. Feb. '81. Up to £1,000 if sold today.*
3. *Pretty set of German dolls' house furniture. Aug, '81, £130.*

Miscellany

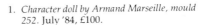

1. *Character doll by Armand Marseille, mould 252.* July '84, £100.

2. *Character doll by Gebrüder Henbach, stamped 9085.* July '84, £80.

3. *Character doll by Armand Marseille, mould 320.* July '84, £180.
   These three delightful 7 in. character dolls all have painted faces and eyes glancing to the side.

4. *Fine quality character doll, modelled as an oriental.* June '84, £650.
   Although only the mould number 220 is marked, because of his closed mouth he was sold for a high price.

5. *Shoulder-headed Parisienne.* June '84, £1,000.
   Early shoulder-headed Parisiennes are much rarer than the later swivel-headed types. This one was possibly made by Madame Rohmer and has finely modelled arms.

6. *Charming musical jester doll with closed mouth.* Sept. '84, £600.
   The tune is played by pressing his tummy, also causing him to bang the cymbals.

7. *Jester doll.* June '84, £160.
   A cheaper version of the jester doll, this time with a wax over composition head. He has a squeaker in his body, which when pressed bangs the cymbals and closes his eyes.

8. *Doll by Kammer and Reinhardt, mould 101.* 7½ in. June '84, £550.
   Mould 101 is currently one of the most fashionable, as it has a pouting mouth.

9. *Another jester doll, known as a folie, marotte or poupard.* June '84, £220.
   When the doll is twisted on the stick the music plays. The pretty French head has a closed mouth.

10. *Diving belles of bisque with wigs and net bathing dresses.* June '84, £300.

11. *Two bisque figures, one modelled as a ballet dancer, the other sitting on a powder puff.* June '84, £320.

12. *Three chubby bisque babies, one by William Goebel.* June '84, £190.

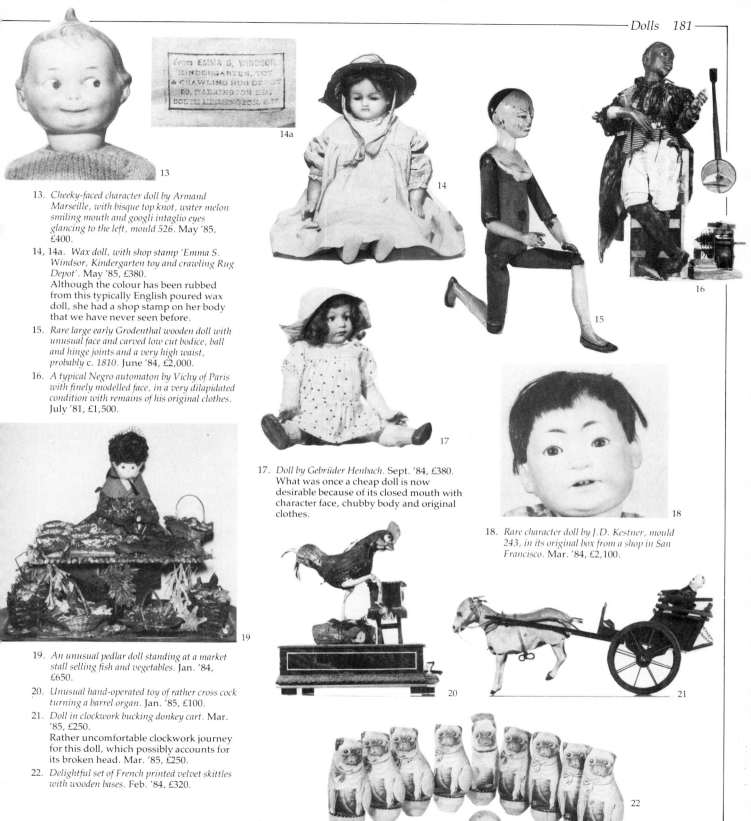

13. *Cheeky-faced character doll by Armand Marseille, with bisque top knot, water melon smiling mouth and googli intaglio eyes glancing to the left, mould 526. May '85, £400.*

14, 14a. *Wax doll, with shop stamp 'Emma S. Windsor, Kindergarten toy and crawling Rug Depot'. May '85, £380.*
Although the colour has been rubbed from this typically English poured wax doll, she had a shop stamp on her body that we have never seen before.

15. *Rare large early Grodenthal wooden doll with unusual face and carved low cut bodice, ball and hinge joints and a very high waist, probably c. 1810. June '84, £2,000.*

16. *A typical Negro automaton by Vichy of Paris with finely modelled face, in a very dilapidated condition with remains of his original clothes. July '81, £1,500.*

17. *Doll by Gebrüder Henbach. Sept. '84, £380. What was once a cheap doll is now desirable because of its closed mouth with character face, chubby body and original clothes.*

18. *Rare character doll by J.D. Kestner, mould 243, in its original box from a shop in San Francisco. Mar. '84, £2,100.*

19. *An unusual pedlar doll standing at a market stall selling fish and vegetables. Jan. '84, £650.*

20. *Unusual hand-operated toy of rather cross cock turning a barrel organ. Jan. '85, £100.*

21. *Doll in clockwork bucking donkey cart. Mar. '85, £250.*
Rather uncomfortable clockwork journey for this doll, which possibly accounts for its broken head. Mar. '85, £250.

22. *Delightful set of French printed velvet skittles with wooden bases. Feb. '84, £320.*

14. *Mechanical Music*

Introduction
by Christopher Proudfoot

Regular Mechanical Music sales have been a feature of the specialist sales at South Kensington from the start in 1975, and looking back over those ten years prices can be seen to have moved upwards in a series of steps and plateaus. Towards the end of 1984, an already apparent move upwards took a leap, confirmed by the first sale of 1985, the first dramatic move in several years. No doubt the dollar exchange rate had much to do with this, although it is interesting to see that, even now, very few musical boxes are bought at auction by American collectors, even though their phonograph-seeking countrymen have always shown an interest in the rarer items to appear in London.

The December 1984 sale was notable in several ways: firstly because of the high prices achieved, with only two very small lots unsold, secondly because of the number of unusual and rare items on the phonograph and gramophone side, and thirdly because of its proximity to the Christmas break, which some had feared would affect the sale adversely. The price trend of this sale continued in March 1985, and the similarity of the sold totals (£52,000 for 209 lots in December, and £49,000 for 150 lots in March) disguises the very different character of the two sales. The difference lies in the fact that a phonograph worth £500 or more is equivalent in rarity to a musical box at three or four times that figure. The March sale saw new levels for regular stalwarts like the 19 inch upright Polyphon without stand or pediment (£2,400) which a year ago would have made perhaps £1,000, and a particularly good example of the double-comb 15⅝ inch table model made £1,900 – probably nearly £1,000 up on what it might have made 12 months earlier (No. 1 – see also p. 184 No. 7).

The main problem in buying musical boxes is (and has always been) the difficulty of assessing damage and the cost of repair. True, there are probably more repairers now

1

1. *15⅝-inch Polyphon disc musical box with twin combs, in panelled walnut case.* Mar. '85, £1,900.
   This model has always sold well, both because of its double combs and its attractive case. The single-comb version, using the same size discs, normally comes in a much plainer case, and even these have been around the £700 mark recently. An important consideration with both models is the condition of the lead under the bass teeth on the combs. This often corrodes, and when this decay is advanced the bass teeth become totally 'dead', leaving only a thin treble sound. The disease can be cured, at considerable cost, by expert musical box repairers.

2. *Forte-piano musical box by Bremond, playing four operatic airs.* Dec. '84, £2,200.
   The broad plinth moulding is typical of good quality boxes of the 1880s and later, and the fact that *Aida* and *Tannhaüser* both received their first Covent Garden performances in 1876 confirms that this is a late example of a forte-piano musical box. Although the cylinder is of a common standard size (13 × 2½ in. diam.), the combination of four airs (instead of six or eight) and the forte-piano effect are signs of quality, and explain this price.

2

The extra-diameter cylinder was the most satisfactory answer to the problem of increasing the number of tunes on one cylinder, since it did not increase the number of endways shifts – a cylinder with six positions could play twelve tunes on a comb with as many teeth as a six-tune musical box. The extra-diameter cylinder partly compensated for the shortness of the tunes. No. 3 is a good quality example of this system from the last quarter of the nineteenth century.

Overture boxes have always been eagerly sought after by collectors; they usually have the dual appeal of rarity and outstanding musical quality. Most date from the 'golden' age (approximately 1840–60), when the art of musical box making reached its zenith, musically speaking. An example in the April 1984 sale was unusually late, and, as overture boxes go, disappointing in sound (it played six, which itself was a disadvantage). It was nonetheless an overture box, and of very good quality for its period, which explained its price of £1,700. Even that is about half the price that could be expected for a good overture box of the 1850s.

than at any time since the First World War, but the work is necessarily very expensive and the cost of repairing a badly damaged musical box can be about the same as the eventual market value. With this in mind, the difference between the auction price of a damaged box against one in good condition is often surprisingly small. This is all the more difficult to understand in those cases where the movement is jammed or otherwise incapable of playing at all, since this makes it almost impossible to assess how well it will play when restored.

The quality of a musical box depends not on how pretty the case is, or how many tunes it plays. With certain exceptions it is true to say that, for a given length of cylinder, the fewer tunes a movement plays the better will be its quality. This is because, with fewer tunes, the cylinder has fewer positions to shift between tunes, and this allows closer spacing of the comb teeth – hence more notes and richer sound. Equally important is the musical arrangement: the arrangement of tunes to fit the notes on a given comb (which would not be a simple chromatic scale) was an art in itself. Discerning collectors listen for this aspect more closely than any other, and a good arrangement can push up the price of a musical box considerably.

Particularly attractive arrangements are achieved with the aid of special effects such as 'mandolin' and 'forte-piano' (No. 2). The former involves repeating each note of a treble melody up to eight times in rapid succession, and this in turn means that each note is represented by up to eight teeth in the comb. Mandolin movements can be recognized, even if they are not in playing condition, by the pattern of pins in the cylinder (No. 3). Forte-piano boxes have two combs, representing the soft and loud passages, with the former usually at the treble end and occupying about one third of the total length. On a good forte-piano box, the alternating soft and loud effect is very attractive, and can increase the value by as much as 100 per cent compared with a standard comb.

Another factor which can indicate quality is the diameter of the cylinder. The average cylinder is about 2–2½ inches in thickness (anything less will either be cheap and nasty or very early, rare and collectable – in either case, it is unlikely to sound impressive). A cylinder 3 inches or more in diameter will usually play two tunes for each revolution (No. 4), or will play a small number of operatic overtures.

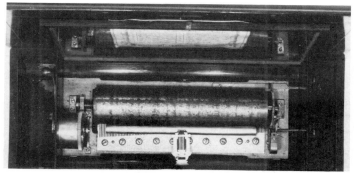

3

3. *Mandolin musical box by J.H. Heller, Bern, playing 16 airs.* Mar. '85, £1,600.
This birds-eye view shows the slanting rows of pins in the treble (right-hand) half of the cylinder, characteristic of mandolin boxes. (The word 'Mandoline' also appears on the tune-sheet in the lid, but this is often missing). The cylinder is also very fat (3 in. diam.), as this is an unusual late-19th-century 'two-tunes-per-turn' movement.

4. *Key-wind two-tunes-per-turn musical box by Nicole Frères.* Mar. '85, £850.
A more typical two-per-turn movement, dating from the late 1850s (towards the end of the key-wind era) and made by the most famous manufacturer of all. In the photograph it appears to be in immaculate condition, but in fact many of the comb teeth had been inexpertly replaced or de-tuned by overcleaning. For this reason, it fetched only about half its likely price in first-class order.

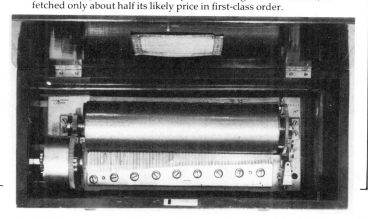

Musical Boxes

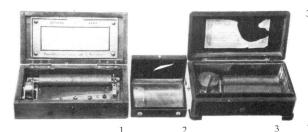

1   2   3

1. *An unusually small 'full-size' musical box, with the spring in a 'going barrel' (with horizontal axis) and of good quality, c. 1840. 7½in. wide. Dec. '84, £500.*

2. *Musical 'snuff' box, mid-19th century. Dec. '84, £200.*
   Typical of its kind, this plays two airs and has a horn translucent covering over the movement. The case is of black embossed horn – a thermoplastic material.

3. *Musical 'snuff' box, late 19th century.* 5 in. wide. Dec. 84, £170.
   In the late 19th century (and into the 20th) these small boxes lost all pretence of being connected with snuff, and were cased in larger wood boxes, with a fixed glass inner cover. Prices range upwards from about £50; this one, larger than usual and cased in amboyna with brass and mother-of-pearl inlay, was a particularly good example.

4. *Britannia disc musical box, Swiss, c. 1900.* Dec. '84, £700.
   The Britannia was one of several rivals to the Polyphon and Symphonion boxes. As with several of the others it differed in that the musical part of the movement was set low down in the case, with the motor at one side instead of underneath. This made a more rectangular case, though few were as heavily moulded as this one. Very unusual, but also ungainly, thus the price was not much above the current level for orthodox boxes.

4

5

5. *Musical box playing 12 sacred airs with bells and bee-shaped strikers. Mar. '85, £1,700.*
   This may seem a high price for a 12-air box, and not everyone likes sacred airs. However, sacred air arrangements (normally of hymn tunes and oratorio arias) are often of very good quality, and bells are also a good selling point. So is abnormal size – the cylinder in this case was just short of 20 in.

6

6. *Stella 14 in. disc musical box.* Mar. 85, £1,400.
   The Stella was a Swiss rival to the German Polyphon, of very good quality and notable for the fact that there are no projections on the discs – this makes them easier to handle and store, and much less easily damaged. Although the price realized was high, it represented a much less dramatic increase in recent months than the less-known 15⅝ in. Polyphon (see p.182).

7. *24½ in. coin-slot Polyphon in Art Nouveau case.* Dec. '84, £2,000.
   This at first seems relatively cheap when even the smaller 19½ in. models are making similar prices in more conventional cases. The reason: this was a conversion. The case had various redundant holes all carefully plugged, on the inside, and probably started life with a mechanism that changed its own discs. In that form, it might have made £5,000 plus, but as a non-original single-disc machine, it was neither the one thing nor the other.

7

Pneumatic Instruments

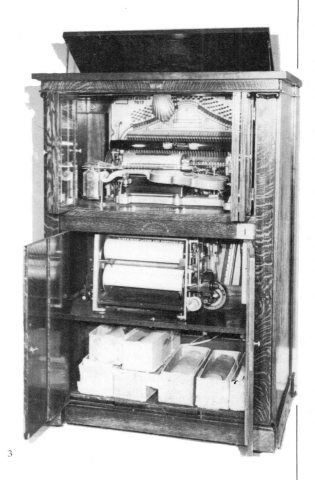

1. *Chamber barrel organ by H. Bryceson c. 1820.* 60 in. Mar. '85. £1,300.
   A barrel organ is not, as many think, a honky-tonk mechanical piano with a monkey on top, but an organ operated from a pinned barrel instead of a keyboard. This was a typical instrument from the period when they were in fashion (before musical boxes took over), in unrestored condition and in need of an overhaul.

2. *Barrel organ by William Hubt van Kamp, Holborn, c. 1770.* 89 in. Mar. '85, £1,500.
   Compared with the Bryceson organ, this was earlier, larger and rarer. However, it had been extensively, and not very sucessfully, restored, and did not play well. This accounts for the small difference in price between the two, and well illustrates the attraction to auction buyers of an object that looks as if it is straight out of the attic, untouched by inhuman restorer's hand.

3. *Mills violano Virtuoso piano and violin orchestrion.* June '84, £6,200.
   One of the most sophisticated of the paper-roll operated instruments of the early 20th century, this American machine regularly sells at this price level on the rare occasions when it appears at auction in this country. By contrast, the most basic Pianola pianos often fail to bring even £100.

4. *Musical box with 15-note organ section, by Nicole Frères, 1890–1900.* Mar. '85, £1,000.
   With a cylinder only 8 in. long playing 8 airs, this movement breaks the rules about fewer tunes and bigger cylinders, and the price reflects the interest now shown in organ boxes when the organ section (operated by the levers in the centre) is in good playing order. Organ repairs can present problems, and a longer organ box (with 11 in. cylinder) in the same sale, needing attention in that department, managed only £950.

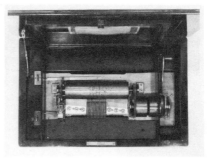

Phonographs

'One of those old record players, the sort that play round records' is a regular Guess-what-I've-got description meted out to telephone answerers in auction houses. One soon learns not to ask if they've seen any square records, and to assume that what they have is a phonograph, playing cylinders rather than discs. As there is a generation now that does not know what a gramophone is, it is hardly surprising that the name of a device that was effectively obsolete by 1914 is not familiar to all.

If you have a phonograph, the chances are that it will be an Edison Standard or an Edison Gem. The Gem was small, cheap and cheerful, the Standard everything that its name implied. Both sold in vast quantities, and have lasted well, though often without the horn. Gems have stuck at around £100, Standards around £150, for a long time, but they started to move up in 1984, especially towards the end of the year, and £150 and £200 are now typical for average examples. Extra interest is added by, for example, exceptional original condition (a tatty one polished up is never the same), early or late models (before 1901 or after 1909) and a large horn. The Standard which realized £700 in the March 1985 sale was a 'clean' but very standard Standard, and in this case one has to assume the buyer felt the five-foot copper horn was worth £450–£500 (No. 1).

Other Edison models include the Home, the Fireside and the Triumph (in ascending order of rarity), but very few bring more than about £500. Real rarities (of which there have been all too few on the market since the blockbuster sale of the E.M.I. Collection at South Kensington in 1980) include tinfoil phonographs from the 1877–86 era and the earliest wax cylinder models of 1888–95. Columbia Graphophones ('Graphophone' is the same as phonograph, the other way round) tend to bring slightly less than the equivalent Edison models, although many are visually more attractive.

Many European phonographs were based on the cheaper Graphophone models, but only exceptional examples bring more than about £150. 1984, however, did see what is probably the rarest phonograph to appear at auction since E.M.I., in the form of a Lioret 'Eureka' (No. 2). All Lioret phonographs are rare, and sufficiently idiosyncratic in design to attract wide interest, but the Eureka, which plays cylinders almost as long as those of Edison (and giving a longer playing time) is very seldom seen indeed.

If all you ever seem to find are Edison and Columbia models, do not despair; remember that £700 Standard, and keep looking for large or elaborately shaped horns. *Christopher Proudfoot*

3

2

1

4

1. *Edison Standard Phonograph with 55 in. copper horn, 1898–1908.* Mar. '85, £700.
   Like many Edisons of the date this was originally capable of playing only 2-minute cylinders, but it has been modified with extra gears to the left to take the later 4-minute cylinders. It also has a Diamond B reproducer (mounted horizontally over the record rather than angled to the front) which can add £20–£30 to the price. Even so and allowing for the large horn, this price was exceptional.

2. *Lioret 'Eureka' Phonograph, 1898.* Dec. '84, £4,500.
   Apart from the aluminium horn and reproducer the entire mechanism is brass, with original lacquer intact. Superb original condition and rarity make an unbeatable combination in an established collecting field.

3. *'Polyphone' phonograph attachment for an Edison Standard Phonograph, patented 1898.* Dec. '84, £420.
   This strange early attempt at stereophony used two reproducers, each with horn, tracking in the same groove with one stylus slightly behind the other. Examples (made for Edison by a Chicago firm) are very scarce.

4. *Edison Standard Phonograph and Bettini attachment, c. 1899.* Dec. '84, £380. The Bettini sold separately for £850.
   This was the earliest form of 'Standard': the speaking tube was for recording – most wax cylinder phonographs could record as well as play back. In exceptional original condition this made a good price; another example in the same sale, in quite good but restored condition, made £160.
   The Bettini, consisting of horn, reproducer and carriage, was the Rolls Royce of reproducers, and although not quite as rare as the 'Polyphone' is of greater historical importance. Many Bettini attachments, however, are copies, with the carriage made largely of diecast alloy; they are less desirable.

Gramophones (1)

Unlike phonographs, which only play fragile and relatively difficult-to-find cylinder records, gramophones appeal to a market beyond the rarified world of specialist collectors. Appearance has much to do with it – horn gramophones have a visual appeal which is lacking in most phonographs, which when not in use tend to resemble sewing machine cases. Many horn gramophones on the market today are of doubtful age, because the fact that even the most uninteresting models (from the collector's point of view) make £150 and upwards at auction has fostered the assembly of complete gramophones out of parts from varied sources. An increasing number of these parts are being made new – brass horns, for example, and the 'elbows' by which they are attached to the machine. Most new elbows are made of cast aluminium, a material seldom used originally, except in Columbia machines.

Another warning sign is the length of the tone-arm; most gramophones were designed so that the needle reached the centre of the turntable spindle, but as many recently assembled machines use tone-arms from cabinet or portable gramophones, there is often a large discrepancy in this respect.

There is surprisingly little difference in auction prices between these assemblies (No. 1) and original horn gramophones, unless the latter are of real interest to collectors. Into this category falls any HMV model (including those by 'Gramophone & Typewriter Ltd.' or 'The Gramophone Company', before the HMV trade-mark was adopted) and also those by Columbia. Even the most common HMV models, like the Junior Monarch, are seldom much below £300, and if the horn itself is of wood, £600 is normal. For ordinary, unnamed gramophones with metal horns, the usual price range is from £120 to £250, visual appeal and original condition being important factors in reaching the upper end of this range. Original paintwork on the horn is always important.

When it comes to gramophones with internal horns, there is not a lot to look for – very few make more than £100, and most are below £60. Exceptions are the larger HMV 're-entrant' models of 1928–30 – Models 193, 194, 202 and 203. These are large and very heavy, and have two doors enclosing a fretwork grille which occupies the entire front of the cabinet. Prices range from £150 up to £250 for the 193 and 194, and the 202 and 203 appear so seldom that no typical figure can be quoted. Cheapest of all are the black portables – but some coloured versions can sell well. The HMV 102, around £20 in black and good condition, is about £50–£60 in red, and £100 has been known for a particularly well-preserved example. Miniature portables, which fold up to look like cameras, make £60–£100 in the main, and the smallest of all, the Mikiphone, which looks like a giant pocket watch, currently brings around £170.   *Christopher Proudfoot*

1

1. *Typical 'assembled' horn gramophone made up from salvaged parts. Mar. '85, £160.*
   The base is a Zonophone hornless model (open-topped with internal horn). The internal horn has been blanked off, the tone arm inverted – the soundbox is back to front – and the supporting bracket at the back made up of welded scrap metal. The horn is a perfectly genuine Continental tinplate example, *c.* 1910, but it is connected to the machine by a modern aluminium tone-arm. So a surprisingly good price.

2. *HMV Junior Monarch Gramophone with oak horn, 1911. Dec. '84, £650.*
   Although this is one of the most common HMV horn models, the oak horn can double the price against a standard metal version.

3. *Symphonista horn Gramophone, c. 1910. Dec. '84, £400.*
   This was in very good original condition, and like many German models had embossed brass panels all round the case, adding visual appeal to its originality. This combination made the exceptional price, rather than any particular technical or historical importance.

2   3

Gramophones (2)

1. *'His Master's Voice' – a copy of the famous picture, 1930.* Dec. '84, £600.
The original picture was completed by Francis Barraud in 1899, but the Gramophone company had copies painted in later years, both by Barraud himself and others. This is one of the latter, but very few of the copies have come to light.

2. *'Nipper' – a papier-mâché life-sized model of the dog, made for display purposes,* c. *1950.* £550.
Various Nipper models have been made since 1899, this one being distinguished by its electrically wagging tail.

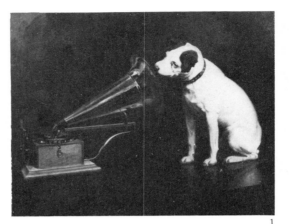

1

2

3

3. *'Camera' gramophones and a home recorder. Sold as 3 lots.* Dec. '84.
In the 1920s and early '30s, many portable gramophones were made in size and shape to resemble cameras of the Kodak type. At the back is a Mignonphone, made in France and distributed by the Paris branch of W.H. Smith. It sold for £85. In the centre, a Peter Pan – one of the best-known makes in this class, but a very unusual version, slightly larger than normal and with a flared metal 'horn' in the lid. This made £150. (Standard Peter Pans, with 'telescopic aluminium horn' attached to the soundbox, or a folding bellows affair in the lid, are in the £60–£100 bracket.) The gadgets in front, including the conical horn on the left, make up a 'Homophone' home recording device, for recording your own voice on a wax disc. These never really caught on, but this was an unusual one and brought £60.

4. *HMV 'Trademark' (or 'Dog') gramophone with black horn,* c. *1899.* Dec. '84, £700.
These tiny gramophones (the turntable is only 7 in. diam.) have always appealed to collectors. This one was in excellent original condition, even to the optional leather carrying case, although the brake had been broken – probably early in life since the replacement was only slightly later.

5. *HMV 'Trademark' gramophone with brass horn,* c. *1899.* Dec. '84, £900.
This had no case, and the metal fittings had been replated at some time with chromium rather than the correct nickel. Without these equalizing factors the price difference between the brass and the black horn might well have been greater.

6. *'Style IV' cheap version of the HMV 'Trademark' gramophone,* c. *1900.* Dec. '84, £650.
These are very seldom seen in the U.K. thus the high price even though the horn, arm and soundbox were replacements and the brake missing altogether.

4

5

6

Radio

1

2

3

4

5

6

1. *Baird Televisor.* Mar. '84, £2,400.
   One of the star items in the sale of the Ritman radio collection. This was the first complete Baird televisor to appear at auction for several years. The underbidder acquired the next one to appear, a month or two later, for several hundred pounds less.

2. *Kit-built Baird televisor.* Dec. '84, £1,100.
   Even with the two March bidders out of the running, this version of the televisor (even less attractive in appearance than the factory version) still raised a fine price. Many amateurs built their own televisors either from complete kits or by buying the essential components and assembling them from scratch. The Baird system became obsolete after the BBC trials of 1936 showed the EMI system to be the more practical.

3. *Marconi V2 two-valve receiver.* Mar. '84, £220.
   Although far from rare, the V2 is a 'must' for collectors, being the first popular valve broadcast receiver, contemporary with the crystal sets of the 1923–6 period.

4. *Loewe single-valve radio receiver.* Mar. '84, £280.

5. *Crystal set with single-valve amplifier, City Accumulator Co.* Mar. '84, £100.
   Two more items from the Ritman sale. This very simple looking Loewe set is based on the Loewe multi-valve – a single valve that did the job of two or three ordinary ones, and a collector's item in its own right. The crystal set is an unusual hybrid by a little-known British company, having a single-valve amplifier for use with a loudspeaker instead of the usual headphones. The case looked very restored, and the price might otherwise have been higher than the £100 realized.

6. *'N.8' 3-valve receiver with horn speaker, by the Non-Aerial Wireless Mfg. Co., London,* c. *1927.* Mar. '84, £100.

15. Cameras and Photographic Equipment

Introduction
By David Allison

Interest in the field continues to be high, although the dearth of early material, and of later rare cameras, has quelled the buying activities of a few of the major collectors. A greater appreciation of the more middle market apparatus is evident, i.e. in field and tailboard cameras, hand-and-stands, studio cameras, quality reflexes and folding plates, serviceable Leicas and Contax etc., where prices have escalated over the past year.

As in any category, new collectors are always welcome and it is refreshing to witness a revival in interest from Japan, and new contacts in Australia, America and Europe. Several new venues for camera fairs have been established in the United Kingdom, mostly with the co-operation of the recently formed Camera Collectors' Club of Great Britain. In short, collectors of cameras and photographic equipment, in their intense interest in the subject, typify all that is best in an established collecting field.

1. *A quarter-plate Benetfink twin-lens reflex camera, c. 1910. Feb. '85, £140.*
2. *A rare whole-plate Marion's mahogany sliding-box, twin-lens reflex camera, 1890s. Feb. '85, £1,000.*

3. *A New Design American Stereoscope by Langenheim, Lloyd & Co. 1880s. Jan. '85, £1,800.*
4. *An Ive's Kromscop stereoscope with eight Kromograms, 1890s. Jan. '85, £750.*
5. *Houghton's Ticka Watchpocket camera with viewfinder, c. 1905. Apr. '85, £85.*

3   4

1

2   5

Wood and Brass

Daguerreotype, wet-plate, transitional, field, hand-and-stand are the general terms used to describe the various Victorian designs of wood camera, and should be recognized if one is to understand the price differences.

Owing to the scarcity of pre-1880s daguerreotype and wet-plate equipment, a greater appreciation of the popular late nineteenth-century wood and brass cameras is evident. The few wet-plate cameras of the more desirable sliding-box type that have surfaced have fared well – two French examples selling in March and May '84 for £650 and £420 against estimates around £300–£500. Also in March, a British wet-plate studio camera by Meagher, with repeating back for multiple exposures, sold for £500. The magic name daguerreotype, however, did not seem to help a mid-1850s Knight's No. 3 sliding-box camera in October '84, which failed to sell against a reasonable mid-1970s estimate of £3,000–£5,000. The design was possibly too similar to the contemporary wet-plate models, pushing its price down to wet-plate price levels. Daguerreotype outfits are still in demand, however, an early and very rare 1841 example by Charles Chevalier selling in April 1983 for £11,000.

The majority of wooden cameras found today were produced after the introduction of dry-plates, c. 1880. Bellows became the norm, allowing makers to construct less cumbersome cameras for both studio and field work. The tail-board type, focusing via bellows away from the front lens panel, were the transitional cameras from wet to dry-plate. Those manufactured by established instrument makers such as Meagher, Ross,

Dallmeyer, Hare and Sands Hunter, possibly brass-reinforced and with a good range of accessories, achieve the highest prices in this category, around £150–£300, a particularly complete outfit being bid up to £600 in June '84. Don't be confused by the inferior Continental walnut tailboard cameras mass-produced early in this century and of a rather simplistic upright design, which are still rooted around £50 or so.

Indeed, British is still best for wood and brass apparatus of this period. The most common type, the field camera, focuses forward from the ground glass screen after opening from its flat folded state. Popular makers such as Lancaster, Thornton-Pickard, Underwood, Lizars and Sanderson produced thousands of field cameras for the early twentieth-century photographer. Prices have picked up considerably over the past year with a good condition triple-extension Sanderson or Thornton-Pickard selling for £100 plus.

Similar period leather-covered hand-and-stand cameras with polished mahogany interior and brass fittings have followed the same price trend, with high-quality Newman & Guardia or Sinclair models selling around £200–£300. Tropical, non leather-covered versions, in brass-strapped teak or mahogany cases made to order to withstand humid colonial climates, are still much sought – a tropical Sinclair Una selling for £800 in June '84.

Finally, across the board remember stereo! Any model described will at least double in price if fitted with two matching lenses, to take the 3-D stereoscopic photographs popular throughout the wood and brass era. *David Allison*

1. *Half-plate Watson's field camera and accessories, 1890s. Apr. '83, £140.*
   A good condition early dry-plate field camera. Note the 'square' cornered bellows normally found on pre-turn-of-the-century cameras.

2. *Half-plate wet-plate camera with Petzval-type portrait lens, c. 1870.*
   A typical sliding-box type. Wet-plate cameras with period lenses are rare, and in good condition range from £400 to £800.

3. *10 × 8 sliding-box wet-plate studio camera by J.H. Dallmeyer on studio stand, c. 1860. Aug. '83, £1,500.*
   Early studio cameras of this type are not too common, hence prices are high. Later dry-plate examples are still rooted below £100 or so.

4. *Dallmeyer sliding-box wet-plate stereoscopic camera and accessories, 1860s. May '84, £1,800.*
   Any wood and brass camera fitted with stereo lenses will normally double in price against its mono counterpart.

Pre-Cinema Optical Toys

2

1

3

Any early pre-cinema toy ending in the letters '–ope' – Thaumatrope, Phenakistiscope, Praxinoscope, Zoetrope, Filoscope – always attracts considerable interest at auction today, with prices for the rarest well into four figures.

The past year, as with most others, has been marked by a shortage of these weirdly named toys, so popular in the Victorian drawing room. In January 1985 two 1860s London Stereoscopic Company Wheel of Life Zoetropes were sold for £220 each. The Zoetrope is arguably the most commonly found animated-picture toy, consisting of a metal drum revolving on a turned-wood pedestal. It is worked by inserting a paper strip of sequential drawings into the drum and then spinning the same and viewing the movement of the drawings through the side slots. The illusion of animation depends on the basic principle of the persistence of vision, in that a moving object is retained in the eye for a fraction of a second, after being removed. The importance to collectors of early animation toys is that they demonstrate this fundamental cinematographic phenomenon, in some cases over half a century before the birth of the movie camera.

A similar machine to the Zoetrope, an 1890s Kinematofor hand-cranked Praxinoscope by Ernst Planck, sold in May 1984 for £280 (No. 3). This was a fairly battered variation of the rare Praxinoscope Theatres, invented by Emile Reynaud in 1877, and identifiable by the central drum of mirrors and range of cardboard accessories for superimposing images. In better condition this should have sold for around £600, and a Reynaud model might easily top £1,000.

Another tongue-garbler is the Phenakistiscope invented by J.A. Plateau in 1833. This is a slotted cardboard disc with a selection of slightly smaller diameter picture discs. When mounted together on a handle the operator rotated the two discs before a mirror, viewing the reflected moving picture through the slotted disc. Phenakistiscopes are rare, especially complete with handle, instructions and box, and can make up to £400 or £500 (No. 1). In April 1985 one missing its handle sold for £280.

The earliest of all pre-cinema toys and the easiest to mis-identify is the Thaumatrope. Introduced by J.A. Paris in 1826, the Thaumatrope is a 2½-inch circular disc with hand-drawn illustrations on each side, e.g. a bird on one side and a cage on the other. By spinning the disc using two side-mounted threads the bird appears resident in the cage. The last set I can trace sold way back in May 1981 (No. 5). Beware of fakes, however, as later printed examples make no more than a few pounds each.

As a yardstick, if it is Victorian and you cannot pronounce the name, buy it! If you cannot afford to, you have permission to illustrate the page corners of this book with a series of matchstick men drawings, which will give you a wonderful Filoscope-type flick-picture toy (see No. 4).

David Allison

1. *Magic Disc Phenakistiscope optical toy with eight discs, in maker's box, French, c. 1840.* Apr. '85, £480.
   A fairly good example of one of the earliest pre-cinema toys. Had it been complete with handle, the price might have doubled.
2. *Tin-plate Zoetrope with animated strips and discs, 1860s.* Apr. '81, £750.
   A very high price due to the unusual all-metal construction (instead of wood base and tin drum) and the large quantity of strips and discs.
3. *Praxinoscope with strips, c. 1880.* A typical model at around the £300–£500 mark. If of more elaborate design with superimposing effects or even steam driven, prices will rise steeply.
4. *Filoscope flick-picture toy by Henry W. Short, 1890s.* Apr. '85, £190.
   An almost 'throw-away' toy of the late Victorian era, hence few survive today.

4

5

5. *Ten hand-coloured Thaumatrope discs, c. 1830s.* May '81, £800.
   The earliest of the accepted pre-cinema toys, original 1830-50s Thaumatropes are very rare.

Leica

1. *Leica I, Model A, late 1920s.*
   The Leica I does not have a rangefinder housing on the top plate and is in black-enamelled finish. Model A has a fixed lens (£200–£400) and C a detachable lens (£150–£200).

2. *Rare I B Compur-Leica, 1930.* Dec. '83, £1,900.
   As a variation of the Leica I, Compur-Leicas are much sought after. This example has a rim-set Compur shutter; dial-set versions are much rarer.

3. *Leica 250 Reporter with accessories, 1942.* Jan. '83, £1,600.
   As with the Compur-Leica, any factory-made special-purpose Leica is of greater value than standard versions. The Reporter, designed to take 250 exposures on one loading, is a case in point.

4. *Leica IIIG, 1957.* Apr. '85, £480.
   The ultimate in screw-mount Leicas. Prices during '84 for the very finest – up to £800.

5. *Leica M3 body with instructions and maker's box.* Apr. '85, £350.
   A good unscratched example with instructions and factory packaging (always a bonus to the collector). With a lens it would have made more.

From its introduction by the German instrument makers Leitz, Wetzlar (*Leitz Camera = Leica*), in the mid 1920s, the Leica camera dominated the quality 35mm market until the 1960s. Indeed, the Japanese, who challenged this supremacy, are today the most feverish of Leica collectors.

Virtually any Leica will sell at auction today. Popular camera types are divided into two eras: those with screw-thread lenses, 1931–60; and those manufactured with bayonet-fitting lenses, 1958 to date. Production cameras over the whole period carry a factory number which can be used to date and identify the model from detailed listings released by Leitz. Condition is everything – any scratches, etc. will lower the camera's value.

Prior to 1931 about 54,000 cameras were made with fixed lenses: the Leica I (model A) and Compur-Leica. These are in black-enamelled finish and have five-digit numbers or less. The IA has the standard Oskar Barnack focal-plane shutter and will generally sell at around £250–£300. Those cameras fitted with an around-the-lens Compur shutter are much rarer – one selling in December 1983 for £1,900. In each case the earlier the number the higher the value, based on the smaller yearly production runs. Some pre- No. 70,000 IA's were updated during the 1930s, which can devalue them, so beware the adaptations.

Post-1931 fixed lens cameras gave way to interchangeable-lens models: I (model C) and Standard cameras. The overall look is the same as the Leica IA, although the Standard with a production run into the 1950s is also found in chrome finish. Model Cs and Standards generally fetch between £120 and £200 at sale, but prices for World War II Standards can be higher owing to the fewer models manufactured. In fact any Leica made during the war years with military markings will generally make over £300.

Leica III A, B and C series cameras fitted with coupled-rangefinder facility are the most common. They are normally finished in chrome with a slow-speed dial and a range of faster shutter speeds dependent on the model purchased. Prices range between £80 and £120 for a camera with lens, but look out for combination outfits with additional lenses, filters, viewfinders etc., as the price will rise sharply – a IIIA outfit sold in January 1985 for £400.

The IIIg, made at the end of the screw era with all the refinements developed over thirty years, has sold increasingly well over the past year. A fine example with instructions and maker's carton (both a major plus factor) sold for £800 in June 1984 against a £400–£600 estimate.

Of the bayonet-type models, the M series cameras are most in demand. These are slightly larger and heavier than their screw counterparts and have the model type stamped on the top plate e.g. M1, M2, M3 etc. Outfits are again most desirable although the camera with lens alone is eminently saleable at around £300 or £400. *David Allison*

Wood and Brass Apparatus

1

2

3

4

5

7

9

8

1. *Quarter-plate wet-plate camera, c. 1870.*
   Feb. '85, £420.
2. *Lancaster's No. 3 four-lens, multiple exposure camera, c. 1890.* Feb. '85, £1,900.
   Two examples of sliding box focusing cameras. No. 1 is a typical wet-plate camera with Petzval-type lens and quite rare owing to the specialist nature of photography in pre-Kodak days. No. 2 is designed to take four simultaneous, or separate photographs on one quarter-plate, and again was used in specialist areas, such as portrait studios.
3. *Bi-unial magic lantern, c. 1880.* Feb. '85, £400.
4. *Triple-lantern with accessories, c. 1870.* Feb. '85, £2,400.
   Two lanterns for special effects work including colour anaglyphs and superimposing. No. 4 was a much more complicated piece of apparatus than No. 3 and hence few were made for use by the professional lanternist.
5. *Birtac 17.5mm cinematograph camera/projector by Birt Acres, c. 1905.* Jan. '84, £1,600.
6. *Biokam 17.5mm cinematograph camera/projector by Alfred Darling, with accessories, early 1900s.* Feb. '85, £1,800.
   Two very rare wood-cased ciné outfits. Any movie camera with an unusual film gauge (as opposed to 8mm, 9.5mm, 16mm, and 35mm) will be of interest, as will any wood-cased hand-cranked models.
7. *Half-plate Lancaster's 1890 Instantograph and accessories.* Estimate £80–£120.
8. *10 × 12 Gandolfi mahogany field camera, c. 1930.* Estimate £250–£300.
9. *5 × 4 Shew Eclipse brass reinforced folding-strut camera, 1890s.* Apr. '85, £160.
   Three dry-plate wood and brass cameras. Nos. 7 and 8 are of field type. The Gandolfi, manufactured until fairly recently, is a more sophisticated camera and is often bought at auction by professional photographers today. No. 9 is more attractive than its plain mahogany counterpart, being heavily brass-strapped.

Popular Cameras

1

2

3

4

5

1. *'The Kodak', a factory-load roll-film box camera by George Eastman, 1888 or later.* Estimate £800–£1,200.
2. *Redding's Luzo roll-film camera in ever-ready case, 1890s.* Jan. '85, £600.
3. *Kodak Beau Brownie box camera, c. 1930.* Estimate £15–£30.
4. *Kodak Brownie box camera, c. 1915.* £2–£5. No. 1 is the original Kodak camera with a cylindrical string-cocked front shutter. It is the rarest of all Kodak box cameras. No. 2 shows the first British equivalent; although not quite as rare as No. 1, it is somewhat more attractive in brass-strapped mahogany casing. Nos. 3 and 4 are typical of post-1900 Kodaks, which survive in good numbers.

5. *Two Voigtlander Prominent coupled-rangefinder cameras, early 1930s.* Mar. '84, £220 (left) and £420.
6. *Early model Folding Pocket Kodak camera, c. 1900.* Estimate £20–£30.
7. *Six-20 Kodak camera, 1950s.* Estimate £2–£5. Four various folding roll-film cameras. No. 5 shows variant models of the rare roll-film Prominent – that on the right with a side-mounted extinction type exposure meter. Nos. 6 and 7 show an early model of the Folding Kodak with leather-covered lens panel and ubiquitous Six-20.

8. *Quarter-plate Butcher's Carbine camera, c. 1910.* Estimate £10–£20.
9. *Quarter-plate Newman and Guardia's Sibyl camera, c. 1910.* Estimate £80–£100. Two folding-plate cameras. No. 8 is an example of a typical popularly–made camera. No. 9 is a better-quality model, with lazy-tong side struts, fine focusing and soft leather covering – other models by Adams, Sinclair, Zeiss, Voigtlander, Ica and Contessa–Nettel are also sought..

10. *Rolleiflex T twin-lens reflex camera, and accessories, 1950s.* Apr. '85, £115.
11. *Tele-Rolleiflex twin-lens reflex camera and penta-prism, c. 1960.* Aug. '84, £380. Two very similar Rolleiflexes. No. 11 however, is a special purpose telephoto model, sold in far fewer numbers.

11

6

7

8

9

10

16. *Scientific Instruments*

Introduction
by Jeremy P. Collins

Collecting scientific instruments is now no longer the preserve of the Universities or the well-heeled gentry. Instruments can be purchased at auction or from any one of the many good dealers now specializing in them, prices are keen and suit all pockets. The range of instruments available is enormous, from simple nineteenth-century compasses to fine binocular microscopes by makers such as Andrew Ross.

The Golden Age of scientific instrument making lasted from the mid-sixteenth century to the late nineteenth. Of the great sixteenth-century English makers perhaps none is known better than Humphrey Cole (1530–91). Cole's instruments are remarkable for their fine engraving. No. 1 is a late sixteenth-century quadrant-dial in silver sold recently for a record £62,000. Compare the engraving to that on the brass quadrant made perhaps 100 years later (No. 2) and finally to the crude signature on the even later dial by the famous Augsburg maker Johann Schrettenger (No. 3). The latter, when compared to the work of Cole, appears to have been engraved with a chisel!

Fakes do exist as well as copies – the latter often made for instructional purposes to demonstrate the mathematical principles involved. No. 4 shows a fake mariner's astrolabe dated 1535 and with an extremely crude engraved scale, the date incidentally being earlier than the earliest instrument of this type so far identified and recorded.

Sadly, many instruments have been ruined by the ignorant, mostly by the lavish use of metal polish combined with the buffing wheel. Compare Nos. 5 and 6. The ring dial by Butterfield has sharp edges and clear numerals, while No. 6 has worn edges and some numerals almost polished out.

The world of the scientific instrument is fascinating, and in many ways the subject is in its infancy as far as collectors are involved. The next few pages give some idea of the variety and scope available.

1. *Silver quadrant dial by Humfray Colle (or Cole), c. 1570. Dec. '84, £62,000.*
   This was a great rarity and of superb quality, with a long and valuable provenance. No other quadrant-dial by Cole is known, and no other instrument in silver. It came with a probably original case.
2. *Brass quadrant by Joseph Richards, 17th century. Dec. '84, £4,600.*
3. *Detail of the signature of Johann Schrettenger.*
4. *Fake mariner's astrolabe. Not included in a sale.*
5. *Universal equinoctial ring dial by Butterfield, Paris, late 18th century. 5in. diam. Dec. '84, £2,700.*
6. *A sadly polished ring dial. Worth perhaps £150 in this condition.*

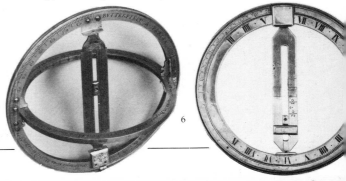

Microscopes

When talking of scientific instruments it is the microscope that first springs to mind, primarily because most of us have used one either at school or in the home. From the most simple student's microscope to the more complex binocular instrument, all now have a place in the collector's cabinet.

Quality must be the goal. If in any doubt as to originality the Oxford Museum of the History of Science, the Whipple Museum in Cambridge, the Science Museum in London and many others will be pleased to help. Museum staff will not, however, give values. Having decided on the type of instrument to collect, then compare item for item and price for price. Remember, the higher the quality the higher the price is a generalization, as many fine quality late nineteenth-century and early twentieth-century instruments can be bought today at a fraction of their original cost.

There are of course a large range of accessories to a microscope: lamps, slides, and specialized apparatus in fitted cases, all of which make a collection more comprehensive.

No. 1 is a delightful type of instrument made for naturalists to satisfy their curiosity about botanical specimens gathered during country walks. In one form or another these remained popular for most of the nineteenth century alongside more complex boxed instruments such as the 'Cary' type.

No. 2 is a Jones 'Most Improved' compound monocular microscope compendium. This elaborate microscope and collection of accessories is contained in the usual late eighteenth-century mahogany case and provides just about everything that the gentleman microscopist might need.

Microscope illuminating lamps (No. 3) are very popular and the collector would do well to add this spidery confection to his collection. Signed 'Ross, London', this superb instrument just shrieks out the word quality, which after all is what one would expect from such an eminent maker.

No. 4 is the school type, made by the thousand. Examples can be found for under £100 – a good starting point for any collection.

Jeremy P. Collins

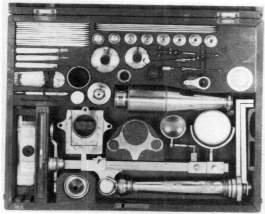

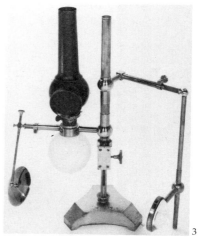

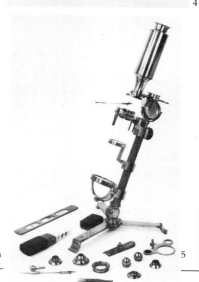

1. *Late 18th-century simple 'screw-barrel' type botanical microscope, with various objectives, slides and accessories contained in the original plush lined fishskin covered case.* About £250. Photo Phillips.

2. *Magnificent 18th-century Jones 'Most Improved' microscope compendium, of the highest quality.* Sold at Phillips, Apr. '83, £1,500. This would now make about £2,000.

3. *A rare and desirable late 18th-century illuminating lamp by Andrew Ross, an essential accessory in its day.* Dec. '84, £800.

4. *A fine quality but simple compound monocular microscope by Carl Zeiss.* About £150. Photo Phillips.

5 & 5a *Compound monocular microscope by J. Bleuler, London, with accessories and case, 18th century.* Dec. '84, £2,000. The trade label may well have added as much as 20% to the price of this microscope.

Telescopes

Commercially telescopes were in the doldrums, until the last year. There were of course exceptions, but only recently have auction prices moved up.

Telescopes divide neatly into, 'refracting', and 'reflecting', and the hand-held types commonly used by seamen, hunters, soldiers, and others. The earliest refracting telescopes seen in any quantity today are eighteenth-century examples with vellum-covered card body tubes often tooled in gilt and with ivory and ebony mounts. The outer tubes are sometimes covered in shagreen.

No. 1 is a plain but useful six-draw brass refracting telescope. Telescopes of this type are plentiful and can be found signed by a number of makers including Dollond, Harris, Chevalier, Tulley, Ramsden, Adams and others. Auction prices vary from £40 to upwards of £400 for excellent examples. One of the more unusual types of refracting telescopes recently sold was a rare eighteenth-century double-draw two-power instrument invented and signed by the optician James Ayscough. Despite being in extremely tired condition it sold for £1,100 at Phillips in 1984 (No. 2).

Christie's New York offered two magnificent late seventeenth-century leather and gilt metal refracting telescopes by Paolo Belletti of Bologna in October 1984. These two sold for $4,800 (£3,810) and $5,500, (£4,365), which underlines the strengthening market.

Reflecting telescopes of the type shown in No. 3 are sometimes called the Gregorian reflector after James Gregory who developed the parabolic reflecting mirror surface as a correction for spherical aberration. Telescopes of this type are very popular, not only for use, but as decorative antiques. The most popular size is from 2 in. to 5 in. diameter. A number of makers produced these, including Sterrop, Bird, Martin, Cuthbertson and Champneys, Nairne and Dollond. Prices have begun to recover of late provided that the instrument, in particular the speculum, is in good condition. Two-inch reflectors by makers such as Dollond will fetch £400–£600.

It is as well to be aware of the many nineteenth-century and later copies bearing the name Dollond. Those in No. 4 are signed 'Dollond London' and 'Dolland London – Day or Night'; the lower example is not a fake, but a clever nineteenth-century attempt to cash in on the good name of John Dollond.

Finally, as if to underline the increase of interest and prices of telescopes generally, an interesting 5-inch Astronomical refractor by T. Cooke of York (No. 5) recently sold for £3,400; three or four years ago it might have scraped a price of say £800 to £1,200.   *Jeremy P. Collins.*

1. *A fine quality six-draw refracting telescope by Lerebouers of Paris* – representing good value at £150–£200. Photo Phillips.
2. *Refracting telescope by James Ayscough, c. 1750.* Sold at Phillips, July '84, £1,200.
3. *This 18th-century reflecting telescope by Nairne and Blunt with tripod stand shows its age and certain careless usage – much original lacquer now being absent.* About £400–£600. Photo Phillips.
4. *A 19th-century telescope signed 'Dollond' and one of a similar date signed 'Dolland' – note crude engraving on the lower example, a sample of the sort of workmanship never passed by John Dollond. The 'Dollond' example would make perhaps £100–£120, the 'Dolland'.* £60–£80.
5, 5a. *5 in. astronomical refracting telescope by T. Cooke, York, late 19th century.* Mar. '85, £3,400. Lee Observatory is near Manchester.
6. *Fine brass 3 in. astronomical refracting telescope, signed A. Ross, London, 19th century.* Mar. '85, £3,200.

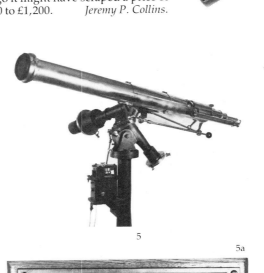

Surveying Instruments

Irrespective of use, most surveying instruments are works of art in their own right, but they have been generally ignored by collectors until recently. However, all is now changed and the fine workmanship and mathematical precision of these objects is being appreciated. Unfortunately, because of their basic materials – brass, copper, silver, and platinum – a vast quantity of surveying instruments has been consigned to the melting pot as scrap. Happily those days are over, and the would-be collector, whatever the range of his pocket, has a fair selection from which to choose.

Of all scientific instruments, the surveyor's are the most varied. They include the magnetic compass in all its forms, mining dials (No. 1), surveying levels (Nos. 2, 3), circumferentors, graphometers, theodolites (Nos. 4, 5),

surveyors' sextants, clinometers and a host of miscellaneous instruments. The theodolite and the level are probably the most common of the larger instruments. Prices are rising steadily for good original instruments by eminent makers. Early examples are notable for simplicity and elegance, and as they developed they became more complex in order to solve the mathematical problems for which they were designed.

Early compasses can be found in fitted mahogany boxes. The rose may be of printed paper, silvered brass or even mother of pearl. Signatures are important, but not mandatory, but a 'signed' instrument will be more expensive than a similar unsigned example. Likewise cased instruments complete with accessories are more desirable than uncased examples.

Many late instruments (post-1900)

have been available until recently at a few pounds. No more. The collector should now take a long hard look at many late instruments – theodolites for example – which have been far too inexpensive for far too long. Once again quality is the watchword, allied to original finish, condition and completeness.

These instruments are beautiful things – made by craftsmen and designed by engineers. Seventeenth- and eighteenth-century instruments for the surveyor are often superbly engraved with flowers, animals and landscapes, and are a joy to behold! Sadly, however, surveying instruments have suffered badly from the dreaded polisher! One must remember that to perform correctly they must be fully maintained and serviced, and handled with great care. Being mostly brass with glass levels, delicate compass needles and finely divided scales, these instruments are easily damaged. Instruments polished up purely for decorative reasons are as good as useless, and a collector would do well to avoid these, however strong the visual temptation.

By following the basic rule of quality, a collector can soon build a most worthwhile collection – so much is still available. *Jeremy P. Collins.*

1. *A simple miner's dial by Troughton & Simms with silvered compass and balanced edge bar needle with fore and aft sights, c. 1840.* Dec. '84, £220.

2. *A simple but high quality surveyor's level with compass and cross-bubble by W. & S. Jones of London, late 19th century.* Dec. '84, £150. Good value today.

3. *A more complex level by E.R. Watts & Son incorporating their patent 'constant' bubble, c. 1925.* Dec. '84, £120. A good instrument, ignored by the trade and collectors until recently.

4. *Rare Cornish miner's simple theodolite, the compass dial signed by William Wilton of St. Day, incorporating bubble levels and with separate fore and aft sights for use as a miner's dial, mid-19th century.* Mar. '85, £800.

5. *Six-inch theodolite by Stanley, c. 1890.* Mar. '84, £650. A magnificent piece of the instrument maker's art. Unpolished and in superb original condition, complete in every detail with case and accessories. This represents marvellous value at anything between £500 and £1,000.

Drawing Instruments

There is a growing awareness of the simple beauty of drawing instruments, and an increasing number of people are beginning to collect them. The basic form of many of these instruments has remained static since the sixteenth century with few modifications and improvements, the principal reason for this being that the mathematical functions required of them did not change. As the epic voyages of exploration and discovery gathered momentum from the sixteenth to the eighteenth centuries it became necessary to produce instruments to record their findings. Instruments such as the protractor, sector, ruler and parallel-rule were generally included in drawing sets, many of which came in elaborate cabinets, pocket cases or even leather rolls.

The lack of evolution in instrument making has been put down to the fact that there were few manufacturers, but many tradesmen selling instruments on which they signed, engraved or stamped their names. The collector therefore must be wary of signatures as these are often not of the maker. Many instruments are unsigned, but that should not deter the studious who will in time probably be able to ascribe a maker to the item. Furthermore, the collector should be aware of difference in the quality of instruments by the various makers, the materials employed and in particular the accuracy of the divided scales on rules, etc. (No. 1).

No. 2 is part of a very superior set of mid-19th-century instruments, of ormolu and gilt brass with steel points, beautifully engraved with scrolls and foliage and contained in a large leather despatch box known as the Dudley Despatch Box. The maker is not known but they are possibly by Elliot. No. 3 is a simpler drawing set, in a mahogany box with ivory rule and parallel rule and two boxwood scales by George Rowney and Co. Sets of this kind are very numerous and if complete and in fine condition are of interest to collectors, at prices of £60–£120. At more dizzy heights are No. 4 by Search of Soho, with a case of tortoiseshell bound in silver, and No. 5 by C.W. Dixey, 'Mathematical Instrument Maker to Her Majesty', with a case of shagreen also bound in silver.

Lastly, the drawing instrument 'par excellence'! (No. 6). It is really quite amazing what continues to turn up in corners and cupboards. It was in the latter that this magnificent late eighteenth-century brass circular drawing protractor by George Adams was found. This was in the most splendid original lacquered finish and original shaped mahogany case. The vendor was no doubt delighted when it sold for £1,900, being bought for the nation by the Science Museum. *Jeremy P. Collins*

1. *Part of a brass sector by John Rowley, 18th century.* Mar. '85, £400.
   This was a fine example by a well-known maker. Run-of-the-mill examples would fetch £180–£250.

2. *Various superb quality drawing instruments from the Dudley Despatch Box.* Sold at Phillips, July '83, £1,100.

3. *Comprehensive drawing set by G. Rowney with ivory and boxwood scales,* c. 1900. About £80–£120. Photo Phillips.

4, 5. *Two similar gentleman's pocket drawing sets,* c. 1830. Mar. '85, each set £250.

6. *Large 12 in. drawing protractor, signed 'G. Adams Instrument Maker to His MAJESTY, Fleet Street, London', in original specially shaped mahogany case,* c. 1790. Mar. '85, £1,900.

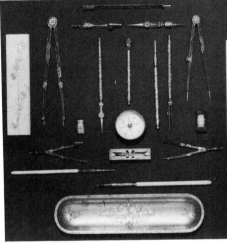

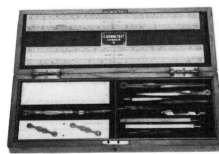

3

Meteorological Instruments and Globes

1

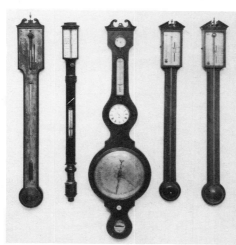

2

3

4

5

6

7

8

1. *Simple mass-produced desk thermometer, 19th century.* Around £30.
2. *Barometers by (left to right) Gregory, Bassnett, Balsany, Donegan and Stampa, all 19th century.* Dec. '84, £1,500, £1,300, £480, £420, £250.
   Prices of barometers vary widely and depend on the makers, the quality of the engraved scales, the choice of case veneer, complexity of the movement, and originality.
3. *Barograph, unsigned, c. 1910.* Dec. '84, £700.
4. *Weather Telegraph by Lambrechts, 19th century.* Dec. '84, £300.
5. *Alloy and nickel plated brass anemometer by Jules Richard, Paris, in fitted case with accessories.* Dec. '84, £140.
6. *Miner's brass air-flow meter with silver dial, in leather carrying case.* Dec. '84, £140.
   Meteorological instruments are arousing increased interest, and once again the shapes and purposes are very varied.
7. *Pair of table globes published by Woodward, 19th century.* Dec. '84, £600.
8. *Star globes for nautical and instructional use (left to right): Xela by E. Bertaud, Paris, late 19th century; English's Patent Star Finder by Cary & Co., London, late 19th century; Star Globe by Heath & Co., London, c. 1940.* Mar. '85, £190, £550 and £260.
   Star globes are erratic in price, but those by Cary always find a ready buyer. Damaged globes sometimes sell surprisingly well.

Miscellany

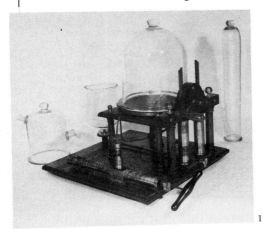

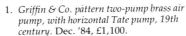

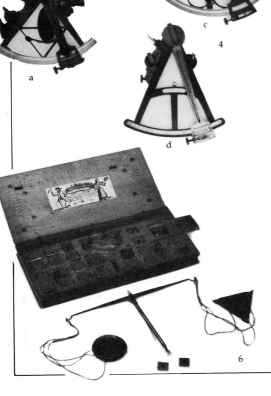

1. *Griffin & Co. pattern two-pump brass air pump, with horizontal Tate pump, 19th century.* Dec. '84, £1,100.

2. *Wimshurst electrostatic induction machine for demonstration purposes, with Leyden jars, on ebonized base.* Dec. '84, £150.

3. *Rare French electrostatic machine with gold foil filled Leyden jar.* Dec. '84, £1,100.
   Laboratory apparatus is now becoming popular.

4. *Three sextants and one octant.* Mar. '85, (a) £320, (b) £700, (c) £280, (d) £340.
   Prices range from £200 to £1,200 for good sextants, and up to £1,500 and more for special instruments such as Troughton 'double' framed instrument at the top.

5. *Military pattern black lacquered brass gun director, with accessories in mahogany case.* Mar. '85, £190.
   Little was considered of such instruments until recently. Price range £150–£350.

6. *Weight and scale box by F. R. Breurer, Germany, 1730.* Dec. '84, £800.
   Even without the dated trade label this would be a rare and desirable item.

7. *Lacquered and anodized brass dip-circle by Dover, Kent, 19th century.* Mar. '85, £280.
   Prices range from £150 to £300.

8. *Fine ivory azimuth diptych dial by Charles Bloud, Dieppe, late 17th/early 18th century.* Dec. '84, £260.
   Prices range from £200 to £800. On a sunny day this could serve as a pocket watch among other functions.

9

10

9. *Anonymous 19th-century oil painting of a scientific inventor holding letters patent, before a reflecting telescope and large mirror.* Mar. '85, £500.

   This is a jobbing portrait in artistic terms, but the buyer should be able to identify the sitter and perhaps the artist.

10. *Crooke's Tubes, late 19th century.* Mar. '85, £400.

    A Dustbin Trove! These four Crooke's Tubes are the survivors of a laboratory clearout in Northern Ireland. Perhaps fifty of their fellows perished at the hands of people who should have known better.

11. *Brass 'Butterfield' type dial by Lordelle, Paris, 1738.* Dec. '84, £4,600.

    Compare the fine engraving on this to the crudity of No. 1 below.

12. *Laboratory demonstration gyroscope by Elliott Bros. with accessories and original case.* Mar. '85, £460.

    Popular toys and now popular with collectors.

11   12

Fakes, forgeries or copies?

1. *Copy of ring dial, 19th century.* Not offered at auction.

   Note the un-18th-century engraving, which is not only sloppy by comparison with a precision instrument maker's work, but is also recognizable on a wide variety of copies. Compare to No. 11 above.

2. *Brass pillar dial, 20th century.* This fake was not offered at auction.

   Note again the poor and inconsistent engraving. This is made from brass tubing and is entirely unconvincing.

3. *Silver equinoctial ring dial, modern.* Approx 3 in. diam. Not offered at auction. Sold today as a souvenir, and nice enough from that point of view.

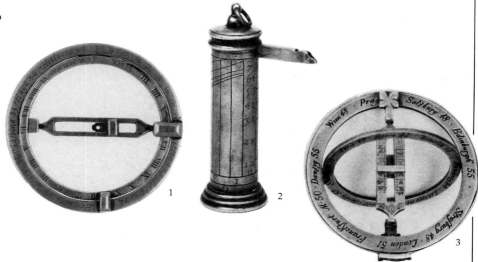

1   2   3

17. Tools

Introduction
by Christopher Proudfoot

To the layman, tool collecting is probably as arcane as any collecting subject, and there are no simple rules about what to look for. Many tools that exude an air of quality, made of exotic woods with brass fittings, are so commonplace as to excite only a yawn from the hardened collector. The classic example of this, the Ultimatum brace which is worth more in beech or boxwood than ebony, is discussed on p. 206, but it is no easier to explain to normal mortals why most moulding planes are worth £2 but some can be nearer £200.

An inquiry during the past year about a box of sixty or so moulding planes led to a decrepit deal chest which produced, once its dusty contents were sorted, a full 36-piece set of hollow and round planes by the late 18th/early 19th-century maker John Green; this realized £450, and another surprise was a set of eight side-bead planes most of which had 'nicker' irons for cross-grain work – virtually unheard of on bead planes, and of doubtful advantage thereon, but the set made £160.

The magnificent painted and inlaid tool-chest shown here, on the other hand, had a more obvious appeal, not least for its possible connection with Nelson, whose coat of arms was painted on the front.

1. *Bronze chariot plane of unusually large size (5⅜ × 2¼ in.), with mahogany case, late 19th century.* Jan '85, £300.
   A particularly elegant tool from a cabinet-maker's kit. Smaller examples in bronze are usually in the £70–£100 range.

2. *Stanley 110 block plane ,* c. *1876.* Jan. '85, £180.
   The ornate, shoe-buckle-like clip holding the cutter in place is the only difference between this and the Stanley 110 in the tool shops today – but this version was made for a very short time, hence the price.

3. *Bronze thumb plane by Norris,* c. *1930.* Jan. '85, £350.
   Norris planes have always been highly esteemed by cabinet-makers, but the limited production numbers of this model make it even more desirable to collectors (cf. the adjustable version on p. 205).

4. *Painted and inlaid tool-chest, early 19th century.* 43 in. wide. Oct. '84, £3,000.

Groovy Tools

1. *Plough by Madox (1748–75).* Apr. '85, £90.
Madox planes are the most numerous survivors from their period, but ploughs by him are scarce even so. Brass caps to the stems are seldom, if ever, seen on ploughs of this date.

2. *Plough with unusual screw-adjustment stamped 'Stiven, Dundee'.* Apr. '85, £200.
One of the many variations on standard plough designs to come from Scotland, this would have gone even higher had it been in better condition and by a recorded maker.

3. *Rare sash fillister by Greenslade,* c. 1900. Apr. '85, £600.
Screw-stem sash fillisters are relatively uncommon, but brass screw-stems are very rare indeed. The larger nuts are of rosewood. This plane was in exceptionally good original condition, even allowing for its late date. Compare the shape of the scroll at the top of the wedge with that of the Madox plough: this was usually round in the 18th century, and became progressively more elliptical towards the 20th century. Ordinary wooden screw-stem sash fillisters tend to be around the £40–£50 mark.

4. *Wedge-stem sash fillister by Charles Nurse, Maidstone,* c. 1840–60. Apr. '85, £40.
A typical, standard 19th-century sash fillister, datable by the maker's address. Apart from having all the wedges replaced, it was in very good condition, with particularly good patina, and this and the interest of a Kentish collector combined to bring the price up to £40 – twice the price of many seemingly identical examples.

5. *Rare Scottish handled rosewood plough with similar adjustment system.* c. 1890–1900. June '84, £320.

6. *Rare beechwood plough with steel adjusting screws in the stems.* c. 1790–1800. June '84, £450.

Before the advent of the power-driven routers and spindle-moulders which make the modern joinery shop sound like an aero-engine testing shed and treat wood as if it were metal, the task of forming mouldings, grooves and rebates in wood was allotted to a whole range of planes, most of which could do one job only.

An exception was the plough, possibly the most expensive tool in most joiners' kits, and certainly the most elaborate. True, it could only make grooves, but at least it could make several (usually eight) different widths of groove, with adjustments for both depth and distance from the edge of the wood being worked. Since every joiner had to have one, ploughs are by no means rare (though less numerous than moulding planes of which most joiners had at least 30). The standard nineteenth-century article, with edges to fix the fence stems in position, brings only around £10 at auction. Brass ends are normal on nineteenth-century ploughs. The cheaper, uncapped models are relatively uncommon – and always worth a second look, as they could be of earlier date (No. 1).

Apart from the possibility of finding an eighteenth-century plough, there are a number of 'extras' to look for on those of the nineteenth century, which can dramatically affect the value. Most of these incorporate some form of screw adjustment for the fence – adjusting and then locking the normal sliding-stem and wedge system is a tedious business. A number of such screw-stem systems have appeared in the past year, and serve well to illustrate the sort of features that interest the seasoned collector.

There was a handled plough which was doubly unusual, for it was made entirely of rosewood instead of the normal beech, and had a system of adjustment by metal threads concealed within the stems and controlled by brass knobs at the end. It had no maker's name but came from Scotland – interestingly, Scottish joiners seem not to have shared their contrymen's proverbial meanness, for they often opted for 'de luxe' versions of ploughs, with extras like handles and screw or other patent adjustments. In rather scruffy condition, it still realized £320 (No. 5), and in the same sale another one with a very similar adjustment made £450, (No. 6). This was obviously early (probably c. 1800) and also unnamed, although a very similar 1790s plane is known by the London maker Gabriel. In April 1985, another 'Scottish peculiar' appeared, with a central metal adjusting screw *and* traditional wedge stems. This had a name, albeit one not recorded hitherto, of a maker (or possibly a dealer) in Dundee (No. 2). The same sale saw the splendid *brass*-stemmed sash fillister by Greenslade of Bristol (No. 3). Sash fillisters are closely related to ploughs, but are specifically designed to form the glass rebates in window frames. 'Extras' available are the same as for ploughs, but less often found on such specialized tools.

Christopher Proudfoot

Boring tools

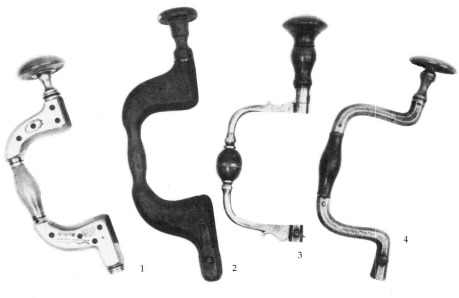

1. *Ultimatum brass-framed brace with boxwood infill.* Apr. '85, £750.
   In 'cleaned' condition, but suffering from loose joints (the hole visible just below the handle on the left remains from a previous attempt to cure this), this example did well to achieve £750 in the current state of the market in such braces.

2. *Brace, probably late 18th century.* Apr. '85, £160.
   By contrast, this almost rustic looking brace, with a badly rusted chuck, is a rare early version of what was to become the standard English joiner's brace in the 19th century. In spite of its condition, it made a good price.

3. *Steel brace, probably French, 18th century.* Apr. '85, £420.
   This beautifully made steel brace is more recognizable as an ancestor of the modern steel brace. Cf. No. 10.

4. *Horton's patent brace,* c. 1855. Apr. '85, £400.
   Also closer to the modern brace, these braces were made of brass or bronze, with a rosewood handle. This example is less than perfect (it is visibly bent slightly out-of-true), and a better example made £450 in Jan. '85.

It is unusual to have to record a dramatic drop in prices in a specialist collectors' field – a halt in the rate of increase is the most that is usually apparent. The brass-framed brace, particularly in its rarer manifestations, has suffered such a set-back. It could be argued that for a boxwood brace to be worth £2,300 (as one was in 1982) when an identical one in ebony could be had for around £150 was an example of collection mania at its worst, and if so, sanity has returned. The boxwood Ultimatum in the April 1985 sale (No. 1), admittedly not a brilliant specimen, made only £750, and an even rarer brace (No. 9) seemed relatively cheap at the same price in October 1984. The latter was in very good condition, an uncommon variation on the 'Ultimatum' type of brass frame, with an equally uncommon rosewood covering. Another rosewood-filled brace, closer to the 'Ultimatum' in design but with a different method of releasing the bit from the chuck, made £550 in January

1985, however, which indicated that all was not lost in the brass-framed world. Indeed, in view of comments heard from dealers recently about the numbers of such braces in stock and the difficulty of selling them, it is remarkable that prices for the standard ebony 'Ultimatum' have remained fairly stable in the £100–£200 region. The latter would be for one in near mint condition (i.e. with the original lacquer on the brass, not polished up to see your face in). Any serious defect (the lack of the chuck-ring, with the end of the spring broken off, for example) takes the price down to £60 or so.

The Ultimatum, made by William Marples, is the most common of the brass-framed braces, and carries a legend stamped into the brass, 'William Marples sole manufacturer of the Ultimatum metallic framed brace' (No. 7). Nearly all of this pattern, whether graced by Marples's name or not, have a Royal coat-of-arms and a movable ring at the end of the chuck to release the bit.

The Howarth rosewood filled brace mentioned above was an exception in this respect.

Apart from ebony, rosewood and boxwood, beech was also sometimes used for the infill: beech Ultimatums (often at first sight difficult to distinguish from boxwood) at one time commanded up to £500, but recently have made no more than those of ebony. Admittedly, most that have appeared have been in poor or restored condition.

Not to be confused with brass-*framed* braces are the brass *plated* variety. These are simply wooden braces (usually beech) with extra reinforcement in the shape of brass plates screwed (and usually inlaid) into the sides of the webs, where the short grain creates a weak spot. Most of these have stuck around the £30–£40 mark for several years now, although a particularly well-preserved specimen will always make more, as will one in a different timber, such as boxwood or ebony.   *Christopher Proudfoot*

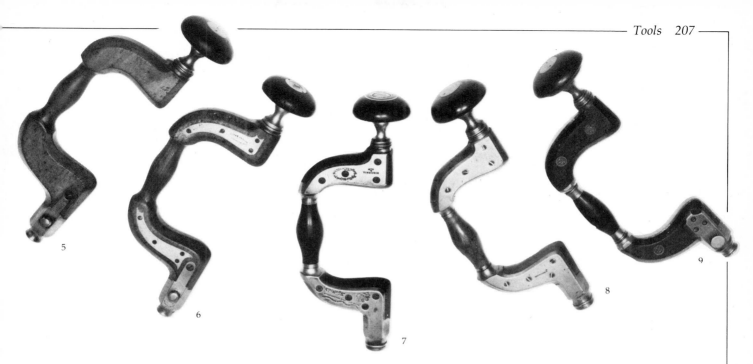

The Range of British mid-19th century wood braces:

5. *Unplated beech brace.* Apr. '85, £35.
   A good example of the most basic type, with its original varnished finish and, again, the luxury of an ebony head. £25–£40 is the normal price range.

6. *'The Mechanics Patent Brace'.* Jan. '85, £60.
   This was also a typical plated brace with button chuck. An ebony and brass head again, which was a step up from all-wood (often lignum vitae) heads on the most basic beech braces.

7. *Typical Marples Ultimatum brace in ebony, with ivory-inlaid head.* Jan '85, £180.
   Good original condition took the price over the normal £100 or so for average examples.

8. *Brass-framed brace of the Ultimatum type, filled with beechwood, by H. Brown & Sons.* Apr. '85, £170.
   This brace has an ebony head, but without the ivory ring inlaid in Ultimatums.

9. *Brass-framed rosewood and ebony brace.* Oct. '84, £750.
   Although this looks like a wood brace, it has a brass frame, in this case sandwiched between two wood faces rather than vice versa. Such braces are rare, and this was especially unusual both for its very original condition and its use of rosewood for the 'scales' but ebony for the handle. (Ebony heads are quite normal.)

10. *Common iron brace, often called a '6d' brace.* The cheapest and simplest form of brace in the 19th century, this still is of small value, and invariably appears at auction as part of a large lot.

11. *Three special-purpose braces.* Sold as one lot. Apr. '85, £50.
    On the left is a chairmaker's brace (or bitstock): the bit is a permanent fixture, and only one size of hole can be made. In the centre is an all-iron brace, probably used by a smith. Right: wagon-builder's brace.

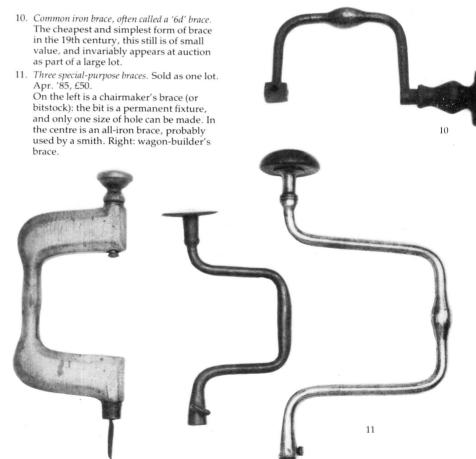

18.   Arms and Armour

Introduction
by Melvyn Gallagher

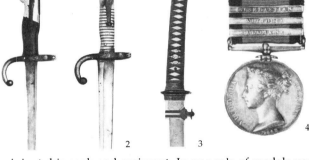

Interest in Arms and Militaria has never been greater, and there is still a wealth of material to choose from at all price levels, with many hitherto unregarded items being now avidly sought and researched.

For example, certain vintage air weapons of the type that grandfather or father used as a boy (No. 1) can now realize £100 or more, and bayonets too are attracting more interest after long years of conversion into chi-chi fire irons (No. 2). At the top end of the market the traditional price leaders such as cased pistols and military headdress continue to rise in price, but only the best pieces in the best original condition. Collectors should be wary of rarities at seeming bargain prices, which may indicate a heavily restored or refinished piece.

Items of American interest, especially firearms and Bowie knives, are at a premium, as too are all Japanese weapons and fittings. Even in poor condition early signed Japanese swordblades fetch high prices, many of them returning home (No. 3).

Lovers of artillery can seldom afford the space to house a full-sized example, so good period miniatures are in demand. These were made either as signal guns, rather lethal children's toys, or demonstration pieces in Military Schools (No. 5).

Rarity is enhancing the prices paid for early military uniforms and militaria, an area where museums are keen buyers if the items have survived the ravages of moth, damp and amateur theatricals.

Historically interesting are medals and decorations; again condition is important but so too is the number issued, the recipient, his rank and regiment. In one sale of medals you can see 200 years of British history from Trafalgar to the Falklands, and in March 1985 a pewter Boulton's Trafalgar medal realized £190, and a Falklands pair £130.

Medals awarded to native recipients, Jubilee, Police, Nursing and Coronation medals are still cheap but are beginning to rise in price, as too are foreign orders, many made of silver or even gold.

1. *.22 'service' air rifle Mark II, Webley & Scott.* May '85, £100.
2. *French sword bayonets for the Gras rifle (left) and for the Chassepot rifle (right), late 19th century.* These are common and now worth about £20 each.
3. *Japanese Shingunto with regulation mounts, c. 1940.* Nov. '84, £210.
   Swords carried by officers in World War II often had inherited blades signed by the 16th- and 17th-century smiths. These are naturally more valuable than modern versions, as good swords are now scarce. Most return to Japan. As the price indicates, this was a 20th-century blade.
4. *Military General Service Medal (1793–1814), 3 clasps, Salamanca, Vittoria, St. Sebastian; to B. Burton, 1st Foot.* Extremely fine. Mar. '85, £220.
5. *A 6-bore bronze signal cannon, on truck carriage.* Barrel 19½ in long. Mar. '85, £400.

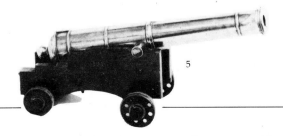

Selecting Swords

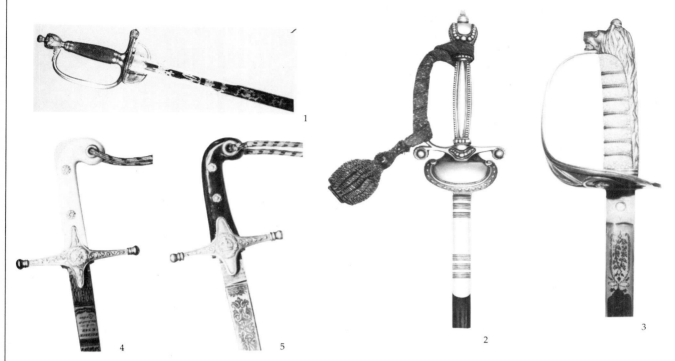

1

4   5

2

3

Most swords available today date from the period after 1796, when British military patterns were standardized. With the Napoleonic wars they were produced in vast numbers, and many have survived. The 1796 light cavalry sabre with its wide blade and stirrup hilt can be bought for under £50 as a wall hanger. Collectors can, however, find better ones with blued, gilt and etched blades, for £100 if worn, and £250 or more if in near original state. Common, too, are 1796 pattern infantry officers' swords with copper gilt hilts and 'urn' pommels (No. 1), for which the same price levels apply.

Swords come in two types, those made for action and those for dress wear. Many of the former proved inadequate in use and so a plethora of new designs appeared. The cavalry sabre caused most problems, and it was not until 1912 that the design was finally perfected. Although still in use, these realize from £100 in good condition.

Also common are the 1897 infantry

officer's sword with a solid nickel plated hilt, and the Royal Artillery pattern with plated three-bar hilt. Most date from the Great War, and although of small value in poor condition, better examples fetch £60–£80, and more if with an interesting presentation inscription on the blade.

Court swords with decorative hilts and slender blades (No. 2) and military dress swords are undervalued, the former often having a good provenance. They were and still are used by the diplomatic corps and ceremonial bodies such as Yeoman Warders. Look for blades with the cypher of Edward VIII, which are at a premium. Plated steel court swords are scarce in good condition as many were relegated to damp cellars and attics and have rusted badly.

Naval swords and dirks are popular at £100 or more, and again blades are usually rusty, possibly owing to the corrosive sea air. Of the many derivatives of the 1827 pattern, the Royal Naval Air Service is the rarest (No. 3).

Collectors are attracted to the 1831

1. *A 1796 pattern infantry officer's sword, the copper hilt with original gilt finish, the blade with much blue and gilt decoration, c. 1800. Sept. '84, £240.*
2. *A Victorian civil dress sword with etched blade retailed by Poole & Co. Dec. '84, £70.*
3. *Royal Naval Air Service sword. May '83, £400. A rare sword in good condition, bought by the Imperial War Museum.*
4. *A Victorian 1831 pattern General Officer's scimitar with etched blade and ivory grips. Jan. '85, £250.*
5. *An Edward VII Police pattern scimitar with horn grips. Jan. '85, £260.*

pattern General Officer's sword (Nos. and 5) sword selling for £150 or more, but a word of warning: there are convincing Eastern fakes of these and other types being imported, including the Highland basket hilted broadsword.

Melvyn Gallagher

The Law of the Gun

Ignorance is no excuse in the eyes of the law, and by collecting firearms and sporting guns you can easily fall foul of legislation. Both the Firearms Act 1968 and the Gun Barrels Proof Acts 1868/1978 are concerned with buying and selling small arms and are designed for the public safety.

Under the Firearms Act is is an offence to possess, purchase or acquire a firearm without holding a Firearms Certificate, firearms being defined as all modern small arms (excluding smooth bore guns with a barrel length exceeding 24 inches, for which a Shotgun Certificate is required). Section 58 (2) of the Act states 'Nothing in this Act relating to firearms should apply to an Antique firearm which is sold, transferred, purchased, acquired or possessed as a curiosity or ornament.' This sounds straightforward enough – but is it? What is an antique? The law is vague on this point, as recent court cases have proved, so be careful.

No problems arise regarding original old muzzle-loading firearms which can be bought and sold freely. The problems arise with early breech-loading arms, many of which are over 100 years old, and as such are deemed to be antique by many thinking that no licence is needed. No definition of 'antique' is given in the Act, and it is left to individual Police Forces to decide exactly what they think antique or modern. Many use as a guide the idea that if it fires a self-contained metallic cartridge then it is modern. There are, however, many small arms well over 100 years old which used such cartridges of a type or calibre long obsolete.

In some parts of the country such weapons can now be collected without licences as the police rightly consider early pinfire, teatfire and some rimfire arms to be 'antique', and prices have doubled for many types since this change.

The modern reproductions of antique arms used by battle re-enactment groups and some target shooters are regarded as modern by law, requiring the appropriate licences, and the barrels must be 'proved' too.

Everyone is aware of gold and silver hallmarks which protect the buyer against fraud, but gun barrel 'proof marks', which have similar intent, are not so well known. No modern firearm or shotgun can be legally sold or otherwise disposed of unless 'proved', which involves testing the weapon with a more powerful charge than the norm. If it survives without damage it is stamped with a series of punches which can be read like a hallmark. However, the presence of such marks does not always mean that the gun is safe to use. On the contrary, it should always be examined

by a gunsmith to ascertain as to whether it can be safely used with modern nitro cartridges. Shotguns may be damaged, have repairs, thin barrels or other faults which render the marks invalid. At Christie's South Kensington all arms are examined using special measuring apparatus, advice is given where repairs are needed, and the 'proofing' of items is undertaken for clients when required before sale. Some foreign arms, including all American weapons, must be proved before sale, but other countries being signatories with Britain of the International Proof Commission, accept each other's marks so that their guns do not require retesting.

Melvyn Gallagher.

1. The Eagle surmounting an N indicates a modern West German proof for nitro cartridges, the antler mark being that of the Proof House of Ulm.
2. The crowned crossed sceptre mark of the Birmingham Proof House established in 1813; BPC, for 'Birmingham Proof Company'; and the V or view mark, both commonly found on arms proved for black powder.
3. A Canadian .280 Ross Sporting rifle. Nitro proof marks at the London Proof House.
4. The underside or 'flat' of a modern Spanish double-barrelled 12 bore gun nitro proved at Eibar, to a higher pressure for magnum cartridges indicated by the CH mark.
5. The flat of a shotgun with two sets of proof marks, indicating a later 're-proof', the BNP for Birmingham nitro proof, the 12 and .729 being the bore size and 2½ in. the length of cartridge.
6. Black powder proof mark for Liège, also found crowned, a common mark, as Belgium was a major exporter of small arms.

It is an offence to sell modern guns and firearms which are unproved or with the marks rendered invalid through alteration or damage to the weapon concerned. A fully equipped gunsmith can advise you. An informative booklet explaining proof and describing the international marks is available from the The Worshipful Company of Gunmakers, The Proof House, 48 Commercial Road, London E1 1LP, or the Guardians of the Birmingham Proof House, The Gun Barrel Proof House, Banbury Street, Birmingham B5 5RH.

Swords, Etc.

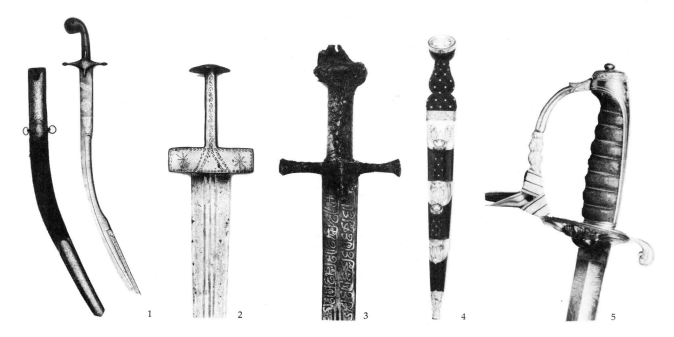

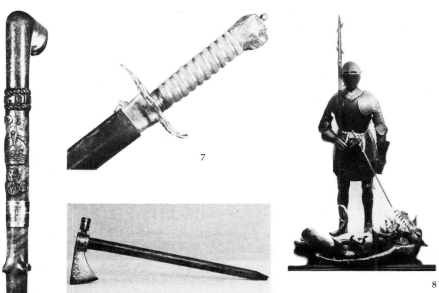

1. *Turkish Kilij with damascened decoration and scabbard, 19th century.* Nov. '84, £750.
   Eastern weapons (if not modern) are very popular at present. Damascening and watered steel blades are signs of quality and boost prices.

2. *North African Tuareg sword, 20th century.* These are worth about £20.

3. *Sudanese Kaskara with calligraphic blade and crocodile hilt and scabbard.* Dec. '84, £70.

4. *Victorian pre-1881 pattern dirk of the Black Watch, with gilt metal mounts.* Mar. '84, £750.
   A quality item with much decorative appeal. Look for hallmarked silver mounts and good etched blades with regimental decoration.

5. *Sword of the Hon. Artillery Company.* Jan. '85, £220.

6. *Gold mounted Royal presentation walking stick given to Sir John French by King Edward VII, 29 Sept. 1907.* Oct. '84, £260.
   Items related to personalities plus the Royal connection are especially popular.

7. *A silver hilted hanger with German blade and slotted hilt, London hallmarks, late 18th century.* Nov. '84, £380.

8. *An armour of mid-16th-century style emblematic of St. George, probably 20th century.* Oct. '84, £650.
   Copies are popular with the decorator market. This suit was exported to America.

9. *Tomahawk pipe, 18th century.* Apr. '85, £2,500.
   Good American pieces always sell well.

Pistols

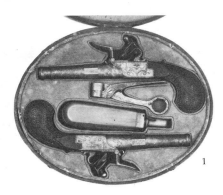

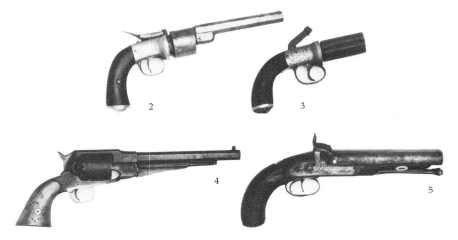

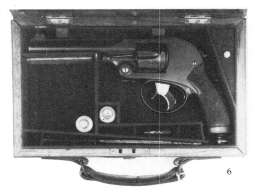

1. *Pair of boxlock flintlock travelling pistols, De Bouberl, Paris, in fitted case with bullet mould and brass mounted powder flask.* Apr. '85, £1,900.
   Not of top quality, but in original condition with an unusual and pleasing shaped case.

2. *Six-shot Baker Patent transitional long spur single action revolver, dated 1852.* Barrel 5½in. long. Apr. '85, £210.

3. *Six-shot bar hammer pepperbox pistol, mid-19th century.* Apr. '85, £160.
   Nos. 2 & 3 have bar hammers, the final stage of pistol design before the development of the modern frame.

4. *Six-shot single action 'New Model' revolver, Remington barrel.* Barrel 7⅞in. long. Apr. '85, £400.

5. *Double-barrelled percussion holster pistol, Westley Richards, London.* Barrels 7in. long. Apr. '85, £400.

6. *Rare .476 Schlund Patent concealed hammer, double trigger revolver, Kynoch, Aston, 1885–90.* May '85, £680.
   Kynoch, the ammunition makers, briefly tried revolver production, but with little success. Fewer than 600 of this model were made.

7. *Boxed pair x46 bore percussion pistols, Jno. Manton, London, 1812.* Apr. '85, £2,500.
   These have been converted from flintlocks. Otherwise the condition is original and the price shows the demand for quality pieces by the best London makers.

8. *.22 Tranter's Patent pocket revolver, S. Grant, London.* Barrel 2½in. long. Apr. '85, £230.
   The case with trade label is a bonus, but the pistol had rusted and its frame had cracked. Hence the low price.

9. *.54 bore five-shot double action Tranter's Patent revolver, J. Blanch & Son, London, with bullet mould, Hawksley flask and accessories.* Barrel 10in. long. Mar. '85, £900.
   A popular revolver with collectors, and in mint condition.

10. *.22 model 1911 single shot target pistol by Webley.* Barrel 9in. long. Oct. '84, £55.

11. *.41 rimfire Colt 'Cloverleaf' House pistol with nickel plated frame.* Oct. '84, £310.
    Arms using obsolute .41 rimfire ammunition are now widely accepted as 'antique' by many police authorities, and have risen in price as usually no licence is required (see p. 210).

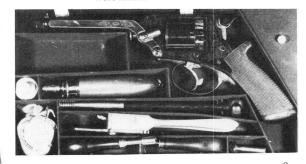

Medals and Long Arms

1

2

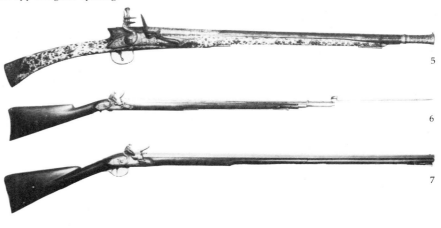

3

1. *Brass stall-plate for a Companion of the Order of the Bath, 1815.* Mar. '85, £190.
2. *Badge on a silk mantle of the Royal Victorian Order, c. 1905.* Mar. '85, £650.
   This splendid blue mantle belonged to the Russian Ambassador to the Court of St. James 1903–17, Count Alexander Benckendorff.

4

3. *The awards to Capt. H.E. Davis, J.P., Captain of the Fire Brigade and Mayor of Gravesend, Kent, between 1903 and 1912; includes a Fire Brigade Medal for bravery for his courage in saving 14 girls from fire in 1876, and various English and French Fire Brigade, Jubilee and Coronation medals, enamelled mayoral collar and two badges.* May. '85, £460.
   Bought by Gravesend Council. It is unusual to find such a complete collection, as many are split up. This had obvious local interest to the town, and the Council was immediately informed it was on the market. It was most gratifying to see it go home. This is a case of the group being worth much more than the sum of the individual parts.
4. *One of a pair of Khairpur State presentation collars embroidered in bullion cord and sequins, in cases, 1927.* Nov. '84, £230.
   Note the appealing mis-spelling.

5

6

7

5. *Indo-Persian flintlock gun.* Barrel 25½ in. long. Sept. '84, £580.
   The damascened barrel and painted flowers on the stock helped to boost this price.
6. *Flintlock cadet musket engraved brass furniture and socket bayonet, Jackson, London.* Barrel 28 in. long. Sept. '84, £380.
   This was a miniature musket for a boy.
7. *Flintlock gun with a brass barrel by Cahtman, London, and lock by Mortimer.* Barrel 37 in. long. Sept. '84, £480.

Pictures

Introduction
by Nicholas Lambourn

A Times columnist, reporting a sale in New York recently, dubbed the incessant flow of world record prices 'meaningless'. Dumbfounded, the writer signed off.

In the saleroom a more reverent silence has greeted the new high. Familiar faces, normally twitching significantly to the end, frown or raise eyebrows in defeat. Victory to a voice unheard on a telephone or to the anonymity of a porter's raised hand furthers the intrigue. The presence of invisible bidders has added a mysterious dimension in the saleroom which can be sensed at all levels of the picture market.

New buyers and simply more buyers have come to the rooms in the last year, and estimates have been pushed to allow for their influence. The exciting increase in demand has coincided with a shortage of good pictures. Prompted by this shortage, a discovery and promotion of so-called minor artists is in vogue. In May, Charles Napier Hemy's 'Oporto' (No. 3) soared above the pre-sale estimate to a record £16,000. In the same sale, a good example by Henry Redmore (No. 2) sold for a record £18,000. Redmore, like Hemy, stands as a typical example of the minor artist in vogue. If the high price for an atypical work by Hemy points to the occasional qualities of an artist well received in a major exhibition recently devoted to his work in the West Country, the success of Redmore's picture, a typical work by an unchanging artist and one who could certainly not sustain a major exhibition, points to the strength of the market and its ever more fixed liking for standard works that fulfil a constant and uncomplicated demand.

Whole categories of pictures as well as individual artists are attracting attention. The interest in watercolours has multiplied in the past season. A once modest domestic market is now attracting an international public. Arabs pick and choose amongst sunsets on the Nile, Americans are led

1. *Antoine Dury, 'Ressemblance Garantie', French, late 19th century, signed, oil on canvas.* 26 × 23 in. Nov. '84, £1,700.

up the paths of English cottage gardens, Italians are drawn to bright Neapolitan views, and a Parisian may be seduced by Russell Flint's resplendent nude 'Olearia'.

2. *Henry Redmore, 'A Calm, Vessels Taking in Provisions', signed and dated 1870, oil on canvas.* 20¼ × 44 in. Apr. '85, £18,000.

Nineteenth- and early twentieth-century drawings seem underpriced in this colourful and now inflated company. A fine collection can still be formed at reasonable expense. Good artists are still accessible to the majority (No. 10). Prints, like watercolours and drawings, remain an interesting option for buyers unable to compete in the market for oil paintings. Prints still easily fit the bill for the fashionable interior decorator and provide effective decoration for Chelsea flats and City offices alike. The supply of albums of eighteenth-century engravings and bulging folios of loose etchings continues, and appears not to have been properly exploited as yet. June 1985 saw the first international fair to be devoted to prints in London, and in January 1986 a

3. *Charles Napier Hemy, R.A., 'Oporto', signed and dated 1900, tempera on canvas.* 45 × 83 in. Apr. '85, £16,000.
This was unusual in that it was a very large and finished exhibition picture. Much of Hemy's work, particularly from the later part of his career, is in pure watercolour, and is much more impressionist.

4. *John Alexander Harington Bird, 'Breaking Cover', signed and dated 1904, oil on canvas.* 18 × 30 in. Nov. '83, £2,400.
Lesser-known sporting artists are growing in popularity as works by the major names in this field become more expensive (cf. No. 7).

6. *John Alexander Harington Bird, 'Arab Stallions at a Watering Hole', signed and dated 1899, watercolour.* 13 × 20 in. Apr. '84, £6,000.
Watercolours normally fetch less than oil paintings. Exceptional demand from Arab buyers for Arab subjects continues and pays little attention to convention (cf. No. 8).

5. *John Alexander Harington Bird, 'The First Chukka', signed and dated 1898, oil on canvas.* 15 × 30¼ in. Nov. '83, £5,000.
Polo subjects are rare and consequently attract higher prices than otherwise comparable hunting scenes.

7. *John Frederick Herrings, Sen., and James Pollard, 'The Doncaster Gold Cup of 1838 with the Earl of Chesterfield's Three-Year-Old Bay Colt, "Don John" Beating Mr Orde's "Beeswing", Mrs S.L. Fox's "The Doctor" and Mr Robinson's "Melbourne"', signed, inscribed and dated 1839 by J.F. Herring, oil on canvas.* 36 × 72 in. King Street, July '84, £777,600.

similar watercolour fair will take place, which suggests that the market is organizing properly for the first time.

Posters have advanced once again, satisfying by their very nature the demand for decorative material. As decorative items inflate in price, so here as elsewhere, a new premium is paid for important works (No. 10).

The large market in oil paintings, which subdivides into so many different and individual areas, has fared better than ever before. As fine examples appear less and less often, and as foreign buyers are excited by favourable rates of exchange, prices shoot up and up.

At more modest and well-supplied levels too, prices inflate as buyers explore and exploit areas overshadowed just a few years ago by the boom in all things Victorian. The growth in international demand has undoubtedly contri-

buted to the end of the recent pro-Victorian prejudice, and has stirred interest at home in many neglected areas of English painting. Eighteenth-century portraits have been overlooked for some time, but are benefiting now from the craze for smart decoration at home (No. 11). The majority of pictures removed from the studio of the late Tom Keating went straight from the saleroom to living rooms in the Home Counties rather than to dealers (No. 12).

At the lower end of the market, where supply is always over-generous, prices are mercurial, subject to those chance meetings of picture and admirer in the saleroom.

While buyers appear more mobile and adventurous in their taste, specialized fields remain the preserve of devotees, who price their chosen markets out of popular contention (Nos. 7 and 8).

8. *John Frederick Lewis, R.A., 'An Intercepted Correspondence, Cairo', signed and dated 1869, oil on panel, 30 × 35 in. Christie's King Street, May '79, £220,000; Sotheby's New York, May '85, $1,150,000.*

9. *Walter Greaves, 'Seated Nude', from a folio of twelve drawings by the artist. Feb. '84, £180.*

0. *Koloman Moser, 'Ver Sacrum', lithographed printed in colours, 1902, on wove paper. 68 × 23 in. Apr. '85, £62,000.*

11. *Circle of Sir Peter Lely, 'Portrait of a Gentleman', oil on canvas. 30 × 25 in. Dec. '84, £1,600.*

12. *Tom Keating, 'Sunflowers', oil on canvas, 24 × 20 in. Sept. '84, £16,000.*

Still-life

The appeal of still-life paintings in the saleroom is as evergreen as the tradition. From the zenith of the discipline in seventeenth-century Holland, No. 1 is typical of paintings that provided a model for generations to come (Nos. 2 and 3). De Bryer, Ladell, Kennedy, Cradock and Hall all specialized in still-life. For moderns such as Gertler and Wolmark, the subject provides a perfect vehicle for their preoccupation with colour (Nos. 5 and 6).

1. *C. de Bryer, 'Cherries, Grapes, Apricots, Figs, Maize and other Fruit with a Silver Tazza on a Table', signed, oil on canvas. 16¾ × 19½ in.* July '84, £16,000.
   Works by this little-documented 17th-century painter are extremely rare: always an important factor determining a good price.

2. *Edward Ladell, 'Fruit, a Tazza, a Bird's Nest and a Butterfly on a Ledge', signed with monogram, oil on canvas. 14 × 11¾ in.* Nov. '84, £7,000.
   Ladell exhibited regularly at the Royal Academy in the second half of the 19th century. His prolific work appears regularly in the rooms and invariably commands high prices.

3. *Cecil Kennedy, 'Spring Flowers in a Glass Vase', signed, oil on canvas. 20 × 16 in. Mar. 84, £4,000.*
   An obviously derivative composition by a popular 20th-century painter.

4

5

4. *Attributed to Marmaduke Cradock, (c. 1660–1717), 'A Peacock, Peahen, Pigeons, a Turkey and Ducks in a Landscape', oil on canvas.* 26 × 36 in. Dec. '84, £3,400.
The still-life can extend to a variety of subject-matter. Arrangements of game and fowl suited English taste in the 18th century.

5. *Mark Gertler, 'Anemones and Autumn Leaves', signed and dated 31, oil on canvas.* 18 × 14 in. June '85, £2,500.

6. *Alfred Aaron Wolmark, 'Tulips in a Yellow Vase', signed with initial and dated '49, oil on board.* 20½ × 17 in. Mar. '85, £900.
New life to an old tradition in the brightly coloured work of the Modern British school.

7. *George Henry Hall, 'Raspberries in Cabbage Leaf', signed, inscribed and dated 1889, oil on canvas.* 10½ × 14 in. June '85, £17,000.
Delicate still-lifes of fruit by this American painter are much sought after by collectors in the United States.

8. *Vernon Ward: 'Roses and Daises in a Vase', signed and dated 46, oil on canvas.* 18 × 14 in. June '85, £480.

6

7

8

Nineteenth-Century Figure Painting

1

1

Two- and four-legged ragamuffins and country bumpkins, laundered for popular consumption, satisfied the Victorian craving for sweet sentimentality. Popular taste has not changed greatly in the meantime, and the obliging Victorian artists and their many followers continue to meet with great approval in the salerooms.

1. *William Hemsley (b. 1819), 'The Toilet' and 'Perfectly Satisfied', a pair, oil on panel.* Each 9 × 7¼ in. Nov. '84, £1,100.
   Hemsley's eye for a pleasing subject redeems his modest technical skill.

2. *Charles Edward Wilson, 'Between School Hours' one of a pair, both signed, watercolour, late 19th century.* 8 in. diam. Apr. '85, £8,000.
   Technical skill here complements a pleasing subject, a winning combination that will often price watercolours above comparable oil paintings.

3. *William Bromley: 'The Young Hurdy Gurdy Player', signed and dated 1864, oil on canvas.* 20 × 26 in. Nov. '83, £5,000.

4. *Arthur Wardle (1864–1949), 'The End of the Day', signed and dated 99, oil on canvas.* 24 × 30 in. Nov. '83, £4,000.
   One of the most disarming of popular painters, who can make an array of dead game complement a lighthearted subject.

5. *Charles Edward Wilson, 'The Inglenook', signed, watercolour, late 19th century.* 19 × 12 in. Mar. '84, £6,000.

6. *Arthur Wardle, 'The Quartet', signed, oil on canvas, late 19th century.* 26 × 34¼ in. Nov. '84, £6,000.

2

3

4

5

6

Marines and Landscapes

Marine paintings invariably sell well, and not surprisingly English artists figure prominently here as in the field of sporting painting. If both disciplines were latterly considered provincial, a widespread upsurge in interest has been confirmed by dramatic commercial appreciation for major and minor artists alike.

1. *John Wilson Carmichael, 'Shipping off a Coast in a Swell', signed and dated 1857, oil on canvas.* 22 × 29½ in. Nov. '83, £4,900.
2. *Robert Salmon, 'A Coastal Packet, a Brig and a Clipper with other Shipping in an Estuary', signed with initials and dated 1818, oil on panel.* 15¼ × 25 in. June '85, £12,000.
3. *John Schranz: 'H.M.S. Tiger in Valetta Harbour', oil on canvas.* 11 in × 17 in. May '85, £2,000.

The English landscape tradition: of the multitude of followers of John Constable working through the nineteenth and twentieth centuries, the paintings of Benjamin Williams Leader and Edmund Morison Wimperis are representative and rising steadily in value. Demand for conventional landscapes is strong enough today to absorb even the prolific 'furnishing' paintings (those all too familiar Highland landscapes, setting suns and early morning mists) completely disregarded just a few years ago.

4. *Benjamin Williams Leader, R.A., 'The Common, Burrows Cross, Surrey, signed and dated 1896, oil on canvas.* 12 × 18¼ in. June '84, £900.
5. *Edmund Morison Wimperis: Cutting Hay, signed and dated 91, oil on canvas.* 15 × 23 in. Apr. '85, £1,500.

Topographical Pictures

Pictures and other works of art relating to the Americas, Africa, Asia and Australasia have sold increasingly well in recent years. Their commercial progress can be explained in part by the simple ratio of short supply to growing demand that has characterized much of the art market in the 1980s. This ratio is perhaps most acute in the topographical category.

Supply is limited initially by the small number of professional painters working outside Europe in the first three-quarters of the nineteenth century. Of the few working in Africa, Asia and Australasia in this period, the majority were itinerant, producing in passing a small oeuvre of interest to one or other particular continent. Baines and Bowler in South Africa and Conrad Martens in Australia are fortunate exceptions to the rule. The availability of good topographical work is limited – a little produced by a handful in a relatively short time. Much of this was undoubtedly lost to the elements in the course of precarious travel, and the precious survivors were often consigned to

museums and institutions, so banished from the market place.

A residue is to be found in private collections in the United Kingdom. As the British travelled and colonized extensively thoughout the eighteenth and nineteenth centuries, it is not surprising that material of interest has been found and continues to be discovered in this country. The pictorial diary of a businessman abroad (No. 1) or an unassuming sketch book kept by an army officer as a souvenir of his service in the colonies during the last century have now become valuable commodities.

Once consigned for sale in London, topographical works will, virtually without exception, return to their countries of origin. They are prized today as historical documents, the first records and impressions of life in the New World and colonies. This historical importance takes precedence over technical accomplishment. The 'descriptive' works of amateur artists (Nos. 4, 5, 6) compete favourably, according to the significance of time and place, with the conventional genre of professional artists. A naïve

watercolour by the self-taught convict artist John Eyre of an early settlement on the Parramatta, New South Wales, proves more valuable today than the sophisticated charms of many contemporary works. The significance of place is clearly displayed in the work of John Skinner Prout who visited Australia and Tasmania in the 1840s. Prout's 'From Sandy Bay, Hobarton' (No. 10) raised £14,000 in 1983, well over ten times the price for a comparable English view by the same artist. Similarly, Glover's Tasmanian oils, the work of Baines and Bowler in South Africa, Le Breton in South America and Australia, and of Webber and Hodges in the South Seas will attract prices as heady as their exotic subjects, and quite disproportionate to their domestic oeuvre.

The high performance of topographical works is further explained by considerable developments in demand. Foreign buyers are increasingly in search of works of historic and artistic importance to their countries of origin. Australians now display the national chauvinism initiated in the United States, concentrat-

1

2

ing on collecting works of domestic interest ranging from early topographical sheets to later indigenous material.

While fluctuating economies and changes of regime, particularly in South America and Africa, will make prices of work relating to these continents irregular, recently strong dollar economies have granted foreign buyers omnipotence in London. The appearance of fine pictures over the last few years has tried and tested their resources to the full. Cornelius Krieghoff's 'Huntsman Shooting Moose in Winter' (No. 8), Conrad Martens's 'View of Sydney' (No. 9), Thomas Baines's 'Victoria Falls from Garden Island' (No. 7), and Captain Thomas Davies's 'A South View of the city of New York in North America taken from the Governors Island' (No. 3) demonstrate the real extent of this enthusiasm.   *Nicholas Lambourn*

1. *Rudolf Von Wedemeyer, 'Diligencia, Mexico a Ixmiquilpan', signed with monogram and dated '68, pencil and watercolour. 14 × 10 in. Oct. '83, £900.*
   Von Wedemeyer was a merchant living in Manchester. The drawing comes from an album recording, with humour and accuracy, incidents from his business trips to Mexico in the 1860s.

2. *Rudolph Friedrich Kurz, 'Indians on a Riverbank', signed and dated 54, watercolour. 14⅛ × 10⅝ in. Nov. '83, £6,500.*

3. *Captain Thomas Davies, 'A South View of the City of New York in North America taken from the Governors Island', signed, inscribed and dated 1760, watercolour. 12 × 40½ in. June '85, £110,000.*

4, 5, 6 *French School, from an album of topographical drawings and watercolours of Eastern Quebec and Eastern Ontario, c. 1840s. June '85, £5.500.*

7. *Thomas Baines, 'Buffaloes Driven to the Edge of the Chasm opposite Garden Island, Victoria Falls', signed and dated 1874, oil on canvas. 20 × 26 in. May '84, £90,000.*

8. *Cornelius Krieghoff, 'Huntsmen Shooting Moose in Winter', signed and dated 1854, oil on canvas. Oct. '81, £85,000.*

Topographical Pictures (cont).

9

9. *Conrad Martens (d. 1878), 'View of Sydney Looking from the North Shore', signed, watercolour. 18 × 26 in. Oct. '83, £48,000.*

10

10. *John Skinner Prout, 'From Sandy Bay, Hobarton', signed and dated 1847, watercolour. 15 × 22½ in. Oct. '83, £14,000.*

The Orientalists

The last year or so has seen a renewed surge of prices in the market for Orientalist paintings. The fascination of the Near and Middle East for European artists dates back to the 1830s and the French conquest of Algiers, and one of the first painters of romantic Arab scenes, as opposed to topography, was Delacroix. The British soon followed, with John Frederick Lewis, R.A., who lived in Egypt for nine years from 1842 and off it for the rest of his life (see p. 216, No. 9). The demand soon became such that the minor watercolourist Henry Warren could build a career on Arab subjects without even troubling to visit the area. At the same time interest in the Middle East, and especially Egypt and the Holy Land, was fuelled by topographical lithographs after David Roberts, R.A. and Edward Lear.

This fashion was by no means limited to the countries with the most direct colonial interests in the area. Well before their invasion of Libya in 1911, the Italians had produced a flourishing Orientalist School, and the Germans and Austrians were also prominent in the field. Leaders include Saloman Corrodi, Octavio Simoni and Giulio Rosati from Italy, the German Gustav Bauernfeind, the Austrians Rudolph Ernst and Ludwig Deutsch, Jean Léon Gérôme in France, and Carl Werner and Carl Haag, the last two working in both Germany and Britain. Later followers in the steps of Lewis include Frank Dillon, Joseph Benwell, Charles Robertson, Harrington Bird, Walter Tyndale, Augustus Osborne Lamplough, Noel Henry Leaver, and Arthur Keith.

During the second half of the nineteenth century and the early years of the twentieth, Orientalist pictures, especially flamboyant canvases of Nubian slaves with cheetahs guarding the doors of harems, and the like, commanded very high prices. As a taste they may be compared to the exotic Roman costume pieces of Albert Moore and Alma-Tadema – with the added frisson that such scenes still existed. However, from the First World War they were utterly despised by collectors and dealers alike in the reaction against Victorian tastes and values.

In the early 1970s there was a tentative revival, part of the wider reappraisal of Victorian painting, and in 1975 a fine Ernst, which had stuck on the London market for months at £1,000 or so, sold for £3,000 in Beirut. However, this was a lonely portent, and watercolours by minor figures, such as Lamplough, could be had for £30 or less. Only the very best artists, such as Lewis, had a ready sale.

The end of 1981 and beginning of 1982 saw a quite extraordinary turn around in the market. A major Orientalist exhibition had been held at the Royal Academy, and subsequently prices rocketed. No. 1 shows a watercolour by Joseph Benwell which we modestly estimated to make £400–£600; it sold in January 1982 for £2,000. Throughout 1982 prices remained strong for both major and minor works, with buyers seeming almost indiscriminate in their choice of subject and artist. It was thought of at the time as a 'Silly Season'. The end of 1983 and beginning of 1984 saw a settling down, and buyers became much more selective. Subject became of prime importance. Troubles in the Middle East made Egypt a tricky a subject to re-sell for many dealers and collectors, and they began to go more to desert views, figure subjects, and views not associated directly with Egypt.

The present time finds the market still buoyant with Lamplough now one of the market leaders, partly because work by the top artists is becoming scarce. Nos. 4–6 illustrate some of the artists and prices current for the early part of the 1985 – which in our opinion are still on the increase. *Jonathan Horwich*

1. *Joseph Austin Benwell, 'Desert Caravan', signed, watercolour.* 9 × 17 in. Jan. '82, £2,000.
   A surprising price marking the beginning of the present revival.

2. *Rappini, 'Moorish Courtyard', signed, watercolour.* 14 × 9 in. Feb. '84, £400.
   An Italian artist whose figure subjects such as this sell well, but whose desert views seldom exceed £40–£50.

3. *Augustus Osborne Lamplough, 'Philae on the Nile, Egypt,' signed, watercolour.* 19 × 29 in. Feb. '85, £1,500.

4. *Augustus Osborne Lamplough, 'Desert Riders', signed, watercolour.* 20 × 27 in. Feb. '85, £4,800.
   Sold in the same sale as No. 3, but as a desert view and not clearly associated with Egypt made far more despite being virtually the same size and by the same artist.

5. *Noel Henry Leaver, 'Merchants at a Mosque', signed, watercolour.* 10 × 14 in. Sept '84, £1,000.
   Another Orientalist artist whose prices are currently strong.

6. *Arthur Keith, 'Desert Riders', signed, watercolour.* 10 × 13½ in. Feb. '85, £750.

3

1

2

4

5

6

Scottish Paintings

It has become apparent over the 1984/5 season that collectors and dealers alike are realizing that the art market in the British Isles does not stop at Watford Gap. It is also apparent that when the term 'Scottish pictures' is mentioned, it should not only build up visions of long-horned animals drinking from a burn with the sun reflecting off the mountains, or the 'Monarch of the Glen standing proudly, head held high'. In fact this type of picture is much more in demand in areas where one cannot drive for twenty minutes from a city centre to find just that scene in reality. The Scots on the whole do not require that form of escapism in art, which for the most part was to decorate the walls of shooting lodges.

Indeed the Scots are rightly proud of the abundance of their own artists. Leaving aside the greats – Raeburn, Ramsay, Wilkie – there are the fine late nineteenth- to early twentieth-century painters. To mention just one group, there are the Colourists, notably four artists: John Duncan Ferguson, Samuel John Peploe, Francis Campbell Boileau Cadell and George Leslie Hunter. This is not meant to read like a saleroom report, but the reasons for giving the following examples from a sale in April 1985 will be apparent.

Included was a marvellous collection of Peploes, running from 1905 to 1928 and in price from £3,800 to £78,000. No. 1 realized the record price of £78,000.

Recently one has read of astronomical prices for pictures of the Newlyn School, and where do the more astute auctioneers market this small, but élite group? Cornwall, of course.

This brings one to 'horses for courses'. Good Scottish pictures sell best in Scotland for two main reasons. Although the population of Scotland is a mere 4 million, it has a very strong buying and collecting tradition; more often than not the pictures are brought to hang on the wall, not purely for investment. Secondly, the international collector, when he or she is seeking to buy Scottish pictures, obviously looks to the two main Scottish cities: that is why we tend to advise our clients, be they in Australia or London,

All these paintings were sold at Christie's and Edmiston's Glasgow; prices exclude the 8% buyer's premium.

1. *Samuel John Peploe, 'The Coffee Pot', signed, oil on canvas, c. 1905. 25 × 33¼ in. Apr. '85, £78,000.*
2. *Edward Arthur Walton, 'Grandfather's Garden', signed and dated '84, watercolour, 15 × 22 in. Dec. '84, £17,000.*

Note: prices exclude the 8% buyer's premium.

3. *David Farquharson, 'Amang the Withies', signed and dated '94–5, oil on canvas. 35 × 54½ in. Apr. '84, £11,000.*
4. *John Duncan Ferguson, 'A Storm round Ben Ledi', signed and dated 1922 verso, oil on canvas. 21½ × 22 in. Apr. '84, £13,000.*
5. *Waller Hugh Paton, 'The Holy Island from above Lamlash, Arran, with a distant view of Troon', signed and dated 1856, oil on canvas. 29 × 49 in. Apr. '84, £9,500.*

7

8

9

to send Scottish pictures to Glasgow, where they are researched, documented and offered to a very appreciative and keen market.

A typical example of the practical sense of selling Scottish pictures in Scotland was given last year when our Toronto agent sent a photograph to Glasgow showing a watercolour by the Edinburgh artist, Walton (No. 2). The picture soon followed and made a world auction record. It now graces a private collection in Scotland. Had it been offered in Canada, who can say that the final buyer and bidders would have been even aware of it? *Alexander Meddowes, Christie's Scotland*

10

11

6. *Arthur Melville, 'Scarlet Poppies', signed and dated 1885, oil on canvas. 24 × 30 in. Apr. '84, £7,000.*

7. *Francis Campbell Boileau Cadell, 'The Persian Tile', signed and dated 1907, oil on board. 11½ × 14½ in. Apr. '84, £8,000.*

8. *John Pettie (1839–93), 'The Rehearsal', signed, oil on canvas. 23¾ × 19¼ in. Aug. '84, £7,000.*

9. *John McGhie, 'Waiting for the Boats', signed, oil on canvas. 30 × 25 in. Dec. '84, £4,000.*

10. *Anne Redpath (1895–1965), 'A Rainy Day in Spain, Ubeda', signed, oil on board. 20 × 24 in. Apr. '85, £5,500.*

11. *Mary Nicol Neill Armour, 'Flowers with Orange Lily', signed and dated 1964, oil on canvas. 32 × 23 in. Apr. '85, £3,500.*

12. *Edward Atkinson Hornel, 'Stewartry Girls amongst blossom', signed and dated 1908, oil on canvas. 30 × 36 in. Apr. '84, £18,000.*

12

Modern British Pictures

Sales concentrating on Modern British pictures have traditionally been the exclusive domain of British buyers. Prices have tended to reflect the relatively conservative means and taste of this domestic market, and the category has remained distinct, as one modestly priced, from immodest categories elsewhere. In 1984 the market has been vulnerable to new interest from farther afield, invigorating prices and stirring a new enthusiasm at home.

Among the many notables, Sickert, Gore, Lavery, Lewis, Bomberg, Roberts, Gertler, Nash and Nevinson at last compete on level terms with their European contemporaries. Auction records have tumbled and pushed individual sale totals past the million mark for the first time.

Foreign competition has not been restricted to artists of such obvious popular appeal as Munnings and Flint. New buyers for Orpen and Topolski, Lamorna Birch and Augustus John have emerged from Geneva and New York, Vienna and Toronto.

At home, competition has been lively for decorative paintings from the 1920s, '30s and '40s (No. 4), reflecting the continuing growth of this period in all fields. Happily this direction is extending to the once 'difficult' canvases of the non-figurative and Surrealist painters of the interwar years and through to the distinctive work of Minton, Ayrton, Colquhoun and Vaughan (No. 5) in the 1940s.

The sun-drenched subjects of the Newlyn painters have appreciated dramatically and are affording new popularity to many deserving though lesser-known painters. In their wake follow the more colourful of the 'Outdoors' painters from Dame Laura Knight to Dorothea Sharp (No. 2).

Many names remained to be discovered, or, as is often the case, rediscovered, and offer the amateur the rare opportunity to form a collection of quality at reasonable expense. Studio sales are becoming more common and frequently bring previously overlooked, but nonetheless good, minor artists to light. Dealers similarly must be attracted by the little-exploited potential of these many artists who can often compare well with their inflated peers.

Nicholas Lambourn

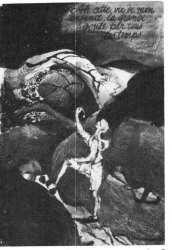

1. *Henry Scott Tuke, R.A., 'Bather', signed and dated 1909, watercolour.* 6¾ × 9¾ in. June '85, £1,800.
   A strong price for a good example of Tuke's speciality.

2. *Dorothea Sharp, 'Toddler with Ducks on the edge of a Pond, signed, oil on panel.* 15 × 18 in. Mar. '85, £2,800.
   A typical pretty, sunny subject by Sharp, growing in commercial appeal.

3. *John Tunnard, R.A, 'Surrealist Landscape', signed and dated 47, watercolour and pencil.* 16 × 26½ in. Mar. '85, £2,000.

4. *Robert Duckworth Greenham, 'Auburn-Haired Girl', signed and dated 45, oil on canvas.* 14 × 10 in. Dec. '84, £1,500.
   Higher prices have been paid in 1984/5 for decorative works with period appeal.

5. *Keith Vaughan, 'L'Impossible' (illustration to Rimbaud's 'Une Saison En Enfer'), signed, brush, ink and wash.* 11 in × 7 in. Dec. '83, £550.

The Work of the Illustrator

Many artists working as illustrators have become household names. The work of Henry Mayo Bateman (1887–1970), 'The Man who', is familiar to many of us as a merciless cartoonist portraying blustering Colonels and outraged ladies. The price of his works has increased dramatically in the last two years and the price realized for No. 1 was probably twice what it would have been a year earlier.

Donald McGill the postcard artist made quite a splash also in December, which may have had something to do with the festive nature of many of the designs (Nos. 2 and 3). There were approximately 20 designs by McGill in the sale, and the prices varied from £80 to £480, the lower prices being for late work *c.* 1950/60 and the higher for earlier work *c.* 1920/30. The illustrations show examples of his earlier work, which is usually of better quality.

The subject includes illustrations from and for cartoon films, such as No. 4. There is increasing interest in this category, especially the work of Walt Disney and his studio. Even a signed reproduction will reach a good price (No. 5).

Illustration from the mid-Victorian period is usually well represented. No. 6 is a typical Cruikshank pencil sketch with touches of watercolour. In the same sale a watercolour sketch of 1831 which was later engraved went for £420, a price reflecting the finer detail and greater interest of the sketch.

The beauty of this market is that although very high prices can be obtained for major works, many things can often be bought for less than £100. Surprisingly, in view of the demand for late nineteenth- and twentieth-century illustrations, eighteenth-century examples are still very cheap. Charming watercolours and wash drawings by considerable artists such as Thomas Stothard, Samuel Wale, Richard Westall and John Masey Wright can also be found at two-figure prices.

At the top end of the market works by Heath Robinson and Arthur Rackham can command prices in excess of £10,000. The mixture of canny dealers and determined collectors will ensure this end of the market's continued growth.

Jonathan Horwich

1   2   3

4

5

6

1. *Henry Mayo Bateman, 'The Cocktail Connoisseur', signed, watercolour.* 12 × 10 in. Dec. '84, £950.
   Our highest price attained for a work by the artist.
2. *Donald McGill, 'Santa Claus', signed, watercolour.* Dec. '84, £420.
3. *Donald McGill, 'Christmas Fayre', signed, watercolour.* Dec. '84, £480.
   Nos. 2 & 3 sold very well and represent rare examples of early works in prime condition, having been stored out of light since being finished. Normally prices fall into the £150–£250 region.
4. *Studios of Hanna Barbara, 'Tom and Jerry's Christmas', bodycolour on acetate original film cel.* Dec. '84, £550.
5. *Studio of Walt Disney, 'Mice Dancing', colour reproduction, countersigned by Walt Disney and dedicated.* Dec. '84, £440.
6. *George Cruikshank, 'Cinderella and her Fairy Godmother', pencil with touches of watercolour.* Dec. '84, £160.

Cottage Gardens

It is obvious that fashions play a part in art auction prices, and a fondness for one artist often affects works by others of a similar nature. In the case of a family of artists this can also be true.

Only a few years ago the works of William Gardener Fraser increased dramatically in price. No. 1 and its pair, both typical subjects for the artist, made £2,400 in May 1981 against a pre-sale estimate of £600–£1,000. (Note that the artist, despite his real name, has signed himself W.F. Garden). This high price and others at other sales prompted an interest in the other painter members of the family, Robert W., George Gordon, Gilbert Baird and Arthur Anderson. Probable prices for the first listed, known as Robert 'Winter' Fraser, fall in the £200–£400 region, whereas the others do not normally exceed £80–£120; however, prior to interest in 'Garden' Fraser their work was very difficult to sell at auction at all.

A similar rise has been among the Stannard family of painters. As far as cottage gardens go, the Stannard family consisted of Henry John Sylvester (1870–1951), his brother Alexander Molyneux, sisters Emily (not be be confused with two Norfolk Emily Stannards) and Lilian, and daughter Theresa. The 1984/5 season has seen a marked rise in auction price of all members of the family. The price paid for No. 2 would have seemed incredible only two or three years ago, and compares favourably with that paid for a work by Henry John Sylvester only a few months previously. Theresa Stannard, I feel, is not far behind her aunt in the market as her work is very similar in subject and quality. Prices for Alexander Molyneux are now starting to creep up, but his work, unfortunately, is not of the same quality as his brother and sister, although the subject-matter is similar. The works of the remaining members are rising steadily, but I see Theresa, Lilian and Henry John Sylvester as the market leaders, with higher prices to come.

Following on from the Stannard family there are many other painters of Cottage Gardens who enjoy healthy prices at auction. No. 4, by Alfred Parsons, follows the same theme as the Stannards, but it is more subtle in handling, and I see his prices exceeding this in the near future. Beatrice Parsons, possibly a relative of Alfred, painted very similar watercolours to his, and her prices usually fall into the £500–£800 bracket. Other notable names and price ranges of interest are as follows: George Samuel Elgood (£600–£800); Ernest Arthur Rowe (£600–£1,200); William F. Ashburner (£400–£600, No. 5); George Marks (£400–£600, No. 6); Lynas Gray (£200–£400); Arthur Claude Strachan (£1,500–£2,000); John Mackay (£800–£1,200); Thomas James Lloyd (£1,500–£2,500); Henry John Yeend King (£400–£600); William Affleck (£800–£1,200); Benjamin D. Sigmund (£500–£700); Joseph Kirkpatrick (£400–£600).

The above does not cover all those artists involved in this school of painting, but I hope it gives food for thought in a decorative and pleasing field of art, which at present gives an opportunity for the modest collector. However, I see a continuing upward trend.

Jonathan Horwich

1

5

3

2

6

4

1. *William Gardener Fraser, 'On the Ouse', signed W.F. Garden and dated 1898, watercolour. 7 × 10 in, one of a pair. May '81, £2,400.*

2. *Lilian Stannard, 'Cottage Garden', signed, watercolour. 10 × 14 in. Apr. '85, £1,700.*

3. *Henry John Sylvester Stannard, 'Woman and Child by a Pond', signed, watercolour. 18 × 20 in. Nov. '84, £1,500.* Compare this price with No. 2, as normally Henry John exceeds his sister in auction price.

4. *Alfred Parsons, R.A., 'Sussex Garden', signed, watercolour. 10 × 14 in. Dec. '84, £500.*

5. *William F. Ashburner, 'A Country Maid', signed, watercolour, 14 × 18 in. Oct. '84, £400.*
The handling here is less accurate than that of the Stannards, but none the less attractive.

6. *George Marks, 'Terrace, Villa Babliacello, Lake Como', signed, watercolour. 9 × 13 in. Jan. '85, £480.*

Modern British Etchings

Most art forms have their market cycles, periods when they are greatly in demand alternating with years of neglect, partial or complete. Probably none has ever showed this more clearly, or provided a better warning against buying for investment, than the school of Modern British Etchers.

The first period of popularity for etching in Britain ran from the 1830s to the 1880s, from the founders of the 'Old' Etching Club through Palmer and Haden to Whistler. The early men are still often surprisingly cheap, largely because their work, although often fine, was mostly illustrative rather than standing on its own. An exception is Charles Keene, best known for his cartoon drawing, whose landscape etchings are among the best of their kind. They are also rare, but many by his Victorian contemporaries are common and well worth seeking out.

Although there was no break in production of etchings after the death of Whistler, what might be termed the 'second' British School enjoyed its brief if dramatic heyday only in the 1920s. It was almost entirely created by investment. Etchings came in limited editions, they had a readily ascertainable market price, and thus were treated by many as shares or securities. A subscriber to an etching might realize up to ten times his investment merely by walking into an art gallery. It is not surprising that this artificial boom crashed with Wall Street in October 1929.

Just as the boom had been artificial so was the collapse illogical in its completeness. While the price of Arthur Briscoe's 'Clewlines and Buntlines' tumbled from £100 in 1926 to £2 in 1955, or 'On the Main Yard' could be found for £3 in 1931 and now £130 (No. 1) the artistic quality – value indeed – was unchanged. It was not until the very late 1960s that any signs of a real revival became apparent, and even today in real terms few prices equal those of the '20s.

The best prices by the best men – for example, Sir D.Y. Cameron's 'Ben Ledi, Ben Lomond and the Five Sisters of York' or McBey's 'Strange Signals and Dawn: the Camel Patrol Setting Out' – are now in three or even four figures, but these are rare. Most dramatic of all was

1

2

3

4

5

the £3,780 paid for an impression of 'Adolescence' by Gerald Leslie Brockhurst in April 1984 (No. 2). Because of the subject, this had never fallen quite as far as the others, but from 1934 to 1960, the top price was £32 and by 1968 it had risen only to £210. Other etchers such as Dame Laura Knight, R.A. (No. 3) or Sir David Muirhead Bone (No. 4) or Arthur Briscoe are all worth seeking out.

This market has now established itself, and despite its slight unpredictability it is a viable area for investment, with ever rising prices.

See also the general introduction (p. 10) for a further comment on the Modern British Etching boom and collapse.   *Richard Barclay*

1. *Arthur Briscoe, 'On the Main Yard', etching heightened with brown ink (unframed), 1939. 9 × 6 in. Nov. '84, £100.*
Another impression sold for £130.

2. *Gerald Leslie Brockhurst, A.R.A., 'Adolescence', etching on wove paper, fifth final state, signed in pencil, from edition of 91, full edition 101, 1932. 14½ × 10½ in. Apr. '84, £3,780.*

3. *Dame Laura Knight, R.A., 'Study of a Girl', etching, signed in pencil. 13 × 9 in. Mar. '85, £95.*

4. *Sir David Muirhead Bone, R.A., 'Trinity Bridge, Cambridge', etching, inframed. 8 × 9 in. Mar. '85, £80.*

5. *Charles Frederick Tunnicliffe, 'The Bull', etching with drypoint, signed in pencil and numbered 42/75. 9 × 11 in. Sold at Phillips, June '85, £400.*

Prints

1

1

2

For many people prints seem a fickle and unpredictable commodity: 'It's only a print, a poor man's painting.' Yes, but then £50,000 for an Edvard Munch lithograph?

Nineteenth-century sporting aquatints are the height of fashion, but the 'same' print may be £10 or £400. There is a simple explanation. A Henry Alken hunting subject issued in 1832 with good contemporary colouring is rare, as only a few would have been printed, the impression would be fine and rich and the result is a high price. The same plate could then be reprinted and republished over the years, and each edition is less sought after as the actual image becomes less clear and crisp.

Some hunts are less in demand with collectors than others, just as some countries and towns are wanted in topographical prints rather than others. Switzerland, Germany, Greece, America, the Middle East, the China Coast, and British towns such as Bristol and Brighton are in vogue, but not, for the moment, France, Spain or India.

With figure subjects an elegant, preferably nude or semi-nude girl will do much better than a man of similar quality (No. 8). Thus certain prints by E.A. Lord, P.C. Heller, G.L. Brockhurst (see page 231, No. 2), or Louis Icart (No. 9), far outstrip portraits by M. Todd, A. Legros, F.S. Haden or J. Simpson.

The effect of a single collector on prices can be dramatic. Over the years Christopher Lennox Boyd has been collecting British portrait mezzotints. He

1. *Henry Alken, 'One of the Wrong Sort', and 'One of the Right Sort', coloured aquatints.* 9 × 12 in. May '85, £100.
   Late reprints 1860/1870. Slightly faded, colours odd: price therefore low. An original impression with good colours could be £500 to £600.

2. *After Henry Alken, 'The First Steeple Chase on Record', plate 3, rare first issue, 1839, excellent condition.* Sotheby's Mar. '85, £3,410 (the set of four).
   The mistake of the unbroken shadow of the gate became so well-known that although it was corrected in the second issue, it was reintroduced in the third. Apart from quality of printing and colouring the first issue can sometimes be told from the third by the dated watermarks 1836 and 1838.

3

4

3. *After Maurer, 'La Ville de Zurich du Côté du Nord', by Hegi, coloured etching and aquatint, unframed.* 10 × 13 in. Mar. '85, £480.

4. *After William F. Austin, 'River Landscape View, Leeds', coloured photogravure.* 11 × 19 in. May '85, £40.

5

6

would be unlikely to pay £5 for a second copy of something that he owns, but if a print fills a gap for him . . .

These are some of the reasons which make the market so difficult to predict, and why two seemingly identical prints may make £100 or £10,000 respectively.

Experience, handling and really looking are the only ways of learning how to tell the one from the other.

Richard Barclay

5. *Thomas Malton, one of six views of Bath, coloured aquatints. 14 × 20½ in. Nov. '84, £1,100.*

6. *William Daniel, 'Indian River Scene', coloured aquatint. 16½ × 23½ in. May '85, £80.*

7. *Sir William Russell Flint, R.A., 'Aragonese String Makers', etching, signed and inscribed L.I. in pen. 9 × 14 in. Mar. '85, £170.*

8. *After Sir William Russell Flint, R.A. 'Rosa and Marisa', coloured reproduction, signed in pencil. 17½ × 24 in. Apr. '81, £380.*
It seems ludicrous that people are prepared to pay much more for mechanical reproductions of Flint's work than for his original prints, but there we are. Prices for them seem solely dictated by the amount of nudity.

7

9. *Louis Icart 'Summer', etching, signed and numbered 91/100 in pencil. 7 × 11 in. Sold with one other similar, Mar. '85, £300.*
Icart could be regarded as a French Russell Flint, but because he has a French and an American following, his prices can be much higher – especially in New York sales.

9

8

Posters

The market in posters varies greatly, and in the past there has often seemed to be little logical connection between prices at one sale and the next. It is very much an American collecting field and sales were pioneered by Phillips in New York. The April 1985 sale was the third at South Kensington, and in some areas did very well indeed.

Posters are obviously attractive and decorative – otherwise there would be no point to them – but equally obviously it is almost impossible to know how many examples have survived. A good artist – Toulouse-Lautrec, Mucha, Hockney and so on – will boost prices. All illustrations come from the April sale.

1. *Alphonse Mucha, 'Zodiac, Savonnerie de Bagnolet', lithograph.* With another, £950.
2. *Marc Auguste Bastard, 'Bières de la Meuse', lithograph, c. 1896.* £190.
   Art Nouveau but not Mucha.
3. *Leonetto Cappiello, 'Vodka Relsky, 1° Kumel', lithograph, c. 1900.* £95.
   There was some wear and damage to this.
4. *G. Massiot, 'Porto & Sherry, Sandeman', lithograph.* £550.
   A fine impression of a very famous image.
5. *Leonetto Cappiello, 'Cognac Monnet', lithograph, 1927.* £300.
   Condition here was much better than in No. 3.
6. *Eugène Charles Paul Vavasseur: 'Huile Rigal, Léon Juillet', lithograph, c. 1900.* £150.
   Motoring is popular, and these national caricatures were amusing.

7. *Delval, 'Fap' Anis', lithograph. £80.*

8. *N.R., 'Dungeness', lithograph. £180.*

9. *Paul Emile Colin, 'Haut de Cagnes, ou la Joie de Vivre', lithograph. £300.*

10. *Charles Gesmar, 'Mistinguett', lithograph, 1925. £350.*

11. *Portefin, 'Théâtre des Champs Elysées, Jonny Mène, La Danse', lithograph, 1928. £500.*

12. *David Hockney, 'Hollywood Bowl, Calif.', lithograph, 1965. £200.*
    A good impression by one of the most popular contemporary British printmakers.

13. *Edward McKnight Kauffer, 'The World', lithograph, 1934.* With four others, £1,000.
    This was not in the best condition, but undoubtedly it carried the others in the lot, some of which were reproductions and others by lesser names.

14. *J.S. Anderson, 'Motorists prefer Shell', lithograph, 1935.* With three others, £380.
    The series of posters for Shell include some of the most striking British work of the period.

8

9

10

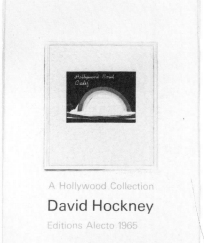

11

12

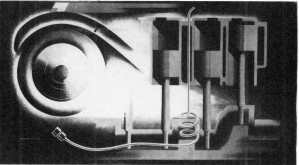

13

14

Index